ALSO BY JULIUS LESTER

*Look Out, Whitey! Black Power's Gon' Get Your Mama!*
*To Be a Slave*
*Revolutionary Notes*
*Black Folktales*
*Search for the New Land*
*The Seventh Son: The Thought and Writings of W. E. B. Du Bois*
*Long Journey Home: Stories from Black History*
*Two Love Stories*
*The Knee-High Man*
*Who I Am* (with David Gahr)
*All Is Well*
*This Strange New Feeling*
*Do Lord Remember Me*
*The Tales of Uncle Remus: The Adventures of Brer Rabbit*

Julius Lester

# *Lovesong*

## Becoming a Jew

HENRY HOLT AND COMPANY
NEW YORK

*To my son*
*MALCOLM*


Published by Henry Holt and Company, Inc.,
521 Fifth Avenue, New York, New York 10175.
Published in Canada by Fitzhenry & Whiteside Limited,
195 Allstate Parkway, Markham, Ontario L3R 4T8.

Library of Congress Cataloging in Publication Data
Lester, Julius.
Lovesong : becoming a Jew / by Julius Lester.—1st ed.
p. cm.
ISBN 0-8050-0588-9
1. Lester, Julius. 2. Proselytes and proselyting, Jewish—Converts
from Christianity—Biography. 3. Authors, American—20th century—
Biography. I. Title.
BM755.L425A3 1988
296.8′346′0924—dc19
[B] 87-16793
CIP

First Edition

Designed by Francesca Belanger
Printed in the United States of America
1 2 3 4 5 6 7 8 9 10

Grateful acknowledgment is given to the following for permission to reprint: From *The Sign of Jonas* by Thomas Merton, copyright 1953 by The Abbey of Our Lady of Gethsemani; renewed 1981 by The Trustees of the Merton Legacy Trust. Reprinted by permission of Harcourt Brace Jovanovich, Inc. From *Contemplation in a World of Action* by Thomas Merton, reprinted by courtesy of Doubleday and Company, Inc. From *God, Sex and Kaballah* by Allen S. Maller, reprinted by courtesy of the author. Article in the New York *Post* by Lee Dembart, courtesy of the New York *Post*. Article from *Katallagete* is reprinted with permission. "The Uses of Suffering" first appeared in *The Village Voice* and is reprinted with permission.

ISBN 0-8050-0588-9

**"All my bones shall proclaim,**
**'O Lord, who is like unto Thee?' "**

—Shabbat and Festivals Morning Service

Lovesong

## December 1982

In the winter of 1974, while I was on retreat at the Trappist monastery in Spencer, Massachusetts, one of the monks told me, "When you know the name by which God knows you, you will know who you are."

I searched for that name with the passion of one seeking the Eternal Beloved. I called myself Father, Writer, Teacher, but God did not answer.

Now I know the name by which God calls me. I am Yaakov Daniel ben Avraham v'Sarah.

I have become who I am. I am who I always was. I am no longer deceived by the black face which stares at me from the mirror.

I am a Jew.

# Part One

# 1

It is summer, any summer in the 1940s. I am with Momma and for two to four weeks we will be here, staying with her mother outside Pine Bluff, Arkansas.

Grandmomma lives with her brother, my great-uncle Rudolph, in a frame house whose unpainted boards have absorbed sun and rain, frost and dew until they are as gray as restless sleep and as weary as the sleeper who awakens to a day for which he has no love.

Grandmomma's house stands alone, removed from its neighbors and back from the main road like the monarch of an impoverished kingdom. To the east is a large field, "the orchard," Momma calls it still, because when she was a girl (and I can't imagine that), rows and rows of peach, apple and cherry trees flowered where now an infinite variety of weeds flourishes like immorality. On the other side of the "orchard," beside the railroad tracks, is another house, smaller than Grandmomma's, and even more weary. Grandmomma's sister, my great-aunt Rena, lives there with her husband, Fate McGowan.

Behind Grandmomma's house is the chicken yard, henhouse and outhouse. Beyond these are deep woods, somewhere in the midst of which is the family cemetery. In all, there are forty acres of fields and woods enclosed by a sturdy wire fence, whose gate no one ever enters and we seldom go out.

Beyond the fence, on the west, is a dirt road leading to and from the main one on the north. It is wide enough for a mule wagon as far as Grandmomma's gate; then it narrows to a dusty footpath and winds into the innards of Pine Bluff's black community. (We were "colored" in those days when Hope was the name some dreamer bestowed on a daughter, when change was what the white man at the store *might* give you when you bought something, and progress was merely another incomprehensible word on a spelling test.)

I sit on the porch each day and watch children go back and forth to the little store on the main road. I am a child yearning to be with children, but these wear dirty and torn clothes. How am I supposed to play with someone whom dust coats like roach powder? They look furtively at me sitting on the porch in my clean and well-pressed clothes, socks and shoes(!). (Only now, looking back, do I realize that in the fifteen summers at Grandmomma's, no child ever came to the gate to ask me who I was, where I was from and did I want to play. I realize only now, too, that I never went to the gate so that they could ask.)

I accept such separateness as unquestioningly as I do the air my body breathes. There is something different about us—Grandmomma, Uncle Rudolph, Momma and me. In the evenings we sit on the porch and watch as trucks, filled with fieldhands who work the white man's cotton, stop on the main road in front of the store. With much laughter and loud talking, they jump or climb off and meander down the side road that leads past Grandmomma's to their houses scattered over the fields behind like neglected thoughts. Their loud voices soften as they near Grandmomma's. "You niggers hush! Don't you see Miz Smith setting on the porch?" (That was Grandmomma's name when she wasn't Grandmomma.) A quietness as stifling as the heat falls upon them, fifteen, twenty, men, women and children, hoes at forty-five-degree angles across their shoulders, fraying straw hats or red handkerchiefs on their heads, and as they pass the gate, that gate they never enter and through which we seldom go out, someone calls out loudly, "How y'all this evening?" We call back, "Fine, and you?" "Tol'able, thank you." Only after the last one passes do their voices rise again like birds from tall grasses.

We are different. Daddy is a Methodist minister and I was robed in a mantle of holiness even before the first diaper was pinned on my nakedness. I cannot do what other kids do—play marbles for keeps, go to the movies on Sundays, listen to popular music on the radio, play cards. Momma cannot wear makeup or pants. Only sinful women do that. We represent Daddy and he represents God.

My brother hates all of it. He is nine years older than me. But he does not come to Grandmomma's and I do not know where he is or what he is doing.

I do not hate holiness. Sometimes I wish I could do what other children do, but Daddy tells me, "God has special plans for you," and I wonder what they are. I cannot imagine, but I will never know if I do not nurture separateness as if it were my only child.

We are different, too, because we do not depend on white people for our economic survival. Daddy does not work for white people and we do not have to talk to them or even see them, except when we go to town. We go to town as infrequently as we can.

There is something else different about us, too. Grandmomma and Momma look like white women. Both have thick, wavy long hair and skin like moonlight.

(Summer 1982. Daddy has been dead a year. My oldest son, Malcolm, and I go to Nashville to help Momma sort through the remains of fifty-seven years of married life, sell the house and prepare her to move in with a relative in Washington, D.C. I cannot imagine being eighty-five years old and Life asking me to begin again. I look at her and learn what it is to submit to Life's requirements and create oneself anew as Death takes your hand in his. For Momma, part of beginning again is to go to Pine Bluff and visit the family cemetery for what might be the last time.

("Your daddy was supposed to bring me down last summer but he died before he got to it," she says several times.

(We drive in silence. Neither Momma nor Grandmomma ever had much use for words. Grandmomma died at age ninety-one more than twenty years before and she never spoke of herself, to her children or grandchildren. Momma is not very different. So I am surprised when into the silence she says, "It was hard growing up looking white. I had a hard time in school. The other kids were always beating me up. And when we went to town, the white people acted like they hated us because we looked white but weren't. I grew up being afraid all the time."

(Silence closes around her again like an enemy. It is a silence I know too well, a silence she has bequeathed me like an antique family ring of dubious value. It is the silence of Grandmomma's solitary house and of how solitary we were in that house, in that community and with each other. We were different, Grandmomma, Momma and me, holding ourselves back from the world and all in it—reserved, polite, formal—acknowledging salutations with the fingertips of white-gloved hands while longing for an embrace.)

At night we sit on the porch and I listen to the sounds of Momma's, Grandmomma's and Uncle Rudolph's voices telling of people now dead, and their dead walk through the silences between their words, and I miss people whom I have never known.

Silence acquires the dimension of space at night. There is no electricity in the black community and the lights from coal-oil lamps flickering in the windows of houses in the distance are like matches before the force night is. Night is an absolute, an irrefutable mathematical equation to which one submits with grateful awe. Night and silence are palpable presences I love.

The only time I go outside the fence is to sit by the mailbox and await the mailman. I am not expecting mail but want to decipher the name on Grandmomma's box. I read almost as well as an adult but cannot pronounce the name painted crudely in black on her box. A-L-T-S-C-H-U-L. Grandmomma's name is Smith. Sometimes mail is addressed to Rudolph A-L-T-S-C-H-U-L, however. Who is that? Uncle Rudolph is Grandmomma's brother, which means that he is Rudolph Smith.

I want to ask Momma who A-L-T-S-C-H-U-L is, but she does not like my questions and generally answers them with "No," even when they begin with "Why?"

One afternoon we are sitting in the porch swing next to each other. She is telling me about the orchard and her voice is soft like moonlight on magnolia blossoms and I want to melt into her and, without thinking, my voice soft like the fuzz on a bee's back, I ask, "Momma? Who is A-L-T-S-C-H-U-L?"

"That's your uncle Rudolph's name," she answers.

"I thought his name was Smith."

She chuckles. "That's your grandmother's married name. She was an Altschul before she married."

Al . . . I try to say it to myself, but can't. I know she hasn't told me who Al . . . whoever is, but if I ask again, she will only say that I ask too many questions.

---

Time at Grandmomma's is like the tall pine tree by the main road. It is simply there—straight and immovable, unbending and indifferent. Day becomes night and night becomes day and the new day is the old one's twin.

One morning every week or so, however, Momma says, "Your daddy's coming this evening." I eat breakfast quickly and hurry to the porch. Daddy never comes until the sun is like fire on the edge of the world, but maybe he will come early today. That is what I think each week.

Daddy teaches ministers in summer school at Philander Smith College in Little Rock. I do not know even now what he taught. I know only that I miss him.

Night is squeezing day into evening before I see the blue Plymouth cross the railroad tracks by Aunt Rena's house. I leap from the porch and race across the yard to unlatch the gate. Before the car turns off the main road, I am standing at the exact place Daddy will park.

There is a big grin on his face when he gets out of the car. "Well, what you saying about yourself?" he chuckles, picking me up in the air, which is fun and scary at the same time.

Anybody can tell that Daddy is a preacher. He always dresses in a suit and tie. They are as natural on him as his black skin. He is a serious and, at times, stern man. Even when he grins and laughs (and he laughs a lot), the seriousness does not change. It is as if his grin and laughter are prayers, too.

Though I am glad to see him, I know that the next morning we will go to town to shop. I don't like to go to town, especially when Momma and I ride the bus. We have to sit in the back, and if Momma talks to me, her voice is small and tight, as if her throat is lined with dust that water cannot wash away. She never talks much on the bus, though. So I sit and read the sign over the bus driver's head:

WHITE SEAT FROM THE FRONT
COLORED SEAT FROM THE REAR

Daddy doesn't like us to ride the bus.

"What was I supposed to do, Reverend Lester?" Momma will say. "You said you were coming Wednesday, and when you didn't, I got up Thursday morning and Julius and I went to town. There were things Momma needed."

"Wasn't nothing so important that you couldn't have waited one more day," he answers.

"How was I to know if you were going to be delayed a day or another week?"

"You didn't. But I don't want you riding on the back of no bus!"

When Daddy takes us to town, Momma's thin lips are not pressed together more tightly than the boards of Grandmomma's house. I still don't want to go, however. It is hotter in town and Daddy won't let me drink out of the colored water fountains in the stores. He won't buy me an RC or Dr Pepper, either. There were no soda machines in those days and the only places to buy cold drinks were at the colored windows of cafés or diners. Daddy says only "common Negroes" go to the colored windows, Negroes who don't care about themselves, who don't have any pride and let the white man treat them like dirt, and he will let me die of thirst before I drink a soda bought at a colored window.

On many of those hot summer days, dying of thirst seemed imminent. Yet I do not recall being angry with Daddy or thinking him mean. His anger taught me that though we were powerless to change segregation, we would not freely choose it. His anger was self-respect and we took pride in knowing that Lesters did not use COLORED toilets, drink from COLORED fountains, walk through doorways with signs reading COLORED ENTRANCE, buy anything from a COLORED WINDOW, and at home, in Kansas City, Kansas, I walked to and from downtown rather than ride in the back of the bus.

We are walking along a street in downtown Pine Bluff one hot summer day. I see a large round clock jutting from a store front. Curved over the top are the letters A-L-T-S-C-H-U-L. Curved at the bottom is the word JEWELERS.

"Momma! That's the name on Grandmomma's mailbox!"

My excitement is met with a long silence. Finally Daddy chuckles softly. "Those are your cousins," he says.

When we are driving back to Grandmomma's he says, "Your great-grandfather was a Jew. Altschul. That's a German-Jewish name. He was married to your great-grandmother. She was a slave. Not when they met, of course. His name was Adolph. Your grandmother was one of his daughters and your uncle Rudolph was one of his sons. That's how come they look like white people. You remember your uncle Charlie?"

I recall being taken to a tiny apartment in Chicago one hot

Sunday afternoon where a tall, white-looking man was introduced to me as "your uncle Charlie." I looked up at his dour face, wondering what he had to do with me.

"He's an Altschul, too. Your aunt Rena was an Altschul before she married your uncle Fate. There was another girl, Julia. She's dead now. Your momma was named for her and you were named for your momma. Then there was Ada and Florence. Florence moved away somewhere, passed for white and nobody has seen or heard from her since.

"Well, the way the story goes is that Adolph came over here from Germany at some time or another and him and his brothers somehow made their way down here to Pine Bluff and Adolph became a peddler. He went around through the countryside selling things off a horse and wagon. That must've been how he met your great-grandmother. This was not too many years after slavery and him and your great-grandmother—her name was Maggie. Maggie Carson. A little bitty woman who looked like she was white. Well, somehow she and your great-grandfather met up with one another. His brothers disowned him for marrying her. But I always respected Adolph for that. Back in them times he didn't have to marry her if he didn't want to, but he did the Christian thing, even if he was a Jew. When he died, his brothers came and got his body and buried him in the Jewish cemetery somewhere here in Pine Bluff. I don't see how come they did that. They didn't want to have nothing to do with him when he was alive. I think sometimes about going and digging him up and burying him out there in the family cemetery next to your great-grandmother. That's where he belongs.

"That store we passed, well, the ones that own it are the descendants of them brothers. They're your blood relatives." He chuckled. "But don't you go marching in the store and call them cousin. They'd pretend like they didn't know what you were talking about. Your mother knew your great-grandfather, you know."

"What was he like, Momma?" I ask eagerly.

"He was a very nice man," she says in that proper way when she doesn't want to talk about something, or doesn't know how she feels about it, and maybe that's the same thing. "I was just a little girl, so I don't remember much. But I remember when my father died, and don't start asking me about him because I remember less about him than I do about Grandfather. But when our father died,

I remember Grandfather came and got us and brought us out here where Momma lives now. And that's where we lived from then on."

My great-grandfather was a Jew, I say to myself. I don't know what that means, not if meaning is confined to words and concepts. But meaning is also feeling and sensation and wonder and questions.

Altschul. I can say it now. Altschul.

# 2

After Daddy's death I find among his possessions a large photograph of the church he pastored in Kansas City, Kansas, and next door to it, the parsonage. They are the only two buildings on that side of the block.

"How bleak," my wife says when I show it to her some months later.

I look again. There are no people on the street. The trees are topped and leafless; the sky is as gray as grief. The church is a massive rectangle of huge stones as dully gray and heavy as the sky. Two stories high, it extends from the corner of Ninth and Oakland for three-quarters of the block up Ninth Street. It looks as impregnable, immovable and eternal as a mausoleum. Next to it the frame parsonage huddles as if recoiling from the prospect of such an eternity. I was taken into that house two years after my birth in St. Louis, Missouri, and we lived there until I was nine.

Looking at the photograph, my wife's comment resounding through me, I see a childhood as heavy and gray as the stones of the church, as bare and lifeless as the trees, a childhood pruned and pruned again until who I might have been is not even a memory in my veins.

The home of my childhood is as if it never was. I remember the twin bunk beds in which my brother and I slept, but not the room. Were there pictures on the wall? Where did I hang my clothes? Where is the dresser which I opened each morning to get a clean pair of underwear? Was there a box for my toys? Did I have toys? Of course I did, but what has memory done with them?

I do not have memories of people in that house—no sounds of conversation or laughter, no odors of food cooking. I see myself sitting at the piano, and on the floor in front of the big Philco console radio listening to "Inner Sanctum," "Beulah," and "Amos 'n' Andy," but where did we eat every day?

Yet I was at Grandmomma's for no more than a month each summer, but every detail of her house, the nuances of the heat of the day, the smell of dust and sounds of bees in the heavy air, the textures of silences from waking through sleeping are integral to my daily journeys through memory.

Was there no separation between life in that house and the church next door? Only now do I understand that there was not. Daddy was not a pious man and our house was not burdened by family prayer meetings and nightly Bible readings. But he was deeply religious and the word *God* appeared in conversations as casually as milk, broom and weather. My children ask me about my childhood, and I am embarrassed and annoyed when images and their attendant emotions slide from memory as if I am being born only when I think of church and Sundays.

Sunday mornings begin with Momma's voice pulling me up from sleep as if I am a fish on a hook. (Momma supervised my getting dressed and recalled to my wife with pride once that she never allowed me to get dirty. It is almost as if the memories of slavery in our blood demanded perpetual cleanliness as expiation. My shirts had creases, and during my first marriage, my wife pronounced me crazy for expecting her to iron my underwear. I hadn't known that the people I passed each day on the street wore wrinkled ones.)

At breakfast Daddy prays for God to protect us "in health and in life, because one of us might not be here next Sunday morning." At nine-thirty I go with Momma next door and into the basement of the church for Sunday school. I am not a child who asks embarrassing questions about the nature of God, or anything else. I believe and accept what I am told, and when my fifth grade teacher tells us about dinosaurs, I am so outraged that I form an after-school study group to "prove" that dinosaurs never existed because they are not mentioned in the Bible. However, I do correct my Sunday school teachers when they are wrong. I know the Bible, or at least the Old Testament, my favorite part.

At ten forty-five Sunday school ends and I go up to the sanctuary where Momma teaches her class. If she is not finished I sit quietly and wait. Sometimes I go to Daddy's study to tell him all the mistakes my Sunday school teacher made. If he is busy elsewhere in the church I sit at his desk as if it will be mine one day, which neither of us doubts.

Church service begins always with the singing of "Holy, Holy, Holy," and, bored by the song, I stare at Daddy. The pulpit is curved and wide, occupying nearly half of the front of the sanctuary. Daddy sits alone at the center in a massive, high-backed chair. In his black robe he looks like an omnipotent prince. Momma and I sit in the third pew to his left, and I believe he sees me even when his eyes are closed in prayer. If I think about being restless it seems that he looks over at me and my body stiffens. There are members of the church, I am sure, who still chuckle about the time my brother was making noise during service. Daddy stopped preaching, came out of the pulpit, took off his belt, beat my brother, and put his belt back on, returned to the pulpit and resumed his sermon in mid-shout! (I am certain I was there that Sunday—where else would I have been?—but that memory, too, has been quarantined in some room which I cannot find and to which I do not have a key.)

In the 1940s a black minister was the recognized and accepted authority in the community—the enforcer of divine law, adjudicator of disputes, provider for the poor, intermediary between the white and the black communities. He knew the words that gave one person the strength to carry a sorrow that could never be relieved and those to scare a sinner out of hell. He was expected to respond to any plea for help, even if it wasn't from a church member. When Jimmy Bell got drunk on Saturday nights and sought to leave the signs of his manhood on his wife's face and body, she ran to our house as if it were a cathedral whose portals the enemy could not cross. It was, because Jimmy Bell sobered instantly when he stood on the porch before my father and promised to treat his wife better. (He always did, until the next Saturday night. One Saturday night she didn't make it to our porch and died in the alley, a knife in her belly.)

The white community regarded the black minister as a tribal leader. I accepted it as normal that Daddy went to court and on his word alone the judge paroled young black men into his custody, or waived bail. No wonder he sat in the pulpit as if he were the creator of life and death.

The black minister embodied—in the way he dressed, talked and walked—the dreams and hopes and aspirations of a people who carried these as if they were illicit contraband that had to be smuggled past hostile guards. That was why I seldom saw Daddy without a suit and a tie on. He exuded dignity as if it were everyone's birthright and people would say, "Reverend Lester, I feels better sometimes just by looking at you."

As his sons my brother and I were expected to be his representatives in miniature. Among my father's belongings I found a booklet commemorating the sixty-fifth anniversary of the church during the winter of 1944. I would have been five years old. In it there is a short section about me and my brother: "Parsonage children have their problems. They have to live with 'One Foot in Heaven,' but these boys find it a source of joy." The paragraph continues with a few words about my brother, and then says of me: "Julius is just fine. He can read a little and count money. He attends Sunday school and stays for church. He knows practically all the members."

I remember going into a back room after church each Sunday, walking in with all the authority I have as Reverend Lester's younger son, sitting down at the table where the men are counting the money from the collection plates, and being given the pennies to count. A normal child would have raced outside after church to play with the other kids. I am the minister's son and I am admitted to the world of men and act like one. Every Sunday someone says, "He's just like you, Reverend Lester!," or "You gon' be a preacher like your daddy!"

In that sixty-fifth-anniversary booklet there is a picture of the Sunday school teachers. In the middle is Daddy in a dark suit and clerical collar. I stand in front of him, my head barely coming to his belt buckle. I have on a dark coat and am staring directly at the camera, intent and serious. It is no expression for a child. I look closely at the photograph and notice both of Daddy's hands on my shoulders. There is no affection in those hands, but control, power, dominance, and I submit gratefully: This is my father, I am his.

I do not enjoy living with "One Foot in Heaven," being God's representative among my peers as Daddy was among us all. But, unlike my brother, I do not hate it. That is simply how things are and to quarrel with how things are is to think you can box with God and win.

Yet I do not like church, do not understand why the people

shout and "get happy" and scream, "Yes, Lord!," do not understand why one old man "gets happy" and trots around the sanctuary muttering, "Thank you, Jesus! Thank you, Jesus!," do not understand the lady who always throws her pocketbook into the choir loft when she "gets happy."

Nor do I like to look at the cross affixed to the wall behind the pulpit. Jesus died on that cross for my sins and I wonder if there is something wrong with me for not understanding. I accept what Daddy preaches about Jesus, afraid I will not be saved if I don't. Yet God knows that I do not understand and when I die I will go to hell anyway where I will burn with all the other sinners.

I hope God is not angry that Jesus is less real to me than the giant in *Jack and the Beanstalk*. God knows that I love the story about David and Goliath and sometimes fantasize that I am Jacob meeting Rachel at the well, or Elijah in the valley of the dry bones, or Joseph putting on his many-colored coat. That should count for something, shouldn't it, God?

I am seven or eight years old when it happens. One night Momma and Daddy are at a meeting in church and leave me in Daddy's office. Mrs. Hilda McIntosh, a church member, brings her daughter, Voynez, to the meeting, and tells her to wait in the office with me. I sit behind Daddy's desk, Voynez in the chair next to it.

She asks me to read from the Bible to her. I open the one on Daddy's desk and turn to the Book of Psalms, my favorite. Whenever I read or hear its wholehearted love and praise I am so happy that my body wants to jump up and down, dance, turn flips, spin around and around until I collapse in laughter as lilting as sunlight on a wheat field.

*O Lord our Lord, how excellent is thy name in all the earth! who hast set thy glory in the heavens.*

Voynez asks me what that means. I look at her, annoyed, wondering why she isn't crying at this beauty that is too great to carry. I tell her she is dumb. As soon as I say it, I am sorry, but don't tell her that. I am too angry and I snap the Bible shut, slam it on Daddy's desk and tell her I am going home.

I rush angrily from the study, down the steps and out the door. Suddenly my head is like a balloon into which helium is being blown, and though it is night, I float languidly into a deeper blackness that comes up from the bowels of the earth and my body bends to meet it, to embrace it . . .

I open my eyes. Daddy is looking down at me. His face is tense, pinched. Next to him I am surprised to see Doctor Love. Momma stands beside him, her face a mirror of Daddy's.

I am lying on the dining room table, my shirt off. I hear someone snicker. Voynez! What is she doing here? Her mother is standing beside her. Why am I on the table with my shirt off? I fold my arms over my tiny chest.

Doctor Love wants to know how I feel.

Fine, I tell him.

Daddy asks what happened.

I don't know.

"I caught you just as you started falling," he says. "Voynez came back to where we were having the meeting and I asked her where you were and she said you went home. I couldn't understand why you'd do that since you knew nobody was there and the house was locked. I rushed out and caught you just as you started to fall."

Mother wants to know if I can sit up.

I do. I ask for my shirt so Voynez will stop giggling.

I go upstairs to get ready for bed.

A little while later, Daddy comes in. "How're you feeling?" he asks, concern in his voice.

"Fine," I say, getting beneath the covers.

He puts his big, rough hand on my forehead. "You don't seem to have a temperature," he says. He removes his hand. "Doctor Love couldn't find anything the matter with you. He and I went over to the church to see if that old gas stove in my study might have a leak, but we didn't smell any gas. Did you?"

"No, sir."

He is silent for a moment. "What were you and Voynez doing in there?"

I know what he is thinking because his voice sounds like he doesn't want to ask and doesn't want me to answer. But I wouldn't do whatever it is boys do with girls, and I certainly wouldn't do it in church, even if I knew what it was. "We weren't doing anything. I was reading the Bible to her and she asked me a dumb question. I got angry, slammed the Bible down and walked out."

He doesn't speak for the longest time. He looks at me and then looks away. When he finally speaks his voice is quiet, almost hollow, and more serious even than when he prays. "Don't ever slam the Bible down again."

His seriousness is like a cold, sharp wind and I can only nod my head and manage a halting "Yes, sir."

He doesn't move to leave but remains standing, as if there is something else he wants to say but the words are outside my window, caught in the darkness, and can't get free to come to him. In the silence a fear crawls over my flesh like a long-legged spider and I understand in the hollows and crevices and caves of my soul: God has chosen me for Himself.

But I don't tell Daddy.

# 3

I am eight or nine years old. I am playing Bach on the upright piano in the living room. Though it is a simplified arrangement of a Bach fugue, the lines of music move away from and back to each other, never merging or separating, like windblown ribbons on the tail of a kite. I forget that I am playing, and I slip through the lines to the other side of the music where I understand all that was, is and will be. When the music ends, however, I return to this side and cannot remember what I understood.

I love Bach's music more than that of any composer, but my favorite composition is in a thick book Momma bought me. There is no composer's name and I do not know how to pronounce the title because it is in a foreign language. Every day after I finish practicing, I play it over and over. It is not lines or chords; neither does it move, but it does not stand still. It simply is. It is happy and sad at the same time. I play and beauty becomes pain and then beauty again and in a half-step is inverted into pain once more until beauty and pain wrap around each other like the braids of a girl's hair, and beauty and pain become a piercing that holds me pinioned and I feel old like "In the beginning," old as if I was never born and will never die. The music winds itself around me and wants to take me somewhere, but I am afraid and do not go. When I stop playing there is a painful yearning in my stomach, a wishing for something I have never had and thus do not know what it is, or a wishing for something which I had once and have forgotten what it was. The name of the composition is "*Kol Nidre*." It is a Hebrew melody.

I am eight or nine and sit on the floor in the living room before the big Philco console. The news announcer says that Sammy Davis, Jr., has converted to Judaism. "I'm going to do that someday," I say to myself.

As I began work on this book, I wanted to know the precise year of Davis's conversion and read his autobiography, *Yes, I Can,* to find it. He does not give one, but mentions that he converted a few months before beginning work on the film version of *Porgy and Bess,* which was released in 1958. Given the time between the making of a film and its release, Davis converted in 1956 or '57. I was a senior in high school, a freshman or even sophomore in college.

Why, in memory, do I see myself, even now, sitting on the floor before that console radio hearing a news broadcaster say that Sammy Davis, Jr., "the Negro entertainer," has become a Jew? I wanted to call up Sammy and tell him he was wrong, that I was a little boy when he converted, not an aging adolescent pestering God to tell me the meaning of life.

Did I think the memory was safer in childhood where I would not have the responsibility to the declaration that Davis's conversion evoked from me? Or was the yearning to be Jewish so confusing and disorienting that I put it in the void of my childhood to shine like a tiny flame over a grave?

There is another memory:

Christmas Day, 1951. I am twelve years old. Momma hands me her present. It is big and thick and heavy. A book! Neatly but quickly, I remove the wrapping paper and stare in wonder at the thick wine and gray-colored volume. Along its spine are the intimidating words *The Complete Plays of William Shakespeare.*

I thank Momma effusively. She smiles. "You might want to start by reading the play called *The Merchant of Venice.*"

Why did she suggest that? If I were recommending a play of Shakespeare's to a twelve-year-old child of mine, it would be *Romeo and Juliet.* But *Merchant of Venice* with its two complex plots? Was Momma thinking of her grandfather?

I stretch out on the living-room couch and begin reading. The language is too complex for me to follow the play's subtleties, or even to appreciate the extraordinary language. I do not know even what a money-lender or interest is, but I know that Shylock is being mistreated because he is a Jew.

I eat Christmas dinner quickly, angry at what is being done to Shylock. I return to the couch, and when I come to the climactic scene in which Shylock is allowed a pound of flesh if he does not shed a drop of blood, I am outraged! I try to imagine a knife blade as thin as the wind and as keen as hope, but when I apply it oh so gently to flesh, lo, blood flows.

Shylock. How odd that in him I encounter myself in literature for the first time. It is odd because I did not grow up unaware of black history and literature. The segregated schools of Kansas City, Kansas, were secret training camps for the black leaders of the next generation. In second grade the teacher played Paul Robeson's records. In fifth and sixth grades we learned about W. E. B. Du Bois, Booker T. Washington, George Washington Carver, Mary McLeod Bethune. In junior high school we memorized poems by Countee Cullen and James Weldon Johnson. Daddy subscribed to *Ebony* magazine and there were books by and about blacks on his bookshelves, books I read.

Yet in Shylock I see myself as I do not in Du Bois, Johnson, Langston Hughes, Robeson or any other black figure. Is it because they are models of success and I need a model of suffering, someone to reflect a child's pain and confusion at being condemned because of the race into which I was born, someone whose anger at outrageous injustice gives me permission to be angry and through that anger begin to defend my soul? Or is it simply that through Shylock I learn that blacks are not the only people in the world who must ponder in their flesh the meaning of meaningless suffering?

# 4

## Summer 1953

We move to Nashville, Tennessee.

Because of my summers at Grandmomma's I hate that land in which blacks working the cotton fields look like slaves, where white men stare with eyes as tiny and unblinking as snakes', where stillness and silence lie on the flat land as if the land itself clutches secrets it can never relinquish because we would die, all of us, black and white, if we knew them.

Each summer when we cross the state line from Missouri into Arkansas, I read the sign that says:

WELCOME TO ARKANSAS
Land of Opportunity

Invariably Daddy says, "Land of opportunity if you're a peckerwood." Invariably Mother protests: "Don't talk that way, Reverend Lester." I am only a child but know Daddy is right, know that whoever created the state slogan was not thinking of me and would not understand if I could tell him that the sign is an official proclamation of my nonexistence. I am only a child, but I know. Now I am to live in that land where my nonexistence is not only assumed but demanded.

I do not want to live where ancient memories of black deaths pull at my clothes with fleshless, bony fingers and slavery clings to my hair like spiderwebs. But Daddy has been offered the position of Director of Negro Affairs for the Board of Evangelism of the Methodist Church, and its headquarters are in Nashville. He will be the only nonwhite there. It is an important job, and I am more than willing for him to move to Nashville, leaving Momma and me in Kansas City.

"I hate the South!" I tell him in an unusual outburst of emotion and candor one afternoon as we carry boxes of trash to the alley preparatory to moving.

He nods. How could he not know? I have grown up listening to his stories of lynchings and brutality, of risks and escapes, of small, unseen triumphs and humiliations vaster than hope. I have witnessed some of the humiliations in our travels in the South and remember sitting in the backseat of the car when Daddy was stopped for speeding, and watched and listened as the policeman forced him to say "Yassuh," words Daddy never said to any white man. His anger burned for two weeks afterward like a fire that could not be extinguished.

For other black men, getting gas may have been a simple business transaction and they were willing to endure a little humiliation. Not Daddy. How I dreaded it when we needed gas. Daddy would drive slowly past several filling stations, looking closely at each one before deciding which appeared to offer him treatment as a human being. When he pulled in and stopped at the pumps, he would say, "I'd like to fill up and my wife and son would like to use the facilities."

"I don't need to go to the bathroom, Reverend Lester," Momma always whispered.

Daddy ignored her. If the attendant pointed toward the rear of the station, or said, "They can go around back," Daddy would say, "Like hell," and press the accelerator. That happened often. He would go to three, four gas stations and sometimes was not able to find one where the attendant said that the rest rooms were inside, indicating he did not have a separate one for blacks.

There were also the occasions when Daddy did not get a chance to ask, because if the white man walked up to the car and said, "How many gallons, boy?," Daddy spat out, "Not a damn one, Sam," and pressed the accelerator to the floor. An incident like that meant only a week of anger singeing my edges.

Now my time has come to talk to white men so they will think I am saying "Yassuh" when I'm not, to say "Yassuh" when there is no alternative, to walk with my head bowed, my eyes on the pavement so no white woman walking or driving past will accuse me of leering at her. (That's what Daddy told me after Mack Ingram was arrested that year. Ingram was a farmer in North Carolina. One morning he was plowing a field. In the distance a white woman walked along the road. Later that day Ingram was arrested for "assault by leering." He was convicted and sentenced to life in prison. His conviction and sentence were later overturned.)

White women are the deepest terror. What a white woman says is truth even when it is a lie. How do I assert my existence if nothing I say is believed as truth, if death has blue eyes, long yellow hair glistening like destiny, and skin as pale as hope?

(Since 1975 I have taught a course on the history of the Civil Rights Movement. When I describe life in the South before The Movement, globules of pain like phlegm come to my throat and tears flare in my eyes, and I am aware of a massive trauma of anger and terror within me. This is not the melodrama of rhetoric; it is the consequence of surviving in a land where terror was as omnipresent as sunlight and starshine.

(You do not make friends with terror. You can defy it, challenge it. There was a black photographer in The Movement who rode all over Mississippi on his motorcycle the summer of 1964, his blond girlfriend behind him, her arms tightly around his waist. One day some white men beat him almost to death, and he left Mississippi. You can laugh and joke with terror, a time-honored technique that Southern blacks refined into an art form. Or you can try to reach an agreement with it, as in the famous blues line: "Got one mind for the captain to see, got another mind for what I know is me." That is most dangerous of all, because it is a statement of functional schizophrenia, of the psyche divided against itself. Ultimately, you become your own victim and never know it.

(I chose invisibility and walked as if I did not occupy my body, and talked in the polite tones of a string quartet. I even practiced breathing so that my chest would not rise and fall as I inhaled and exhaled.

(Nothing could mitigate the ontological terror of nonexistence, the unending trauma of being damned in the flesh. The only salvation was to learn to live outside the terror. Daddy taught me how.)

That day as we stack trash, Daddy brushes off his hands and looks at me. "I know you don't want to move to the South," he says gently. "I'm not too keen on the idea myself. But you don't know what God has in store for you down there."

But who was God? And how could I know that what Daddy said God wanted for me was what God wanted?

## September 1956

I enter Fisk University and the first week of my freshman year I see what I think is the most beautiful girl in all of creation light a cigarette. (Her name was Myrna Rivers.) God, Daddy had said, condemned women who smoke as sinners. After thirty seconds of inner theological debate I conclude that any God who would send a woman that beautiful to hell because she smokes should have His head examined.

Such a mundane beginning for a spiritual journey, but in that instant of rejecting the morality of my father's God, a heretical thought follows: "What if there isn't a God at all?"

Before the end of the first semester I have begun to read Plato and Sartre, to study theories about the origin of the universe, and am quickly convinced that there isn't a God. I dutifully inform Daddy. He asks me where I think the trees and all of nature came from. I respond with a capsule summary of the Big Bang theory. In disgust and anger, he says that all *he* has comes from God and therefore everything *I* have comes from God, too. If I do not believe in God, I am obviously prepared to go out and work for a living.

This is a proof for the existence of God I had overlooked. We stand and glare at each other for long seconds until he asks if I understand that he can't allow me to go around saying I am an atheist. How can he be telling people about God if his son is arguing against God? We reach a compromise. I can believe what I want as long as I go to church every Sunday and don't embarrass him by saying publicly that I am an atheist. I marvel at Daddy's wisdom. My declaration of atheism has been like a knife in his heart, but he keeps his hands off my soul.

The God of my father is dead, but instead of exulting in the freedom of defining my essence, I am surprised to find myself paralyzed by despair and depression. How do I live now that there is not a God?

I do not know, but suddenly I find that I do not know how to live at all because I am learning just how much I am a child of the South.

I watch Northern black students strut around campus as though being black is not a deformed hump between their shoulders. They talk in classes as if they belong in the world of ideas with Plato and Descartes as equals. I have never heard of Faulkner, Cervantes, Mann, Hemingway, Spinoza, Marx. (I am afraid to attempt to say "Descartes," at least not until I know why the "esses" are not pronounced.) My classmates from Detroit, Chicago and New York discuss these writers and thinkers as if they are neighbors who keep an eye on their houses when they go on vacation. My thoughts are like simple sentences in a foreign language, and I cannot speak in classes.

The Northern blacks have gone to school with whites; they come from places where slavery is not even a memory. What is it like, I wonder with awe, to grow up sitting beside white people on buses, to eat in any restaurant, not to see each and every white person as your potential murderer? They tell me about the white girls they dated in high school, and even in their telling I fear for their lives. Why have they come here, to Nashville, Tennessee, and Fisk University, where slavery's echoes shatter the sky with each rising of the sun? They say they have come to be with their people. I don't understand.

One afternoon during the spring of that first year I am walking across campus when I hear a girl call my name. I look up, and there, at the corner by the chapel, is Roma Jones, waving to me.

I can't believe she has called my name. Roma? Roma with dark eyes so filled with intelligence that they are flames that will consume me if I am not careful? Roma who speaks so rapidly and precisely and brilliantly that words leap from her mouth like stars being sprinkled across the deep of the heavens at creation?

She is a senior from Chicago and I am in danger of dying from terminal heartache and galloping acne from love of her. The mere fact that she called my name is consummation of the relationship.

"Hi!" She greets me brightly. "I'm going to visit a synagogue. Want to come?"

I would read poetry to a brussels sprout if Roma asked.

I don't ask why she is going to a synagogue. I don't even ask what a synagogue is.

It turns out to be an unattractive square building on West End Avenue (no kin to New York's street of the same name). To the right of the entrance a large funny-looking metal candleholder is affixed to the brick face.

A disheveled-looking man meets us at the door and introduces himself as the rabbi. I shake his hand indifferently and follow him and Roma into the sanctuary. It is a large room with pews. That is its only resemblance to a church. There are no stained-glass windows, no crosses affixed to the walls and no altar. I don't even see an organ, piano or choir loft.

The rabbi and Roma are quickly engaged in animated conversation. I sulk, wondering why Roma wanted me to come, since she scarcely said a word to me on the drive from campus. She certainly isn't acting like the experienced older woman who is going to relieve me of the indignity of my virginity.

"I'm not supposed to do this, but . . ." I hear the rabbi say.

He walks to the back of the pulpit to where a curtain is closed and draws it aside. "These are the scrolls of our Torah," he says quietly.

The open curtain reveals an incision in the back wall inside of which are three large cylinders in velvet covers. I stare at them and it is like gazing into a mirror. What are those scrolls? I want to ask. What is the Torah? What do you do with the scrolls?

Now I know. I have been called to the *bimah** on Saturday mornings and holy days for an *aliyah** and watched as the *baal korei** chants from the open Torah scroll. I have carried the scroll on Simchat Torah* and on Saturday mornings. I have lifted the Torah while the congregation sang "*V'zot ha-torah asher sam Moshe lifnay b'nai Yisrael al pi Adonai b'yad Moshe.*" ("This is the Torah which Moses placed before the children of Israel, at the command of the Lord.") Yet even now the feeling is the same as on the afternoon in the synagogue in Nashville—a surge of sudden and wondrous love whose name I did not know.

*Asterisk denotes the first mention of words that can be found in the Glossary on pages 245–248.

When the rabbi draws the curtain closed, however, and the scrolls of the Torah disappear from sight, the sudden and wondrous love vanishes, too, and my attention turns immediately back to Roma, who still shows no sign of wanting to seduce me.

She never did.

## Autumn 1957

I cannot make peace with my murder of God. And yet I cannot return to that God of my father who is like some CPA of Morality recording every curse word I say, every evil thought and sinful impulse. So I study other religions and ways of conceiving the universe. I read the *Bhagavad-Gita* and Zen Buddhism; I study Japanese flower arranging and the tea ceremony, read and write haiku. Hermann Hesse's *Siddhartha* is an important companion for a while. The most important book, however, is Aldous Huxley's *The Perennial Philosophy*. In that gentle compendium of quotes from the mystical tradition of the world's religions, I learn that beneath the rituals, beliefs and practices of them all is a common ground, an identical core of experience: the direct apprehension of God. (I did not notice at the time that Huxley omitted any reference to Judaism.)

## Autumn 1958

It is a mouse-gray day, the kind only an English major finds romantic. Rhoda Miller, a fellow English major, thrusts a book in my hand and says, "Read this." I am beginning the third year of a monumental crush on Rhoda, so I read it, thinking it will give me something to talk about with her. The book is called *Exodus*.

When I finish, I tell her, "I think I could die for Israel. If any people deserve a country of their own, it's Jews."

She agrees, but when I ask her for a date, she says no, yet again. I conclude reluctantly that if she won't go on a date with me, she probably won't go to Israel and live on a kibbutz with me either.

Through *Exodus* I learn for the first time about the six million Jews killed during my childhood, killed in places whose names I am not sure how to say—Auschwitz, Birkenau, Babi Yar, Treblinka. How could I have lived for nineteen years and no one tell me that six million Jews were deliberately murdered, with malice aforethought?

*Exodus* is also the story of how Israel was reborn, of Jews transforming stony soil into verdant gardens, of defending themselves with their minds and guns and, after two thousand years, living once more in the land God promised them. I was nine years old when Israel became a state again, and remember a black diplomat, an aristocratic-looking man who negotiated the end of the war that allowed Israel to be, and how proud I was of Ralph Bunche's achievement, especially after he was awarded the Nobel Peace Prize.

What most deeply affects me in the novel, however, is the love story. Not the one between Ari, the Israeli, and Kitty, the American nurse, but the one about a people and God and a land. I feel a part of that love.

## Spring 1959

I am an exchange student at San Diego State College for a semester, living in the apartment of the campus Methodist minister with students from Thailand, Panama and Jordan.

Khalid Tuck-Tuck is a Palestinian who begins each day with an anti-Semitic diatribe. I have never known an individual so tortured by anger and hatred.

One afternoon I am sitting on the couch in the living room, studying. Tuck comes out of the bedroom and sits down at the other end. "You should have seen the orange groves around my house in Jaffa. My family owned acres and acres of orange trees."

I have heard it from him many times by now. In a moment he will start talking about how the Jews kicked his family out, and then he will start crying.

"The goddamn Jews! The goddamn Jews came and took it all away from us!"

I look at him and the moisture of tears is on his eyelashes.

"You don't know the Jews like I do. They want to control the world. All they care about is themselves." He wipes at his eyes.

I stare at him coldly.

"I wish Hitler had finished what he started!" Tuck explodes, springing from the couch to stand over me.

I look up at him. I do not know that I am humming "*Hava Nagila*" until Tuck screams, "I hate that song!"

It is popular at the coffeehouse I frequent in La Jolla. I hum it louder. The next thing I know Tuck's hands are around my neck, his thumbs at my throat. I begin to sing, in strangled tones, "*Hava nagila, hava nagila.*" He squeezes tighter, screaming at me, "Fucking Jew! Fucking Jew!"

Edmundo rushes from the bedroom and pulls Tuck from me. I rub my throat. My eyes are blurry with tears, but I resume singing, "*Hava nagila, hava nagila,*" my voice strained and weak, my throat aching. But the melody is on key and the words distinct.

"Julius!" Edmundo snaps. "Get the hell out of here!"

I pick up my book and with insolent casualness walk past Tuck, whom Edmundo is holding, my voice getting stronger. "*Hava n'ranana! Hava n'ranana!*" The words and melody trail behind me like pink flower petals.

Tuck and I become close friends. He never talks about Jews and Palestine to me again, and if I hear myself beginning to hum "*Hava Nagila*" in his presence, I stop.

June. I am on a train going from Los Angeles to San Francisco. On one side are mountains as rugged and terrifying as death, tumbling down to the skirts of the ocean, which flings itself at the mountains. Between them, two rails of steel as fragile as the fragment of a dream. Suddenly I know that I am nothing. It is not the emptiness of nonexistence in History. This is a Nothingness-of-Relationship, a void so deeply black that it glistens and burns and palpitates until I acquiesce and submit, until I know, with that knowledge for which there is no understanding: I am nothing compared to the merest fleck of froth on the waves, waves that crashed into the mountains before there was anyone to see them, waves that would crash into the mountains whether anyone ever saw them. Who am I in the midst of all that? I dutifully inform Daddy that I believe in God again, but I don't. One believes in what can be known. It is not that I have faith now. I do, but faith is a bridge from the known to the unknown. Belief and faith are not the same as knowing the terror of the Unknown and Unknowable. That infinite aloneness into which I was lowered as a child has returned; it is here I must learn to live.

## Spring 1960

Dr. Rosey Poole is a Dutch scholar of black poetry, but she is at Fisk to speak about a Dutch-Jewish girl she taught and whose diary she translated. The girl's name is Anne Frank. Dr. Poole is not Jewish, but she was part of the Dutch Resistance movement and her parents were murdered by the Nazis.

As I listen to her talk of a child hiding in an attic, my imagination topples from its perch as if it were a boulder on a mountainside dislodged by unseen stresses from the earth's core. I understand her accented words, but they do not make sense. I do not know how to live with the knowledge of such evil and such suffering.

A few days later I sit on the side porch of Robert Hayden's house. He is a poet and teaches creative writing, Victorian literature and early twentieth-century American literature. He has instructed me in the terrors a writer faces, the life lived in the belly of self-doubt, the life that might require you to sacrifice yourself and anyone else to the demon within.

He asks me what I thought of Dr. Poole's talk. What am I supposed to say? It was good? I enjoyed it? "It's hard to believe," I say finally.

"We think we know something about suffering," he says, stuffing tobacco into his stubby pipe. "We don't know what suffering means, Julius." His protruding eyes peer at me intently through the thick lenses of his glasses as he lights the pipe and puffs at it until the tobacco glows red. "We don't know a damned thing about suffering." He pauses. "Well, that's not true. Maybe it's a problem of language." He laughs. "But isn't that always the problem?" There is another long silence. "Maybe I'm not comfortable using the same word 'suffering' to describe what we have gone through and what the Jews have gone through. Do you know I mean?"

I think about riding on the backs of buses, the signs telling me where I can and can't eat, what I can and can't do. I think about being afraid to look white women in the eyes. Then I think about living in an attic, unable to go outside. I think about gas chambers and furnaces into which human beings were shoveled like waste paper. "I think so," I say finally.

"I'm not saying that Jews have suffered more. How can you measure what a human being suffers? But there is a difference, and we need a word to make that difference clear." He chuckles. "Are you sure you still want to be a writer? That's what writing is, you know. Finding the right word."

How can I find the right word when I don't know what that word is to describe? All I have are images of naked bodies stacked in hills beneath sunny skies. Being forced to ride at the back of a bus is not in the same realm of human experience.

Yet I am not wholly comfortable with that formulation. Jews had to wear yellow Stars of David on their clothes to be identified as Jews. My yellow star is in my skin. I am alive, however, and Anne Frank is not.

There is an aura of unreality about our conversation. We sit on his side porch relaxing in the languid and heavy beauty of spring, talking about suffering, about Jews, about what it is to be black while the city of Nashville is undergoing a social revolution. He and I are not part of it.

Since February students from Fisk and the other black colleges have been demonstrating to desegregate the lunch counters and restaurants downtown. But I have not sat-in at one lunch counter, or come close to being arrested for anything, and I am ashamed.

I tried to talk to Mr. Hayden about it. He said, "You're a writer. Anybody can sit-in at a lunch counter. But not anybody can do what you can do, which is write. James Joyce's job was to write *Finnegans Wake*, not write political tracts or go on a demonstration. I'm a poet. I can make a political speech and demonstrate with the best, but that's not my job!"

I was not convinced. Was he saying *Finnegans Wake* was worth the lives of murdered Jews? I knew he was not, but he valued literature in a way I never would.

What I really need to know is: Why do I rage over and mourn for murdered European Jews as I never have for my own people? But I am afraid to ask him, afraid he will not understand the question as I do not.

I sit on a stool in the kitchen watching Momma move back and forth from the stove to the sink to the refrigerator preparing supper. In a month I will be a college graduate with a B.A. in English. At this moment, however, I am a little boy again, needing to tell her something important and able to do so only from within the safety of mixing bowls and flour-dusted hands, a warm oven and the gentle blue flames of gas-stove burners.

"I want to be a monk," I say hesitantly.

"Monks don't do anything," she replies after a long pause, her back to me as she washes her hands in the sink.

"Momma!" I exclaim, my voice rising and cracking, to my embarrassment. "That's all you talk about. 'Do!' That's not everything, you know."

"What else is there?" She turns to look at me as she dries her hands on a paper towel.

Doesn't she know, she who reads the Bible every night before going to sleep?

In the year since God showed me my need of Him on the train going up the California coast, I have read Evelyn Underhill's *Mysticism*, Meister Eckhart, Pascal's *Pensées*, Paul Tillich's *The Dynamics of Faith* and Rudolph Otto's *The Idea of the Holy*. Each confirmed what I learned on that train: Holiness is as solemn and unfathomable as a mountain, as furious and fluid as the sea, and to be lived as if I am as eternal as they. Holiness is the living of the Oneness of Being. How else can I do that if I don't join the Catholic Church and chant psalms of praise as a monk?

Now I am told that is doing nothing.

The question of "doing" surrounds me like angry bees. I am tired of classmates and professors asking, "What're you going to do after you graduate?" I don't know, and when friends show me their job offers and acceptances to graduate schools, I am ashamed. I have not applied for either. Besides being a monk, the only thing I can imagine doing is writing.

On the first Sunday in June I graduate, and for a commencement present Momma gives me a book: *Disputed Questions*, by a Cistercian monk named Thomas Merton. (I still don't know why she gave me a book by a monk after telling me that monks don't do anything.)

Merton:

> ... true contemplation is inseparable from life and from the dynamism of life—which includes work, creation, production, fruitfulness and above all, *love*. Contemplation is not to be thought of as a separate department of life, cut off from all man's other interests and superseding them. It is the very fullness of a fully integrated life. It is the crown of life and all life's activities. . . .
>
> ... what we need are "contemplatives" outside the cloister and outside the rigidly fixed patterns of religious life—contemplatives in the world of art, letters, education, and even politics. This means a solid integration of one's work, thought, religion, and family life and recreations in one vital harmonious unit with Christ at its center. ["Poetry and Contemplation"]

All the words in the passage excite me except the last, "Christ at its center." I still do not know who Christ is, and I have tried to understand, tried, even, to love him. Since my experience on the train last spring I have striven for piety like an athlete in training. I wear a cross around my neck; I have read *The Imitation of Christ*, but to try to be as good and holy and perfect as Jesus is to condemn myself to wearing shame and inadequacy like a hair shirt. Yet this insistence on holiness claws at me. But if I do not believe in Jesus, how can I be holy?

Sometimes I wonder if I am as crazy as Momma has told me more than once that I am. Sometimes I do not know what is real. Is it this holiness that only I seem to believe in, or is it the sit-in demonstrations my friends went on with religious fervor? Is it the deep quiescence of night when I sit alone in my room, reading and listening to classical music on a Chicago radio station, or jazz on one from New Orleans? Only when I am alone am I not divided against myself, Mind arguing with Soul. When I am alone, I am as uniform and indivisible as the night.

God is real, but more so than the demonstrations and beatings and arrests in the streets of downtown Nashville this past spring? Isn't it selfish to want to be a monk when my friends risk their lives to make mine easier?

The sit-in movement has been victorious and the downtown merchants have agreed to desegregate all public eating places. There is a victory rally at a church near the Fisk campus, and I go.

I sit in a back pew, alone, listening to the joyous singing of freedom songs but not loosing my voice to join the others. I want to belong to the joy in the church, want to be a part of the camaraderie shared by those who have been arrested and jailed. I cannot. I must hold myself apart to know what God wants of me, or what I think He wants.

Is that arrogance, madness or faith?

## May 1961

On the front page of the *Nashville Tennessean* is a picture of Jim Zwerg, a white exchange student at Fisk last semester. He is slumped against a wall, head bowed, blood streaming down his face like ribbons. Quickly I read the story to learn that students from Nashville were beaten in Montgomery, Alabama, protesting segregated seating on buses traveling between states.

I stare at the picture of Jim's bloody face. How can I justify myself? How can I say nothing matters but God, especially when I don't live as if God matters; I don't go to church; I don't study the Bible, pray daily or even once a year.

I want to go to Alabama and join the Freedom Riders, if only to rid myself of this guilt. I am weary of the aloneness, weary of uncertainty, the not knowing what it is God has called me to do. I want to be real to myself.

I leave Nashville and go to New York. It is not a decision but a desperate fleeing to save myself from being impelled by guilt and isolation to do what I know in my soul I am not supposed to do. God has not called me to risk my life on a Freedom Ride.

## Summer 1961

Working as a counselor at Camp Woodland in the Catskills near Phoenicia, New York, I have my first sustained contact with Jews. Within a week I am calling people *meshugge*,* referring to the camp food as *trayf*,* and muttering *oy gevalt** under my breath. I fall in love with a fellow counselor, a large-eyed Jewish girl with long, dark hair, who tells me stories of her grandparents fleeing Russia, and invites me into her childhood through borscht, bagels, lox, sour cream and herring, and gefilte fish, and at the end of the camp season we unburden each other of virginity and think we are adults, at last.

Many nights I sit in the camp dining room with campers and I play my guitar and sing spirituals and songs from the Civil Rights Movement, which is little more than a year old. They sing Jewish and Israeli songs. I don't know or understand the words, but the songs are familiar, and instinctively I know the odd intervals melodies will take. The simplest Israeli song—"*Shalom Chaverim*," or "Every Man 'Neath His Vine and Fig Tree"—brings tears to my eyes as spirituals never have.

Perhaps that is when I first see myself standing in a synagogue singing "*Kol Nidre*." The centuries of black suffering merge with the millennia of Jewish suffering as my voice weaves the two into a seamless oneness that is the suffering and at the same time the only appropriate and adequate response to it.

The following spring I sit in New York's Riverside Park every evening and watch bearded men walk by in black hats, black suits and white shirts without ties. They are Chasidim.* No one has told me, but I know that is who they are. I stare at the older ones and imagine I see the blue stenciled numbers on their forearms, only noticing later that I am rubbing at my forearm as I stare. It is my suffering and theirs I want to avenge and give voice to—for them and for me.

I want to be a cantor. I sit in my tiny furnished room on West End Avenue in the fall of 1961 and yearn to sing Jewish music—as a Jew. When I pass synagogues, I hear melodies of pain and beauty rising toward heaven.

The following year I move to West Twenty-first Street, and between Sixth and Seventh avenues discover a tiny Sephardic* cemetery amidst the factories. During the thirteen years I live in that neighborhood I go often to stand at the wrought-iron fence of the cemetery, looking at the tombstones, wishing I could be who they had been—Jews.

But, who has ever heard of a black Jew? Few seem to take Sammy Davis, Jr., seriously as a Jew.

## July 1986

I stare through the window at the Berkshires, which look like a bank of low, dark clouds on the western horizon. It is a clear New England day, one of those days that make an English major, at least, want to shout Edna St. Vincent Millay's famous line, "Ah, world! I cannot hold thee close enough."

Twenty years ago on this date I was in Atlanta, Georgia, working for the Student Non-Violent Coordinating Committee. It was the first summer of Black Power. Stokely Carmichael, SNCC's chairman, was crisscrossing the country carrying the message of Black Power, and in whatever city he spoke, riots blossomed like apple trees in Johnny Appleseed's wake.

I remember and yet I do not. In the past few years there has been renewed interest in the Civil Rights Movement and I refuse to be interviewed about it. I did not live the period in a way that my memories have documentary value.

We remember only that which our souls value, only what we experience in and with our souls. Did I live through the Civil Rights Movement and not experience it in my soul?

I experienced the Civil Rights Movement in my emotions, my mind and body, and have an ulcer as documentary proof. But my soul, that faculty in which and through which I apprehend God, was not involved. My soul did not believe in The Movement, even. What I remember of that time is my soul calling for me to tend it. How can I write about the Civil Rights Movement when my woe still cries out from within?

My students at the University of Massachusetts do not hear my woe. They look at me as if they are in the presence of History because I knew Stokely Carmichael, H. Rap Brown, John Lewis, Diane Nash, shook hands with Martin Luther King, Jr., remember the day Malcolm X was killed, can tell them how the fear of death mingled with the smell of honeysuckle on Mississippi back roads on cloudless April days. I see the rapture of nostalgia in their eyes, and shake my head. No one should have to live through a time when History strode across the land like a demented conqueror.

Events that shook the soul happened too often: the assassinations of a president, that president's brother, Medgar Evers, Martin

Luther King, Jr., Malcolm X, Che Guevara. Then there were the martyrs of The Movement itself: Jimmie Lee Jackson, Viola Liuzzo, Jonathan Daniels, Reverend James Reeb, James Chaney, Andrew Goodman, Michael Schwerner, William Moore, and the four girls in that church in Birmingham. And there were those killed in the riots of the long, hot summers in Watts, Harlem, Detroit, Cleveland, Chicago and on and on. The decade which began with the elegiac "We Shall Overcome" ended in angry shouts of "Burn, Baby, Burn!" and "Black Power." That is too long and too arduous a journey to make in a mere ten years.

From 1961 to 1964 I resisted the Siren call of History. I married and wrote short stories and novels which no one would publish and eked out a living as a folk singer and guitar and banjo teacher. A part of me wanted to be in the South, though, on the back roads of Mississippi and Georgia where friends were organizing blacks to register to vote. Though I sang at fund-raising parties and hootenannies for SNCC with Pete Seeger, Judy Collins, Barbara Dane, Gil Turner, Guy Carawan, Len Chandler, Phil Ochs, Tom Paxton, and others, it was not enough to ease the guilt at not being in the South.

My wife and I spent the summer of 1963 in a house at the end of a three-mile-long dirt road in New Hampshire. I wrote a novella which would remain unpublished for nine years while a quarter of a million people marched on Washington. I read Merton but found no solace. I still wanted to be a mystic in the world, but that fall a church was blown up on a Sunday morning in Birmingham, Alabama, and four black girls were killed. Wanting to be a mystic seemed selfish and small.

History claimed me for Itself; I became a revolutionary.

Or did I? When I speak on college campuses and in synagogues and hear myself introduced as "a social activist of the Sixties," I am embarrassed. What did I do? I led singing at mass meetings in Mississippi, took photographs throughout the South, and served on SNCC's Central Committee. I was never shot at, beaten, or arrested. I never confronted a Southern sheriff and certainly never saw the inside of a jail.

I remember leading singing at a mass meeting in Laurel, Mississippi, the summer of 1964 and being frightened and repelled by the intensity of emotion with which the people sang "Ain't Gon' Let

Nobody Turn Me 'Round," "Which Side Are You On?" and other freedom songs. I heard the crowds shout "Freedom Now! Freedom Now!," but my lips remained closed. How could they be so sure they knew what freedom was? How could they be so sure that freedom was what they needed even? I knew Spinoza too well to believe in a freedom one called for as if it were a dog that had wandered from home.

I joined The Movement, but something essential within me remained unchanged, remained separate and apart, like Grandmomma's house, like those of us who sat on the porch of that house.

I envied those who believed with their souls that registering people to vote, teaching in freedom schools and challenging the power structure really mattered. They belonged to something greater than their solitary selves. I was a spirit hovering over my body but inhabiting it only when I was alone.

Mind conspired with Body to make me believe I was a revolutionary. Soul knew otherwise. I worked in twelve-hour stretches in the darkroom of the Atlanta SNCC office to be alone. In the solitary darkness Soul was safe to come out and live with me. It asked me why I was playing revolutionary. I didn't know. Nor did I know what else to do. No one wanted to hear what I had to say—that death is awful, that you should see that my grave is kept clean, that none of us would be free until we learned to love, until we stopped seeking to create the world in our own images and knew that the world was each of our images and that we should cry when another cries, whether that person was in the same room or on the other side of the world. But I was afraid to speak those truths because they seemed alien and irrelevant to almost everyone I knew.

When I emerged from the darkroom there was an aura of unintelligibility around them for me, too. To my Mind revolution was more imperative than God. When I led the singing of freedom songs at mass meetings I could feel the pain and desperation in people's lives as their voices overwhelmed mine. I shed no tears for the pain as plentiful as cotton. I drank. All of us did. We were too young to carry the pain of all those lives, too young to live, day and night, knowing that in any car behind us or coming toward us might be white men with rifles to kill us.

I have told my students that when death is a presence with

which you lie down and with which you rise, you will either be destroyed or become free. That is romantic and sentimental, I realize now. Most of us were not destroyed, and none of us became free. We were simply maimed in ways we cannot afford to recognize, even yet. So we drank and went to places like The Chicken Shack in Selma, or to nameless cabins on nameless back roads where there was a jukebox and a few tables, and someone in the back room sold moonshine, and we shoved nickels into the jukebox and danced and drank and laughed hysterically and somehow made our way back to the Freedom House, where SNCC organizers lived and worked, and we fell across one of the thin mattresses scattered over the floor and the next morning the glare of the sun slapped us awake and somebody said, "Time to get up. Black folks ain't free yet, are they?"

No, they weren't, and we got up because we hated that people lived with bent shoulders and bowed heads, hated that people lived in houses in which they had glued newspapers up for wallpaper, hated knowing that the children in those houses were condemned never to know what their possibilities were and who they could have been. My Mind did not understand why white people killed over something as innocuous as voting, or why hatred was more compelling than love. Yet if I was left alone for more than five minutes my soul surged forward like a tidal wave to remind me that, as compelling and righteous as such emotions were, as right as it was for others to be doing what they were doing, I belonged to the darkness of God.

May 1966. Lowndes County, Alabama. I go to the outhouse. It is a three-sided tin structure without a roof, and a board over a deep hole. I sit, the warm breeze soft on my exposed buttocks. In the distance, a man plows a field. In the tree above me, birds chirp. I am whole again, at peace and at One with God. Time drops away like an oversized garment, and the poverty and the pain and the death all around me vanish as if they had never been.

That is my most vivid memory of the Civil Rights Movement.

# 5

## Summer 1968

My first book is published. Since college I have fantasized that I would write highly praised fiction and be hailed as "the black James Joyce." Instead, my first book is a political essay and reviewers call me a "black militant."

*Look Out, Whitey! Black Power's Gon' Get Your Mama!* is the first book explicating Black Power. It is written in the language appropriate to the subject matter, namely, an angry, colloquial black English. Yet the anger is not the deadly ire which seeks to kill, but the anger of love that mocks and pokes fun at whites. *Look Out, Whitey!* is a very funny book, beginning with the title. (It doesn't seem that white people can laugh at themselves. The headline on the review from the Fort Wayne [Ind.] *News-Sentinel* read: WHITE MAMAS IN DANGER, SAYS BLACK MILITANT, SNCC LESTER.)

Reviewers are taking out *Roget's Thesaurus* and looking among the dustballs behind their file cabinets to find adjectives they'd mislaid years before to describe the book's language. "Wry, bitter, passionate, angry," says *Publishers Weekly*. "Lester translates into writing the harsh music of ghetto speech." *Time* calls it "a long harangue that reproduces accurately the black tone of voice at its angriest." (And how would *Time* know?) Dick Reeves on WCBS Radio talks about the book's "unabashed, undiminished, ragged racial anger," while Christopher Lehmann-Haupt in the daily *New York Times* writes that "Lester struts and grimaces and rumbles ominously. He trots out a witty down-South patois." Nat Hentoff in *The Nation* compares the book favorably with James Baldwin's *The Fire Next Time*.

Reviewers can't agree on whether my language is "ghetto speech" or "down-South patois." (Except for the three months I lived in Harlem in 1961, I know nothing about ghettos, and I thought "patois" was something you spread on crackers and munched until the spareribs were ready.) However, I do seem to have aroused people's emotions. *Publishers Weekly* concluded its review with "It is not possible to read this impassioned book without feeling strongly about its author."

Why? Are people really so naïve as to think that I have poured my entire being into a mere book? That is all *Look Out, Whitey!* is—a book delineating the political and cultural "philosophy" of Black Power and the historical context from which it comes. I could have written it in an "objective," academic style, but chose the collective black voice of anger and humor because history is the lives and emotions of those who live it and are lived by it. I did what I thought any good professional writer does—fit subject matter to style to create an aesthetic whole.

To be identified personally with words I have written is frightening. I do not assume that a writer is his or her book. Because I can express black anger does not mean I am angry, and it certainly doesn't mean I hate white people. Because I articulate the experiences of many blacks does not mean I am writing autobiographically. I have never been in jail, lived on a Mississippi plantation, picked a boll of cotton, been beaten by a policeman, but the writer in me knew by listening to Fannie Lou Hamer, Charles Sherrod, Lawrence Guyot, John Lewis, and others. I have never been shot in the head while driving a car, but listening to Jimmy Travis talk, the writer in me knew. I wrote the collective story of a generation and used the collective pronoun "we" instead of "they" because it is my generation, too.

To be seen as the personal emissary of Black Power, a "militant," is confusing, distressing and downright embarrassing. I doubt that militants go to the Brasserie as often as possible for its superb caviar-and-sour-cream omelet, or stay up until four-thirty in the morning to watch a Bette Davis movie on the late show, or until 6:00 A.M. listening to Bill Watson on WNCN reading from Thucydides' *Peloponnesian War*. Not only am I not a "militant," I'm not even political, even if I am involved in a political movement. (Eating Chinese food with chopsticks doesn't make me Chinese.) Writing politically is a function of Mind. Mind is not me. How can others not know that?

But how can they know if I don't tell them? How can I blame

others for believing I am identical with the only voice in which they hear me speak?

There is the Julius Lester who is interviewed on television talk shows, and takes phone calls on his radio show; he speaks dispassionately about the necessity for blacks to acquire the power to control the institutions that govern their lives, and whatever means used to acquire that power is justified.

Am I lying? Not at all. I am simply speaking in that collective black voice.

That Julius Lester is the creation of a History sweeping across the American landscape like a band of cossacks galloping down the steppes. That Julius Lester was a welfare worker in Harlem in 1962 and stepped over junkies sprawled across doorways to walk up unlit stairs and be smothered by the smell of urine and rats and hopelessness and rage-turned-inward; Harlem, where he sat for an afternoon in a room the size of a closet talking to a man whose only friends were the giant faces on the movie screens he gazed at from noon to midnight every day; Harlem, where he did not know what to say to the fifteen-year-old girl pregnant with her third child; Harlem, which was like a prison whose walls could not be seen but they were there and so were the guards in the guard towers and walking the walls, cradling rifles as if they were babies, and Julius had nightmares and after four months quit his job as a welfare caseworker because his rage that any society would call itself just and offer so many a perpetual living death threatened to destroy him. He read Frantz Fanon, Che Guevara, Ho Chi Minh and Mao Tse-tung and found a way to focus and organize that rage—revolution.

Yet Julius is never sure how much of his revolutionary zeal is born from justified rage and how much is created by the fear of loneliness, by the need for a secure and uncomplicated identity to relieve him of the uncertainty and the unknown in which his Soul seems to delight. The revolution accepts all supplicants, and confers a clear and simple raison d'être.

How can he argue with the nobility of sacrificing himself for the good of that mysterious entity called "the people"? That is concrete. It tells him what he is living for and for what he would die. Revolution rescues its devotees from doubt and ambiguity if they relinquish all claims to a life separate from "the people." The collective aspirations and identity of blacks is all; the individual not only ceases to matter; the individual ceases to exist.

I know better, but am afraid to say so publicly. With close friends I speak from my soul and wonder aloud if power can be magically transformed into a good fairy by calling it black. What are black people doing to their souls by making power an end in and of itself? Even the redefining of ourselves as "black" places us closer to those people called white, because we, too, now claim race as identity. Black Power sounds like the roar of independence but it is the whimper of submission. To make our primary definition the color of our skin is to imitate white people, not be free of them.

Persona and Soul. One of the most arduous tasks given by God is to marry the two so Soul can be a luminous glowing behind Persona. My Persona and Soul are not in communication, are not even living in the same countries. They can't be until I write and speak my Soul's doubts about Black Power and revolution.

I am aware that in public appearances and on my radio show I am not living up to people's expectations. I do not have a ten-foot-high Afro and don't eat white people for breakfast—without sugar. I scarcely raise my voice above conversational level, and prefer to joke and laugh rather than prophesy doom as a latter-day Savonarola. I sympathize with white college students who come to hear me; they expect to be called honkies and to be made to lie prostrate with guilt for all of white America's sins, and are pathetically grateful when I speak to them as human beings deserving respect. I ache for the black students who need me to be their whip, flaying white flesh for sins, real and imagined. I can't do it, and often after I speak I am surrounded by white students eager to talk with me while the disappointed black ones drift sullenly away.

I don't know what to do. However, as long as I publicly espouse a black collective mentality, Persona and Soul will exist within me like opposing forces at Armageddon.

# 6

## Winter 1969

Nineteen sixty-eight was a year that not only tried the soul but left it limp, exhausted, twitching spasmodically on a deserted beach, uncertain if it had the strength to flop its way back into the water or even if it wanted to. Martin Luther King, Jr., was assassinated in April, Robert Kennedy in June. Students took over buildings at Columbia University, while in France, students took over Paris. In August, Mayor Daley of Chicago (may God please rest his soul) permitted police to brutalize reporters and demonstrators during the Democratic National Convention, while Russian troops invaded Czechoslovakia. In November, Richard Nixon was elected president.

In black America the agonized and exhilarating cry of Black Power expunged King's dream of nonviolence and the beloved community. The very words—Black Power—were a magical incantation conferring instant enlightenment, telling blacks once and for all that the black condition was not the result of genetic inferiority. (A lie we were never absolutely certain was a lie as we searched our souls in the wells of dank nights because we did not understand why we could not succeed to the degree *they* did even though we tried to make our hair as straight and shiny as angels' dreams and lavished deodorant on our armpits every morning as if it were paint. Maybe we did have a peculiar odor. We remembered to say "isn't" and "aren't" even though "ain't" was more expressive, but the vacant apartments were always "just rented" and jobs were "just taken" the moment before we walked in to file an application.) Freedom rushed forth in cascades when we heard those words—Black Power!—and we knew that we were degraded because we lacked the power to be anything else.

In Jewish America the stunning victories of the Six-Day War

in 1967 and the reclamation of the Old City and the Western Wall in Jerusalem imbued Jews with a new sense of self and pride. The image of the Jew as Western civilization's pet victim was replaced by pictures of Israeli jets bombing Egyptian tanks, of curly-haired soldiers running through the streets of the Old City to put on *t'fillin** and prayer shawls, and with rifles in one hand and *Siddurim** in the other and with tears like rain on their faces, they prayed before that wall, that massive prayer in stone before which Jews had not been able to pray since 1948, and in those soldiers' prayers and from those stones American Jews, even those no longer sure what a Jew was, reclaimed that stone inside themselves, that stone of indestructibility which the centuries of suffering had not chipped, or the oceans of blood eroded. No longer would they sit beside the rivers of Babylon and weep for Jerusalem. The Jewish people lived!

In New York City, blacks and Jews, each singing the same song in different languages, went to war against each other. The hilltop to be captured was community control of schools.

The smoke has cleared and I wander dazed in a no-man's-land between the two.

## March 1968

I begin a half-hour taped show at WBAI-FM, a listener-supported radio station in New York, interviewing black and white radicals. During the summer I am substitute host on the late-night live shows of Bob Fass and Steve Post. I also cover the Democratic National Convention in Chicago that August for the station. In the fall I am offered a live show for two hours on Thursday evenings. I call it "The Great Proletarian Cultural Revolution." The show's title is intended as self-mockery, but in the humorless atmosphere of the late Sixties, it is taken seriously.

As the only black at the station with a live show, I make the airwaves available to blacks who do not have the opportunity to be heard, or are heard only under adversarial questioning from white reporters.

In addition to the Thursday evening show, I am one of the staff people WBAI assigns that fall to cover the strike called by the United

Federation of Teachers over the issue of community control of schools.

The Board of Education of the City of New York has created three experimental school districts in which boards comprising parents and local leaders are given control of the curriculum, budgets, and the hiring and transfer of teachers. One of these districts is Ocean Hill–Brownsville in Brooklyn, a black and Puerto Rican area.

May 1968: Rhody McCoy, the administrator of the Ocean Hill–Brownsville school district, transfers thirteen teachers, five assistant principals and one principal to central headquarters because of their perceived lack of sympathy for community control. Transferring teachers and administrators from a school district is not an unusual procedure. Though it technically violates the union contract, the UFT has never protested such transfers, and, in the past, many teachers had formally complained to the union about its failure to do so.

This time the union protests, and School Superintendent Bernard Donovan orders the teachers returned to Ocean Hill–Brownsville. Parents block the doors of the schools and the teachers reenter the schools with a police escort.

September: The Ocean Hill–Brownsville governing board refuses to assign the teachers classes, or give the administrators duties. The UFT goes on strike, and from September 9 to November 18, 1.1 million pupils in the city's nine hundred schools are without teachers.

From the beginning the UFT has attacked community control with innuendos and slurs. Union president Albert Shanker is quoted in *The New York Times* of February 6, 1968, as saying that teachers have become "targets of a mounting volume of attacks by extremist groups." On February 12 the *Times* quotes him as maintaining that "a sort of hoodlum element" is in control of several schools. After the transfer of teachers and administrators, Shanker claims that teachers remaining in Ocean Hill–Brownsville are being subjected to a "kind of vigilante activity." On May 14 it is reported that children in Ocean Hill–Brownsville are chanting "Black Power slogans." On May 20, the *Times* quotes Shanker as saying that "four outsiders" from Harlem and elsewhere in the city have "come in and taken over" Ocean Hill–Brownsville.

On September 16, Shanker appears on "Searchlight," a public

affairs show on WNBC-TV, and says that "some element of anti-Semitism was involved" in the opposition of Ocean Hill–Brownsville to the reinstatement of the teachers.

The media does not challenge Shanker's racial code words—"extremist groups," "hoodlum element"—by demanding that he be specific and give names. His charge of anti-Semitism is reported as if it is substantiated fact.

Two leaflets appear mysteriously in Ocean Hill–Brownsville. One is allegedly written by a Ralph Poynter and said to be distributed by the Parents Community Council of JHS 271. The text demands black control of black schools but makes no mention of Jews. The other is viciously anti-Semitic, calling Jews "Middle East Murderers of Colored People," among other things.

The UFT duplicates the leaflets on one sheet of paper, distributes them in the hundreds of thousands to union members and the Jewish community, with a caption reading, IS THIS WHAT YOU WANT FOR YOUR CHILDREN? THE UFT SAYS NO! In other words, black community control of schools equals anti-Semitism.

The New York Civil Liberties Union, headed by a Jew, investigates the leaflets and finds that there is no organization at JHS 271 called the Parents Community Council. Ralph Poynter, the alleged chairman of the alleged council, is a teacher in Manhattan with no relationship to the schools of Ocean Hill–Brownsville. The NYCLU concludes that the leaflets are another example of "the UFT's strategy of lying and distorting in order to whip the city into a frenzy of fear of Ocean Hill–Brownsville." New York's Jewish community is unfazed by facts.

The Ocean Hill–Brownsville governing board issues a statement condemning anti-Semitism, saying "Anti-Semitism has no place in our hearts or minds and indeed never in our schools. . . . We disclaim any responsibility for this literature and have in every way sought to find its source and take appropriate action to stop it."

New York's Jewish community is not mollified. On November 26, the NYCLU issues a report on the teachers' strike, which says, in part:

> The UFT leadership, and in particular Albert Shanker, systematically accused the Ocean Hill–Brownsville Board . . . of anti-Sem-

> itism and extremism, and then "proved" those accusations only with half-truth, innuendos, and outright lies.

The report accuses the UFT of whipping up "religious terror, releas[ing] race hatred and open[ing] sores in the community that will not be easily or quickly healed."

The UFT is defending an area of institutional life in New York City in which Jews hold real power, for two-thirds of the UFT membership is Jewish, as is Shanker; a majority of supervisors and administrators in black areas are Jewish; and a majority of the Board of Education is Jewish.

When WBAI program director Dale Minor asks me to go to Ocean Hill–Brownsville, I am unaware of instances of black anti-Semitism but I have heard stories from blacks about Jewish teachers calling black children "nigger" as they enter schools staffed by nonstriking teachers, nonunion teachers and parents. Shanker's charge of black anti-Semitism seems so transparent that I am astounded that any Jews give it credence. Yet I am prepared to report what I find, and that includes black anti-Semitism.

When I go to Junior High School 271 I am surprised to learn that the majority of teachers there are Jews. They are frustrated and angry that their story is not being heard in the Jewish community. My taped interviews with them have no effect, of course.

I tape a history class taught by Leslie Campbell, a black man whom the press and the UFT have singled out as the most "militant" black in the school district. Impressed by his gentleness as well as effectiveness as a history teacher, I invite him on my show.

Thursday evening, December 26. I am sitting in the control room with Les before going on the air. He shows me several poems written by a fourteen-year-old girl in one of his classes. One of the poems begins:

> Hey, Jewboy, with that yarmulke on your head
> You pale-faced Jew boy—I wish you were dead.

"I want you to read this one on the air," I say to Les, handing the poem back to him.

"Are you crazy?" he responds.

"No," I tell him. "I think it's important for people to know the kinds of feelings being aroused in at least one black child because of what's happening in Ocean Hill–Brownsville."

"You don't know what you're getting into."

I shrug.

This is a transcript of the show as transcribed by Fred Ferretti and published as part of his essay "New York's Black Anti-Semitism Scare," in the *Columbia Journalism Review*, Fall 1969:

Campbell: I also brought with me some works by a young sister in Brooklyn who is fifteen years old . . . a sister by the name of Thea Behran. She has written a poem about anti-Semitism and she dedicates this poem to Albert Shanker, and the name of this is "Anti-Semitism":

Hey, Jew boy, with that yarmulke on your head
You pale-faced Jew boy—I wish you were dead.
I can see you Jew boy—no you can't hide
I got a scoop on you—yeh, you gonna die.
I'm sick of your stuff
Every time I turn 'round—you pushin' my head into
the ground
I'm sick of hearing about your suffering in Germany
I'm sick about your escape from tyranny;
I'm sick of seeing in everything I do
About the murder of 6 million Jews
Hitler's reign lasted for only fifteen years
For that period of time you shed crocodile tears
My suffering lasted for over 400 years, Jew boy
And the white man only let me play with his toys
Jew boy, you took my religion and adopted it for you
But you know that black people were the original
Hebrews
When the U.N. made Israel a free independent State
Little four- and five-year-old boys threw hand grenades
They hated the black Arabs with all their might
And you, Jew boy, said it was all right
Then you came to America, land of the free
And took over the school system to perpetrate white
supremacy

Guess you know, Jew boy, there's only one reason you
made it
You had a clean white face, colorless, and faded
I hated you Jew boy, because your hangup was the Torah
And my only hangup was my color.

Lester: I had you read that in the full knowledge, of course, that probably one half of WBAI's subscribers will immediately cancel their subscriptions to the station, and do all sorts of other things because of the sentiments expressed in that particular poem; but nonetheless, I wanted you to read it because she expresses . . . how she feels . . .

Campbell: I'm glad you said that, man, because some of our listeners are going to get hung up on discussing that and they are going to say that that is anti-Semitism, etc., but I don't think that is the question. . . .

[Campbell read several other poems, then the segment began in which listeners phoned in.]

Listener: That was a very ugly poem. What was it about the poem that made you feel we should have heard it? It aroused anger in me.

Lester: People should listen to what a young black woman is expressing. I hope that will properly cause people to do some self-examination and react as you have reacted. An ugly poem, yes, but not one half as ugly as what happened in school strikes, not one-hundredth as bad as what some teachers said to some of those black children. I would hope that you would not have the automatic reaction, but raise a few questions inside yourself. I had it read over the air because I felt what she said was valid for a lot of black people, and I think it's time people stop being afraid of it and stop being hysterical about it . . .

[Listeners discuss other comments on the program.]

Listener: With all of this discussion about racism and the difference between black and white, doesn't it make it hard for a decent person to contact or communicate with a black person?

Lester: All black people are saying is, if there is going to be communication between black people [and Jews], our point of view and our attitudes are going to be a major consideration. In the past they have not been because we have kept quiet, and now we are saying it's a two-way street, and you have to at least come one-half way on our terms. The question is not one of communication but one of justice for black people. . . .

For the next two Thursday evenings I play a tape of the poem and take phone calls on the air about it. I do so to give as many listeners as possible the opportunity not only to express their views about the poem but also to engage them in a discussion of the underlying issue, namely, the need of blacks for political control over the institutions of their communities. I am pleased by the quality of conversation between me and the listeners and feel that people understand why I thought it important to air the poem.

January 16, 1969: I get home around 2:00 A.M., call my answering service and am told to call Lee Dembart at the *New York Post*. I do and he asks for my comments on the complaint the UFT has filed with the Federal Communications Commission against WBAI because of the poem.

The story, written by Dembart and published by the *Post*, follows:

The reading of an anti-Semitic poem on a local radio station was defended today as a stimulus to discussion of the "emotions that have been brought about by the school strike."

Julius Lester, the black author, radio commentator and host of the WBAI-FM show on which the poem was read, said that while "the poem did not express my own personal emotion" he thought the feelings should not be ignored.

He charged that the United Federation of Teachers, which has lodged a formal complaint with the Federal Communications Commission, was "using the station to try to get at" Leslie R. Campbell, a teacher at JHS 271, Ocean Hill, Brooklyn, and reader of the poem.

The incident occurred Dec. 26 during Lester's weekly two-hour program heard on the listener-sponsored station here. Lester said Campbell had shown him the poem before they went on the air but that they hadn't discussed it.

"I recognized at the time that there would be some understandable reaction," Lester said, but added that he had neither "endorsed the poem" nor "made any anti-Semitic remarks" on the air.

The poem, written by one of Campbell's students, a 15-year-old girl, and dedicated to UFT president Albert Shanker, began: "Hey, Jew boy, with that yarmulke on your head/You pale-faced Jew boy—I wish you were dead."

"The sad thing to me is that I feel the UFT is responsible for quite a bit of the feeling that exists among young blacks now in terms of Jews," Lester said. He said the teachers' union had adopted a position that anyone who opposed them was anti-Semitic.

"Regardless of whether the feelings are true or not, they can't be ignored," he said. "They can't be looked at as 'This is wrong.' "

Campbell, 29, was suspended during the strike on charges of interfering with union teachers but was reinstated this month when the evidence against him was declared insufficient. Shanker yesterday asked Mayor Lindsay to suspend Campbell again for reading the poem.

"What does he want, two pounds of flesh?" asked Lester.

"If he wants to make black people and Jews fight, he's doing a pretty good job."

He charged that the UFT had distorted the reading and didn't "mention that Les also read two other poems by the same girl which were not about Jews."

[The story quoted thirteen lines from the poem, then continued:]

Said Shanker last night:

"Leslie Campbell's proud reading of his student's anti-Semitic poem is an indication of his teaching approach. . . . This city is going to have to decide whether it wants its teachers to teach anti-Semitism or understanding and brotherhood."

"He [Shanker] doesn't want Les Campbell teaching black children. So here's another weapon he's using," Lester said.

Frank A. Millspaugh, WBAI's general manager, said the station had received approximately sixty letters about the reading, most critical.

Millspaugh and program director Dale Minor presented a special half-hour program last Friday in which they "supported the station's right to air such things," Lester said.

The author said he was gratified by some fifty letters he had received, both agreeing and disagreeing with the poem, all "in the main very serious."

"If I had to do it all over again, I'd do the same thing," he said. "These things are not going to go away by screaming about them."

Campbell could not be reached for comment.

That morning's *New York Times* carries a front-page headline about the poem and the UFT complaint. The *Times*, however, does not then or ever contact me for comment, though it contacts and quotes Shanker.

Later that morning I am listening to rock music on the radio and the lead item on the news is that I have been fired from the station. The phone rings just as the newscast ends. It is Frank Millspaugh, WBAI's station manager.

"You heard the radio yet?"

"Yeah. I just heard that you fired me."

"You believe it?"

"No," I respond confidently.

"Good. I don't know how that got on the air, but we're going to stop it."

Despite my denials of anti-Semitism in the *New York Post* article, I am branded an anti-Semite by persons who never heard my show. Each day when I call my answering service, the operator informs me calmly, "You had a lot of folks call who said they were going to kill you, but didn't none of them leave a name."

One afternoon I answer the phone myself. It is the FBI.

"Mr. Lester, we've uncovered a plot to kidnap you."

"What're you going to do about it?" I ask.

"We can't do anything, sir, until you've been kidnapped and carried across a state line. We're only informing you and you should contact your local police."

"Thank you," I say politely and hang up. It is safer to take my chances with the kidnappers.

The airing of the poem coincides with the organizing of the Jewish Defense League and the public appearance of Meir Kahane. I become front-page news in his newspaper as well as a target of the

JDL, who campaign to get me fired from the station. Abbie Hoffman gives me a leaflet that was thrust into his hands on the street one day. On it is a picture of me, a crudely drawn swastika next to my head. Beneath is the poem with a headline reading: "This is the Outrageous Anti-Semitic Poem which was read by Leslie Campbell on the Julius Lester Program, Dec. 26 over Station WBAI." To the left of the poem is a picture of a young woman in a fur jacket and fur boots carrying a picket sign reading: "Do Not Use Jews for Scapegoats." At the bottom in bold letters: "Cancel Out Julius or he may cancel out you!" In the event anybody missed the message, at the bottom right is a circle in which are the words "Cancel Julius Lester."

I remain curiously unafraid, even unperturbed. I am angry, though, that the only newspaper to contact me is the *Post*, and WCBS the only television station to send a reporter and camera crew to interview me. Most distressing is that Jewish newspapers across the country carry stories about the airing of the poem, but no editor or reporter from a Jewish paper ever seeks my side of the story. Equally damning, no newspaper or radio or television station asks WBAI for a copy of the tape of the show on which the poem was aired.

On the night of January 23, two students from Ocean Hill–Brownsville are on the show. During the course of the interview, one of them, Tyrone Woods, says Hitler should have made more Jews into lampshades. I want to kill him!

*The New York Times* dutifully reports Woods's remark, and the Jewish Defense League calls for a demonstration outside the station on the following Thursday to demand my firing and revocation of the station's license.

For the first time, I am tired, depressed and discouraged. Naïvely, I thought that airing the poem would facilitate contact between Jews and blacks. Jews needed to know how damaging Shanker's remarks had been; they needed to know the depth of black anger over the UFT's opposition to community control and how they were being exploited by the false accusation of black anti-Semitism. They needed to know that if they wanted blacks to care about Jewish suffering, they had to care about black suffering. As crude and obscene as the poem was, I heard in it an excruciating paroxysm of pain. It was pain expressed as anger at Jews, many of whom found identity by borrowing suffering from the Holocaust while remaining blithely blind to the suffering of black people around them and actively opposing the political means blacks used to alleviate a portion of that suffering.

Yet my strongest supporters during these weeks are also Jews. At the station, Jewish staff members are very solicitous and protective, defending me to parents and friends. Marjorie Waxman, the young switchboard operator, listens to the deluge of phone calls demanding I be fired, the threats on my life, the threats to bomb the station, and yet always has a smile and something funny to say to me when I come in. There is Steve Post, who on the night of January 30, when the Jewish Defense League demonstrates against me outside the station, sees me walking down the street toward the station and the screaming demonstrators, alone, having been refused police protection, and comes out of the station to walk inside with me. Robert and Carolyn Goodman, the parents of Andrew Goodman, who was murdered in Philadelphia, Mississippi, in 1964, and the parents and brother of Michael Schwerner, murdered with Andy, are publicly and privately supportive. And there is Paul Fischer, WBAI's news director, who, on the night of the JDL demonstration, catches someone on the roof attempting to cut the cable of the elevator I will ride, and yells at him in Yiddish, scaring him away.

Ironically, I do not receive one expression of support from blacks, not even a phone call from a single black friend. I begin wondering why I am so eager to risk my life and reputation in the service of black people when they do not seem to care. It is Walter Teer, a white radical who heads an organization that supports the National Liberation Front of South Vietnam, who calls one afternoon and offers to be my bodyguard. And, on that night of January 30 when I get off the air, Dale Minor takes me home in a cab, saying only that he wants to be sure I get there safely. Neither can I forget the administration of the New School for Social Research, where I teach a course on Monday nights, providing a limousine to carry me to and from my class because of the threats their switchboard receives against my life. Most important are the Jewish listeners who call and write to say that they know I am not an anti-Semite.

However, my airing of the poem has made a bad situation that much worse. If I am going to be honest, I have to consider if I am, indeed, an anti-Semite. I cannot categorically deny that I am not, not with thousands of Jews saying the contrary. So what if they did not hear my radio show? I hurt a people I had no intention of hurting, not then, not ever.

But how can I know? If it is difficult for whites to acknowledge their racism (and their too-quick denials are merely confirmation of what they are denying), I cannot glibly assume that I am not anti-Semitic. (I remember walking through Times Square shortly after the Six-Day War and seeing young Chasidim collecting money in a large sheet. I was overcome by anger and jealousy that I did not have a country in which to exult. I remember an essay I wrote for *The Guardian*, a radical paper to which I contributed a weekly column, in which I had defended SNCC's condemnation of Israel and Zionism. I did not know it at the time, but what I had written was a classic example of political anti-Semitism.)

Between January 23 and the following Thursday I spend most of my time at my studio-loft in a factory building on East Eighteenth Street. I sit at my desk and stare at the back of the factory building on the next block, and in the quiet and aloneness I hear an anger within me, an anger that my suffering as a black person is not understood as I feel the suffering of Jews is. I am angry, too, that Jews, the people I thought most able to understand black suffering, do not understand, do not care, even, to try to understand. Once I see my anger staring at me, I cannot deny that part of my motivation in airing the poem had been to hurt Jews as they had hurt me. If such unspoken anger becomes a comfortable habit, there is no way I can prevent myself from sliding into anti-Semitism as if it were a cool lake at the bottom of a grassy slope.

Then I remember my great-grandfather. I have not thought of him since childhood. I wonder what he is thinking of me, if he would claim me as his descendant. I am afraid that I have shamed my memory of him, and shamed my memory of that little boy who played "*Kol Nidre*" on the piano.

That evening of January 30, when the Jewish Defense League is to picket me, I walk to the station, as is my habit. When I get to the corner of Thirty-ninth and Park, Thirty-ninth Street is blocked off and a policeman stands at the corner. I look down the block toward Madison and see a large crowd. Even three-quarters of a block away, I can hear them shouting and screaming. (I did not know then that Jewish counter-demonstrators were there in support of the station and me, and the shouting is between them and the JDL demonstrators.) For the first time I am afraid. I ask the policeman to escort me down the block, explaining that I am the target of the demonstrators. He says he can't leave his post.

All the years of learning to walk as if I were invisible were training for the walk down the block that night, because I am almost at the station before I am noticed. The JDL demonstrators surge against the police barricades, screaming and yelling, when they see me. Policemen move toward the demonstrators and begin pushing them back with nightsticks. Flashbulbs from the cameras of news photographers explode in my face. Steve Post, looking almost as scared as I am, comes out of the station and walks in with me, a policeman leading the way. Five people are taken into custody that night, some of them carrying tire chains and auto jacks. Seventy-five policemen are needed to maintain order.

What I said on the air that evening follows:

> This is a wonderful time to be alive. Very rarely does anyone have the opportunity to be alive at a time when history is so obviously changing. It brings an added intensity to living, as well as an added responsibility. But it also brings a certain joy.
>
> We're involved in history and never has that seemed more obvious than in the Sixties. At times it feels as if we're being pushed along, unable to control or even direct the way we'd like to go because the roots of what's coming out now are so fantastically deep, so fantastically old.
>
> When the teachers' strike began last fall, I thought that the issue involved was community control of schools and that the racism which was exemplified by the teachers' strike and in the teachers' strike was a part of that. Now I realize that when you roll away one layer, there's another one, more vicious, more ugly, and then you roll away that one, and, lo and behold, there's another one. And you begin to wonder, where does it all end? I have no answer because I wasn't here when it began. But I'm here now, which means that I do have a responsibility to do what I can to see that it does end.

It's been very interesting to watch how things have gone from community control, to black anti-Semitism, to Should WBAI be allowed to exist? to Should Julius Lester be on the air? The only real issue involved is the one of community control, but that has been totally obscured by the manufacture of so-called "issues" such as black anti-Semitism. So one must address himself to that and, hopefully, lay it to rest before minds can return to that which is relevant—community control of schools for blacks.

Perhaps I should explain what I see as my function on the air. My primary job is to relate to and speak as a member of the black community. Everybody in New York City has more than enough outlets for whatever they might want to say, however they might want to say it. Black people do not. So I'm here two hours a week, trying to serve as a forum for the black community. Secondly, I'm here to allow those nonblacks who are interested an opportunity to listen and to talk with me, in the hope that they will come to some understanding of the black frame of reference, the black psyche, the black mind. This is not to say that I expect them to agree. They may not and I accept that. They should, however, have the opportunity to listen. In this light, there can be no question as to whether or not WBAI is serving a valuable function. It seems, however, that white people believe in free speech only as long as they agree with what is being said. A black man in the communications media is generally there as a representative of the Establishment, not as a member of the black community. There are a few exceptions and I am one of them, and I think that that may be why so many people are upset. There's a black person on the air talking to black people, not trying to mollify white people. Thus, there was pressure on me to disavow Les Campbell, Tyrone Woods, and what they said, and that pressure came from nonblacks, Jews, and Anglo-Saxons. They looked upon me as an individual, while I have no choice but to look upon myself as a black, who as an individual has certain skills that he is trying to make available to blacks.

You see, I know that anti-Semitism is a vile phenomenon. It's a phenomenon which has caused millions upon millions of Jews to lose their lives. However, it is a mistake, and a major mistake, to equate black anti-Semitism, a phrase I will use for the sake of convenience only, with the anti-Semitism which exists in Germany and Eastern Europe. If black people had the capability of organizing and carrying out a pogrom against the Jews, then there would be quite a bit to fear. It should be obvious to anyone that blacks do not have that capability. Not only do blacks not have the capability, I doubt very seriously if blacks even have the desire. But Jews have not bothered to try to see that black anti-Semitism is different. It is different because the power relationships which exist in this country are different. In Germany, the Jews were the minority surrounded by a majority which carried out heinous crimes against them. In America, it is we who are the Jews. It is we who are surrounded by a hostile majority. It is we who are constantly under attack. There is no need for black people to wear yellow Stars of David on their sleeves; that Star of David is all over us. And the greatest irony of all is that it is the Jews who are in the position of being Germans.

In the city of New York a situation exists in which black people, being powerless, are seeking to gain a degree of power over their lives and over the institutions which affect their lives. It so happens that in many of those institutions, the people who hold the power are Jews. In the attempt to gain power, if there is resistance by Jews, then, of course, blacks are going to respond. And they're not going to respond by saying "it's the merchants who are holding us down" or "it's the schoolteachers who are holding us down"—not as long as they're being attacked as blacks. In the school strike, Rhody McCoy always talked about teachers, not Jewish teachers. Yet the response of Albert Shanker and the UFT was to accuse blacks of anti-Semitism. A good percentage of New York City policemen are Irish. When demonstrators call them "pigs," they do not respond by saying "you're anti-Irish." Yet, when blacks consistently attacked the political position of the UFT, their response was to accuse blacks of being anti-Semitic and to point to their liberal record on race relations and the fact that Shanker marched in Selma. Indeed, Jews tend to be a little self-righteous about their liberal record, always jumping to point out that they have been in the forefront of the fight for racial equality. Yes, they have played a prominent role and blacks always thought it was because they believed in certain principles. When they remind us continually of this role, then we realize that they were pitying us and wanted our gratitude, not the realization of the principles of justice and humanity.

Maybe that's where the problem comes now. Jews consider themselves liberals. Blacks consider them paternalistic. Blacks do not accept the Jews' definition of either the problem or the claim that Jews have been in the forefront. And what can only be called Jewish contempt for blacks reaches its epitome when Jews continually go to the graveyard and dig up Michael Schwerner and Andrew Goodman, "who died for you." That Schwerner and Goodman paid the ultimate price cannot and will not be denied, but blacks pay a high price every day of every week of every year, and every day some of them pay the ultimate price. When you're powerless, you reach a point where you realize that you're all alone. You have no one but each other. Those who said that they were your friends were never your friends, because they unilaterally defined the relationship. Nonetheless, you had a certain sympathy from them, and having that sympathy, you expected that it would remain. But we have learned that sympathy exists only when it is a question of morals. When it was a moral issue, a question of integration in the South, for example, blacks had nonblack friends. But we have learned, in the rivers of blood from thousands of black bodies, that America does not run on morals. America articulates moral principles. It has articulated moral principles in relationship to black people since we have been here, but when it comes to acting; America acts on the basis of power. Power, and power alone. When black people reached the point of correctly analyzing that it was not a question of morals, but a question of power, then it meant that they had to attack those who held the power.

Many people have written me and said that "Jews are not your enemy because they don't hold the real power. There are others, back of them, who hold the real power." And that's true. However, a colonized people, which blacks are, cannot make fine distinctions as to who holds the power. Everyone else, the nonblacks, are the colonizers, and Jews are no exception because they hold only a measure of that power. It is power, and the Establishment maintains its powers partially through Jews. When a powerless people, a colonized people, begin to fight for power, then the first thing they will do is to lash out verbally at the most immediate enemy. In this particular instance, that hurt, the articulation, the demand that the colonizer listen, is accomplished in a violent manner, like the language of the poem. In this particular instance, the language set off a historical response which has no relationship to what black people are talking about.

Many people were very distressed by the remark of Tyrone

Woods that Hitler should've made more Jews into lampshades. And people were doubly distressed when I did not disassociate myself from that remark. And I've been asked many times this week whether or not I am anti-Semitic. To the question of whether or not I am anti-Semitic, I won't answer, because it's not a relevant question to me. The relevant question is changing the structure of this country because that's the only way black people will achieve the necessary power. The question of anti-Semitism is not a relevant one for the black community. The remark that Tyrone Woods made is not one I would have made. It's not my style. I didn't say anything against the remark because I think I understood what he was trying to say. I was aware that he was speaking symbolically, not literally. And I was also aware that he was defending himself. He was also seeking, in a very direct way, to escape the definition of this controversy which others have put on it. Because what we have seen has been a moral response to a political problem.

We've reached a point where the stage is set now. I think that black people have destroyed the previous relationship which they had with the Jewish community, in which we were the victims of a kind of paternalism, which is only a benevolent racism. It is oppressive, no matter how gentle its touch. That old relationship has been destroyed and the stage is set now for a real relationship where *our* feelings, *our* view of America and how to operate have to be given serious consideration.

When I began I talked about living in an age when the processes of history rest upon our very brows, and who we are as individuals becomes, perhaps, totally irrelevant. I recognize that there are Jews who are exceptions to what I say. I recognize that there are blacks who do not agree with what I say. I recognize that there are good Jews, if you want to put it that way, and bad. However, I believe that everybody's good. They have difficulty expressing it sometimes, in fact, all the time, which is what the struggle's all about. If there's going to be any resolution of the problem that will not mean the total obliteration of America, and afterward silence, then it means that Jews and Anglo-Saxons are going to have to examine themselves. They are going to have to relinquish the security which comes from the definition which the society has given them. They're going to have to question themselves and they're going to have to open up, to be, at the least, receptive to what blacks are trying to say.

Yet sometimes I get filled with despair. We talk, and we talk, and we talk, and nothing changes. Perhaps there's only so much that words can do. Perhaps it is an illusion to think that words can do anything. Today I was reading James Baldwin's *The Fire Next Time*, which came out in 1962, and I was astounded when I read it. The truths which he spoke in 1962 are so relevant in 1969. The book was a best-seller, read by, I'm sure, many more liberals and intellectuals, Anglo-Saxon and Jewish, than it was by blacks. And yet, Anglo-Saxons and Jews still don't understand. Baldwin says in there, I quote,

*. . . the social treatment accorded even the most successful Negroes proved that one needed in order to be free something more than a bank account. One needed a handle, a lever, a means of inspiring fear. It was absolutely clear that the police would whip you and take you in as long as they could get away with it, and that everyone else—housewives, taxi drivers, elevator boys, dishwashers, bartenders, lawyers, judges, doctors, and grocers—would never, by the operation of any generous human feeling, cease to use you as an outlet for his frustrations and hostilities. Neither civilized reason nor Christian love would cause any of those people to treat you as they presumably wanted to be treated; only the fear of your power to retaliate would cause them to do that, or to seem to do it, which was (and is) good enough. There appears to be a vast amount of confusion on this point. But I do not know many Negroes who are eager to be accepted by white people, still less to be loved by them; they, the blacks, simply don't wish to be beaten over the head by the whites every instant of our brief passage on this planet. White people in this country will have quite enough to do in learning how to accept and love themselves and each other, and when they have achieved this—which will not be tomorrow, and may very well be never—the Negro problem will no longer exist, for it will no longer be needed.*

Black anti-Semitism is not the problem; it has never been the problem. Jews have never suffered at the hands of black people. Individuals, yes, yes. But en masse, no. The issue is not black anti-Semitism. The issue is what it has always been: racism. And the physical oppression of black people by a racist system. But that system needs instruments and those instruments have been white people, including Jews. If this fact cannot be faced, then there is little else to be said. It is this which black people understand. I guess it just comes down to questions of who's going to be on what side. If there are Jews and other white people out there who understand, never was there a more opportune time for them to let their voices be heard. All I hear is silence, and if that's all there's going to be, then so be it.

On March 26, 1969, the Federal Communications Commission rules on the UFT complaint against the station, and says that WBAI "fulfilled its obligation imposed by the fairness doctrine to afford reasonable opportunity for the presentation of conflicting viewpoints." It cites as evidence the remarks I made on the air the night of January 30 and quotes extensively from those remarks.

Though neither *The New York Times* nor any radio or television station reported what I said on the air that night, the controversy is over, but I am anathema to Jews across the country.

# 7

## Spring 1969

Jim Holloway, professor of religion at Berea College and editor of *Katallagete*, the journal of the Committee of Southern Churchmen, invites me to speak at the college. We had "met" the previous autumn when he called asking permission to reprint a column of mine from *The Guardian*.

It is overcast when I arrive, and as we drive from the Lexington, Kentucky, airport, the grayness and the gentle Kentucky hills wrap me in their quiet. I remember that the Abbey of Gethsemani is somewhere in those hills. I ask Jim if he has ever been there. He has, the last time being the previous December for Thomas Merton's funeral.

Merton. Hearing his name brings faint, barely recognizable whiffs of something of which I'd once loved to partake. Jim seems to have a need to talk about Merton, whom he'd known, and as I listen I am ashamed that my life has veered so far from what I had intended.

When we arrive on campus, I am introduced to a group of black students who call me "Brother" and surround me like Secret Service men. I cannot imagine from what I need protection and as they escort me around campus looking as grim and forbidding as corpses, I feel like a bad actor in a play that should never have been allowed onstage. Because I have not been wholly honest with my words, I have become a prisoner of the black collective.

At dinner, the black students sit at separate tables in the center of the dining hall, me in their midst like a prize orchid they have bred. I am angry at myself for not asking some of the white students looking fearfully at us from surrounding tables to join us. They are Southerners, too, and I share a history and an agony with them, too, and want to talk about it. I do nothing.

As I am being taken to the chapel where I am to speak, a white girl approaches. I stop. She is hugging herself tightly, as if there is no one else to hold her and never will be. When she speaks, her eyes flutter up to mine and down to the ground quickly as if they are a fallen baby bird that will never find its nest again. Her voice quavers, and with a sharp pain I realize that she is afraid of me, phalanxed as I am by unsmiling, hard-eyed young blacks. She thinks I am one of them.

I need her to know that I am not, and want to ask her to unclasp her arms and throw them around me so that I can cry for what is happening to me and to her.

I don't remember what she asks me, but I make a joke in response, knowing that if she will laugh, or even smile, we will join and be free. My joke bounces against her fear and plops at my feet like a dead fish. She looks at me, bewildered, and hurries away.

I want to go after her, to tell her of my shame and sorrow for what I have become. Instead, I watch her hurry into the night as if it is a haven.

---

For Christmas 1968, my wife gives me something I have coveted since reading the English Romantic poets in high school—a human skull.

Holding it, I wonder about this once-human who had been so uncared for, so alone, that at death, his or her head was severed from the body, examined in a medical school for a semester or two, and then made its way to the window of an antiques shop in Greenwich Village, a price tag attached.

Who had this person been? Male? Female? Some fabulous gay queen whose party entrances were anticipated for a week before the event? Had this skull, with its cavity-pitted teeth, been a black genius beaten down by an oppressive, racist society and forced onto Skid Row, where he died of cheap wine and lack of love? Or had it been a white person who would have hated me when he was alive?

How can race, so all-important in life, leave no trace after death and decomposition? An anthropologist friend offers to examine the skull and tell me its race. I decide I want to know only what my unscientific eyes can see.

I place the skull on my desk, next to my typewriter, and reach out often to touch it, tenderly, almost lovingly, tracing my fingers gently around the eye sockets and over the cheekbones. Then I press my fingers against my face, and feel the skull beneath the skin, the hard protrusions of the cheekbones, the rock-solid bone in which the eyes sit. I get up from my desk, go to the bathroom and stare intently into the mirror until the brown skin dissolves like wet tissue and I see the skull I will one day be, the skull I am already.

The skull is an unconscious symbol, too, of what my life is becoming. My marriage of seven years bleeds from wounds that cannot be sutured, or if they can, neither my wife nor I know how. The end is in sight and we wait passively for it to arrive.

That political movement in which I have been involved full-time since 1966 is disintegrating into factions and acrimony. Such disintegration is, in part, a sign of The Movement's success. With the passage of the 1964 Civil Rights Act and the 1965 Voting Rights Act, The Movement effectively put itself out of business. In five short years, the legacy of slavery has been eradicated. Why do we not celebrate the victories that make our slave ancestors weep for joy from their graves?

Perhaps because we resent having had to risk our lives for what white Americans take for granted in the womb. Perhaps because we hate white America for its persistence in clinging to racism as if it is the nipple of a milk-filled breast. And perhaps because we learned, as we risked our lives, that to change the behavior of white Americans does not transform their souls. They still believe that by being white they partake of innate and God-endowed superiority. As long as they do, our souls will be the garbage dumps for all they loathe in themselves. We cannot celebrate the history-making legal victories because we had wanted to make America the beloved community, where the lion would lie down with the lamb and swords be beaten into plowshares. Legislation is not an acceptable substitute.

There was not a specific day on which The Movement ended. People simply drifted away without anyone noticing. Some returned to school; some joined black nationalist or socialist organizations; others are in mental institutions or sit in the offices of psychiatrists, weeping. Many of us opened our eyes to see that we had acquired children who knew nothing of utopia but urgently needed to know how many queen bees there were in the world and could they stay up to watch the Charlie Brown special. It is easier to explicate a passage from the writings of Chairman Mao than to answer the eyes of a three-year-old.

One unnoticed day I went to Washington Square Park instead of the New York SNCC office, and sat around the fountain, or at a sidewalk café in Sheridan Square sipping a bourbon-and-water, watching women in miniskirts go by.

To live with a skull is to confront one's inescapable mortality; if you don't tremble and quail at the confrontation, you begin to live, timidly, fearfully, but you begin. The only certain knowledge we have about our lives is that they will end, and our deaths will be longer than our lives. To live with a skull is to learn that there is no reality except Death. Only there can the journey toward freedom begin.

Imperceptibly, like the grass of spring which no one sees grow, I begin to know that I must live ahistorically, that I must leap, blindly and joyously, into the void of ahistorical Time which is created only in the leap.

Perhaps this had been the peculiar mission of blacks in America. As Outsiders we were to lead the way *from* history. The victim is the only one who can clear the way to salvation, but only by accepting the existential pain of refusing to become an executioner as he ceases to be a victim. Instead of leaping into the void, blacks are jumping to the other side, and in redefining ourselves as blacks, we impose racial definitions on the rest of humanity. Murder is committed when we define others as anything except a variation of ourselves and we of them. And the greater victim of that murder is the murderer.

It is we who are the executioners of ourselves, and our paeans to blackness are like the rouge morticians rub into the cheeks of the dead. Blackness is a cosmetic, obscuring the reality of human existence. After all, one day I might be a skull resting between jars of pencils on someone's desk.

# 8

## Summer 1970

I get into the first cab waiting at the curb outside the terminal at La Guardia, give the driver the address of the apartment in Manhattan and slump into a corner of the backseat. As the cab merges into the traffic I notice the driver looking more at me through the rearview mirror than at the cars he is passing with reckless confidence.

"It's you!" the cabbie exclaims suddenly, grinning.

That was a statement fraught with philosophical dangers.

"It's you!" he repeats. "Remember me?"

I lean forward, puzzled, and look at him. After a minute I conclude that he must be the same cabbie who has taken me from La Guardia into Manhattan twice in the past year. To get the same cabbie more than once in New York is almost impossible; three times makes it worthy of a story in the *Daily News*.

"How've you been?" he wants to know after we finish exclaiming over the coincidence.

"Fine," I lie. "How about you?" I ask, hoping he will answer with equal politeness and leave me alone.

He shrugs and after a long pause, speaks, his voice tentative. "You're a writer, right?"

I assent reluctantly, afraid he is going to tell me that his life will make an exciting book and if I help him write it we could make a lot of money, etc., etc., etc.

Instead he says, "I've got a problem. Maybe you can help me."

"I don't know," I offer as uninvitingly as I can.

After a long silence he says, "I just got a letter from this cousin of mine." He stops. He opens his mouth several times but no words come. Finally, in a gesture of desperation, he takes his right hand from the steering wheel and bends his arm back at me. I look at the numbers stenciled in blue on his forearm. "You know?"

"I know," I answer quietly.

He puts his hand back on the wheel, and the words come rapidly now. "My problem is this. I just got this letter from my cousin in Israel. She's the daughter of my mother's sister. But the problem is that for the past twenty-five years I thought everybody in my family was dead. Then last week I get this letter from her. She'd thought everybody in the family was dead, too, but somehow she heard that maybe I was alive and she got an address and wrote." He stops. "I don't know what to do," he continues finally. "It's such a shock, you know. So, I thought since you're a writer, you could tell me what to write to her."

I slump back into the seat again, my eyes shut against not only the pain and sorrow of it all, but my own impotence before the enormity of his question and the numbers on his wrist. I wish he hadn't asked me, wish I knew why he asked me. Can't he see that I am black? Doesn't he know that Jews consider me an anti-Semite? And so what if I am a writer? Only God knows what one ghost should say to another.

"Were you happy to hear from her?" I hear myself ask after a long silence.

"Oh, yes! It's a shock, but I'm very happy!"

"Well, maybe that's what you should write. Tell her how happy you are."

He thinks for a moment, then looks at me through the mirror. He is smiling and nodding his head. "Thank you. That's what I'll do."

We say nothing else on the drive into Manhattan. I've flown into La Guardia many times since, but have never seen him again. I wonder now if he was real, or was he an angel?

## Autumn 1970

My wife and I have separated. No matter how right the dissolution of a marriage is, the sense of failure is total. Where did the love go that once shone as brightly as a hundred suns? Why did the silence of tenderness become the foreboding stillness of unspoken hurt and anger? Who have I become that the soaring eternity of love I offered you now feels like dust I am eager to wash from my hands? How do

I explain to a five-year-old daughter and three-year-old son what I do not understand? What I do not understand is me.

Me. Such a tiny word to have to describe so much. Me is a voice on the radio trying to get out of the net of blackness in which I have become entangled. Me is a thin image on television screens as I co-host a live talk show once a week on Channel 13. Me is a father wanting my children to know that he has not divorced *them*. Me is a lover who doubts there is any greater holiness than my body with hers (whoever she is) as the sun shines through the windows of strange bedrooms. Me is a lonely child disguised as a man, frightened by suicidal depressions.

Each Me demands center stage. Yet beneath them I sense something as compressed and unchanging as a stone, something with the power to direct all the Me's to their proper places on the stage where they will be relieved to speak their lines at the proper times and then be quiet.

Merton. I return to him in his first posthumously published book, *Contemplation in a World of Action*, which I review for the Sunday *Times Book Review*. In it I find these words:

> What is meant by identity? . . . We are talking about one's own authentic and personal beliefs and convictions, based on experience of oneself as a person, experience of one's ability to choose and reject even good things which are not relevant to one's own life. . . . Identity in this deep sense is something that one must create for himself by choices that are significant and that require a courageous commitment in the face of anguish and risk. . . . It means having a belief one stands by; it means having certain definite ways of responding to life, of meeting its demands, of loving other people, and in the last analysis, of serving God. In this sense, identity is one's witness to the truth in one's life.

To serve God. To witness to the truth in one's life, regardless. How am I supposed to recognize the truth of my life? How am I to know when I am serving God? How do I do that? I do not even know where or how to begin.

So I write and read a lot—Carl Jung, the diaries of Anaïs Nin; I become a good cook; I listen to Bach cantatas and watch old movies on television and begin living with a very gentle, sensuous woman who is kind to me. We laugh a lot, play Frisbee in Central Park, sip *café au lait* and eat croissants while reading the *Times* on Sunday mornings, and make love with wondrous frequency and in wondrous silence.

It is not enough.

## Autumn 1971

There comes another night on the radio show.

I am playing a recording of songs of humpback whales and a young black woman calls.

"Julius? Tell me something."

"What?"

"What are you playing?"

"Oh, these are songs of whales."

"Whales?" she exclaims. "What relevance does that have to the struggle of black people?"

I pause. "None," I finally say.

"Then why are you playing it? We don't have time for that."

"Well, it's beautiful, and if we don't have time for beauty, then I'm afraid we're lost."

Since the anti-Semitic poem controversy, I have been changing the show, primarily by the kind of music I play. Instead of playing jazz exclusively, I add rock—Jefferson Airplane, the Rolling Stones, Santana, Jimi Hendrix—as well as short classical pieces. It is a subtle attempt to express more of my personality without disturbing my persona. I continue to have black artists, musicians, writers and political activists as guests on the show, but I sense that my listeners are uncomfortable with the mix of the familiar and the new. The night I play the whale songs and receive only that call, I know: I have lost my audience.

I leave the radio station. I can no longer be the person my listeners need me to be. (Nine months later WBAI asks me to do a show from seven to nine on Monday and Tuesday mornings. I accept and call the show "Uncle Tom's Cabin." I wake listeners with the sounds of whales singing, Bach cantatas, Gregorian chants, and on occasion, John Philip Sousa marches. I read *The New York Times* on the air and talk about the news with sacred irreverence. For the first time I allow myself to be me in public. To my surprise, people like me.)

There are days I sit before the typewriter, scarcely moving, and don't know why. I stare at my name on the spines of the nine books I have published and wonder who Julius Lester is and what all those words are that he has written. I am not in those books. Yet I thought I was. If I am not in those books, where am I?

I do not know and am ashamed that I don't. I have written books that, while not false, are not wholly true. I have lived the life others needed me to live. By doing so I have sold my birthright and I never knew what it was.

## Summer 1973

I have been invited to speak at a conference at the University of Kansas School of Religion in August and decide to drive across country. I need to disappear from my life, need not to think, even, about myself or my life. Maybe then I will find both.

*July 1–2, Harpers Ferry, West Virginia.* I come to pay my respects to John Brown, "The Old Man," as his black friends called him. He was a man for whom there was no division between appearance and reality. In his fierce simplicity, he accepted the responsibility of loving and being loved by God. Loving God meant loving the slaves. Being loved by God meant freeing slaves. During a snowstorm he took slaves from a farm in Missouri and walked through the snow so a slave could ride his horse. Later, others realized he had also walked barefooted, having given his shoes to another slave. In a curious way, Brown practiced nonviolence, though American history portrays him otherwise. Once he, his sons and sons-in-law rode over the crest of a hill in Missouri. In the valley below they saw sitting on a porch the man who had murdered one of Brown's sons. Someone raised his rifle and took aim. Brown reached out and lowered the rifle, saying, "We're not about vengeance. Let us ride on." I remember, too, how John Brown knew his death might be necessary to precipitate the war to end slavery, and thus refused to escape from jail, which he could have done. Such integrity and knowledge about who one is leave me awed.

*July 3–4, Bird-in-Hand, Pennsylvania.* Amish country. Their one-horse covered buggies trot along the two-lane highways as if my car, eager to pass, does not exist. The black-suited, bearded men, the women in long blue dresses and the children seem oblivious of their oddness. They are like self-contained worlds rebuking me.

I visit the Ephrata Cloister, organized in 1732 by Conrad Beissel, a German Seventh Day Baptist. That sounds as enervating a religious mixture as one could find. The Cloister was a celibate community and a more depressing place I've never seen.

Beissel never knew the joy of God because the Cloister was architecturally designed to make one feel his worthlessness. The hallways are narrow, to remind you of the straight and narrow path; doorways and ceilings are low, forcing you to bend on entering a room, a way of enforcing humility. The rooms are small and constricting and the beds are boards; the pillows, wooden blocks.

What a fearful view of the world they lived to call their lives religious.

*July 5, Waynesboro, Virginia.* I am surprised at how much terror remains. I know the Civil Rights Act of 1964 says I can eat in any restaurant, sleep at any motel; my body is not convinced. It screams No, No, when I walk into Howard Johnson's or walk toward the registration desk at the Holiday Inn. No one seems to notice me or care; my body says that is a trick, that someone has written down my license-plate number and will follow me down the highway until I pass a spot so lonely that even ghosts refuse to congregate there, and then, my body says . . . It dare not finish the sentence.

The worst legacy of having grown up in the South is not knowing how to trust reality; I do not have the capacity even to know reality. There is still that child in me who senses the violence in how white people talked to his parents in stores, who sees the violence in their eyes, in the set of their mouths, who does not know why he is hated, why so many wish he were dead, that child who knows that he didn't do anything to any of them and yet, and yet, I must have because they wouldn't hate me otherwise.

*July 7–10, Berea, Kentucky.* Jim Holloway, his wife, Nancy, and their three children live on a farm at the foot of a mountain, at least what passes for such in Kentucky. Being here I miss my children, miss those odd moments when your child walks through a room and you see him for an instant, not as your child, but as a person separate from you, belonging to you and yet belonging to something you will never know, that is, the future. For the first time I want to be part of a family, which I'm not sure I ever was. As I watch the Holloways go about the chores of their days—feeding the dogs, working in the fields, brushing and feeding the horse—I wonder if the family could be a monastery, i.e., a group of people intent on holiness. Holiness is not the same as piety. Piety is the face one puts on for a priest. Holiness is Being. Jim Holloway, stocky, of medium build, balding, a Southern accent as thick as kudzu, cussing, kicking a dog out of the house, a cigar in one hand, a bourbon-and-branch in the other, is holy because he values the ordinary.

Late one night while we are talking and drinking bourbon, Jim gets up suddenly and starts rummaging through a drawer. "Here it is," he mutters. He hands me a large rock. "You know where that's from?"

I shake my head.

"Obersaltzburg."

"What's that?"

"The name of Hitler's summer place up in the Bavarian mountains. I was up there shortly after Konrad Adenauer had it destroyed after the war, and stuck that rock in my pocket."

I feel as if I am holding evil itself and want to give it back to him. "Why are you giving it to me?" I want to know.

"Hell, do you want it?"

No, no, I don't. But I drop it in my shirt pocket, sensing that as the skull is teaching me Death, that piece of rock which had helped shelter Hitler might teach me Evil.

Jim and I drive to the Abbey of Gethsemani. I am a little apprehensive confronting the place which has overshadowed my life. I am afraid I will regret not having come twelve years ago, afraid to find that my life has been a mistake.

We spend the day with Brother Patrick Hart, who was Merton's secretary. He has secured permission from the Abbot to show us parts of the monastery not usually seen by others.

When I enter the quadrangle behind the gatehouse I feel as if I have come home. A statue of the Virgin Mary stands in the center, her arms extended from her body, palms outward, and I feel embraced by her. I want to stay with her, but afraid of appearing pious, I let myself be taken to the guest house over whose doors are the words GOD ALONE. How simply truth can be stated when one knows it.

We go to the chapel. It is the first in which I've felt God's presence. It is a masterpiece of simplicity, with high, whitewashed walls. At the rear is the monks' choir, long and narrow, opening at the front into the main sanctuary where Mass is celebrated. There, a large marble slab serves as the altar and behind it a small simple cross is affixed to the wall. The windows are high and long, of pale pastel yellows and blues, abstract in pattern, and the light shining through dabs the colors on the whitewashed walls. The chapel epitomizes Cistercian silence, for the monks know that noise is also visual. Thus, the chapel does not clamor with stained-glass windows depicting scenes from the life of Jesus, or with ornate columns. Everything has been reduced to essence. Nothing interposes itself between me and God.

I stand there, unable to believe this place exists, yet knowing its existence more forcefully than anything I've ever known. A few monks drift in quietly, bow toward the cross at the front and seat themselves in the choir to pray. Nothing is more natural than that chapel, those monks and me here with them. This cloistered Cistercian world *is* the world, though the world does not know it.

*July 11–12, Shakertown, Pleasant Hill, Kentucky.* In the nineteenth century this was a large Shaker community. Now only the buildings remain, restored as they were. This is another kind of monastery. What I sensed at the Holloways and at Gethsemani was a joy in existence. The Shakers expressed it in their furniture, agricultural innovations and especially their cooking. The taste of chicken cooked in cider and heavy cream is more sensual than my most creatively erotic fantasy.

Community. Family. Absent from community is the bond of

blood. All too often what is absent from family is the bond of spirit. Yet each is the most intense effort to bring people to live together whereby each is a place of rest and inspiration for the other. The family is a monastery.

*July 13, New Harmony, Indiana.* When I left New York I did not intend to make this trip to American religious sites, but as I pore through the *Mobil Travel Guide* each night, only the religious sites interest me.

In the nineteenth century there were two religious communities here. Unlike Shakertown, however, the buildings of the communities are scattered throughout the town and I don't have the energy to look for them. Quite by accident, I come upon the Roofless Church, which is just that—a "church" with walls but no roof, the reason being that the roof will be put on when there's peace in the world, or some such nonsense. There is something depressingly Protestant about it.

The "church" features a sculpture by Jacques Lipchitz that is thoroughly modern and secular. It stands beneath a dome, whose shadow, says the tourist brochure, creates the shape of a rose. (Cleverness has been substituted for the sacred.) Fortunately, the barn swallows haven't read that and what seems to be Indiana's entire barn swallow population has built nests on the inner ledges of the dome, from where they have rendered numerous critical appraisals of Lipchitz's sculpture and come close to making it an acceptable piece of art.

Paul Tillich is buried in New Harmony and I am eager to visit his grave. I shouldn't be. He is buried a few yards behind a rather good restaurant, the Red Geranium. He would have been better off buried in the restaurant. His gravesite is in what is euphemistically called Paul Tillich Park, a labyrinth of paths bordered by pine trees. Each path leads to a stone tablet on which is carved a quotation from Tillich at his pedestrian worst. The whole place is infuriating because it is a maze, and I wander and wander, stumbling upon these quotes and, finally, coming face to face with a bust of Tillich, beneath which lies the urn holding his ashes. Everything in New Harmony—the Roofless Church, Tillich's burial site—is a perfect example of religion emanating from the mind. It is all very sterile.

*July 14, Nauvoo, Illinois.* The Midwest. The country of my childhood. Every summer we traveled with Daddy to church meetings and revivals in Missouri, Illinois, Iowa and Nebraska. What I remember most are the rivers, especially the Mississippi, and though I am older now, that child in me still yearns to penetrate the mystery of the broad, muddy water and its barely perceptible movement. Where has so much water come from, and where is it going? I know the geographical answers, but to say Minnesota and Louisiana does not satisfy the child. The child does not understand even his own question, but he knows it is the right one.

I take a small ferry across the Mississippi at Bachtown, cross back on a seldom-used country bridge somewhere else, and recross again at Louisiana, Missouri, over the imposing bridge I remember from childhood. I had planned to stop for the night in Hannibal, Missouri, remembering the time Daddy took me there to see Mark Twain's house and the fence Tom Sawyer tricked the others into whitewashing for him.

It is late afternoon when I drive into Hannibal. As I walk toward the motel desk, there is a noticeable hush among the people in the lobby and a tightening of many razor-thin white lips. I am not surprised when the motel clerk says there are no vacancies. The same scenario is repeated at a second and third motel. As I drive away from Hannibal I hear my daddy's voice saying what it had said many years before: "Hannibal is rough on Negroes."

Unintentionally, I spend the night in another religious community, at least a former one. Nauvoo, Illinois, was established by the Mormons. Joseph Smith and Brigham Young had almost succeeded in creating an autonomous state here, but their frontier neighbors decided otherwise and murdered Smith and many other Mormons. Brigham Young moved the survivors to Utah. Today Nauvoo is capitalizing on its Mormon past, as well as its wine-and-blue-cheese industry, but without mentioning too loudly why the Mormons are no longer here.

It is a depressing little town, but maybe that's because I imagine I hear Mormon ghosts moaning. But any trip across America has to be depressing if one recognizes how many Indian names remain and how few of the people. Illinois, Iowa, Mississippi, Peoria, Keokuk, Sioux City—and on and on and on. The settlers took their land and their lives but retained their words. Why? To do so was to make a contract with the dead.

I bought a framed piece of calligraphy at a gallery. It reads "Come, come, ye saints . . . All is well." I had to have it. Maybe one day I'll understand what it means.

*July 15, Sioux City, Iowa.* On a gravel road to Boonesport, Iowa, a ghost town, I stop at a barn filled with junk, which advertises itself as an antique shop. It is run by two old women, a mother and daughter, and I have never seen a more incredible collection of old farm tools, bottles, jars, chairs and the unidentifiable.

In the back is a pump organ. Seeing it, I remember I was sixteen when I went with the church choir to a small country church in McMinnville, Tennessee. When we arrived I was dismayed to find that the only instrument was a pump organ, but after the minister explained that all I had to do was pump the two pedals to keep air flowing through the pipes, I had a good but tiring time.

"Do you play?" one of the old women asks, seeing me staring at the organ.

"Oh, I haven't touched a keyboard in almost twenty years."

"Well," she says, coming over and opening the hymnbook resting on the organ, "there's nothing like a good hymn on Sunday morning, especially when you can't go to church."

I sit down on the bench. Surprisingly, my fingers remember more about the keyboard than I do, and we have church as the rich tones of the old organ fill the barn and my legs pump the pedals as if I am still a young man.

*July 15, Rapid City, South Dakota.* The world changes to wheat. Everywhere, wheat shines beneath a wide sky, and I am embarrassed to hear myself muttering, "They really are amber waves of grain!" The skies are spacious, too. Now I'm looking for the fruited plain.

I feel at home in South Dakota because it is impossible for Man to dominate this world of land and sky. Houses, cars, trains and grain elevators at ground level look as if they are being seen from a plane. Everything human is reduced to the insignificant. If Shakespeare had lived in South Dakota, he would have known that Man is not akin to the angels. Man is not even in the same category as a kernel of wheat. I feel like a grain of sand on an infinite beach and I am so happy.

I decide to go to Wounded Knee, which, on the map, looks to be at the junction of two gravel roads. I see thunderheads piled on the horizon, lightning flashing in them, and I know that the storm is over Wounded Knee. I don't know how I know, but I do, and I am reluctant to risk being caught in a storm on a gravel road in a part of the country noted for murderous flash floods. Then a strange but certain knowing floods my body and a voice says: "Do not be afraid. The Lord is with you." I do not know if I am to trust the words. Are they words of wishful thinking? The voice repeats itself: "The Lord is with you." I press the accelerator and drive toward the ominous thunderheads.

Two hours later I turn onto a gravel road. The thunderheads hover on my right. I follow the road up and down the hills for ten miles, through pastureland where the cattle are as likely to be standing in the middle of the road as in the fields. There are few houses. Only me, the cattle staring with vacant eyes, and the thunderhead.

As I shift into second gear and start slowly down a steep hill, the sky darkens and the thunderhead rumbles. I come to the bottom of the hill, and suddenly there is no sun. Ahead I see a junction of three roads and a large signboard announcing that this is the site of the Wounded Knee Massacre.

I stop the car at the junction. The lightning flashes, thunder reverberates and the rain comes down in rock-hard torrents. I tremble, but it is not the storm of which I am afraid.

I get out of the car and stand in the rain, visualizing the cavalry riding out of the soft hills to sow blood into the land where I stand.

On a rise across from the junction is a cemetery and I drive to it. It is so dark now that I have to turn on the car lights. I get out and stand at the graves of the murdered Sioux. Flowers lie on each grave, but it is a moment before my mind translates what my eyes are seeing; the flowers are plastic.

I leave. There is an anger in the rain and the car lights cannot penetrate the darkness. I drive slowly, hoping I am not headed toward a water-filled ditch. I drive less than a mile, and suddenly the rain stops. The road is dry and the sun shines with languid evening light. I turn off the car lights.

For several hours I drive through the deserted lands of the

Oglala Sioux. No cars come toward me; none are behind. Occasionally I pass a house or trailer, or see a wrecked car at the bottom of a gully. I am alone and my fear is palpable in the car. I want to believe that the storm was a coincidence. I know better and I tremble with a knowledge I cannot comprehend and do not want to accept.

I wish I were an Indian shaman, a priest of the Great Spirit, accustomed to going off into the hills and being spoken to by God. Then I would understand what God wants me to know.

I want to cry because I do not.

*July 18–21, Little Big Horn, Montana.* I am here to celebrate Custer's defeat, but the first evening when I go to the battlefield and stand at the top of the rise where Custer fell, that is suddenly unimportant. I look down toward the trees behind which is the Little Big Horn River. Beyond are the mountains on the horizon. I look out at the rolling prairie and the blue-curved sky, and it is the same world as at Gethsemani and Shakertown. I am alive as part of the land and sky. I am a clump of sagebrush! What a wonderful thing to be, for didn't God choose to speak to Moses through a bush?

Now that I am here, I know that it was to this place God has been leading me since I left New York. I spend the days listening to the winds in the tall grasses. At evening, to hear the wind whistle gently out of the north is to know holiness, all-pervading yet solitary, awesome yet ridiculously ordinary, mysterious but devoid of mystery. This land, this sky are Truth, which is merely the simple recognition of what is and the acceptance of it. I accept and give myself to it.

The monastery is the world.

*August 3, Lawrence, Kansas.* After five days of listening to theological discussions, I am ready to become an infidel. I do not belong among religious professionals—ministers, teachers and seminarians—who can't talk without quoting Bonhoeffer, Barth and others with whom I am not familiar. I wonder if they lack their own words because they have not experienced God. Tell me about *you*, I want to yell at them.

Eventually they do, but not with words, and not intentionally. I listen to their emotions and perceive that they are people without hope, and thus are in despair. They feel abandoned by God. This is not surprising because their religion is a politicized Christianity. They think Christians are supposed to save the world.

What gives them the right to think they should save the world? And what do they want to save the world *from*? Or for? Christianity seems to find its raison d'être in good works—feeding the poor, marching in Selma, giving money to Indians—all of which is fine, but these are not things that atheists don't do. But when "good works" don't change the world, many Christians fall into despair and wonder, what's wrong with the world? Nothing. The world hasn't changed since Adam.

I speak on the third day of the conference and tell them that there is no hope, and as long as you think there is, you are saying that life is valid only to the degree that one's impact on the world is for the good. The meaning of life is not found in the effect we have on the world, or what we think to be the world. We are called to live our lives and be instruments of God. We are merely human, curls on the waves, clouds that billow at midday and disappear at sunset. As long as Christianity thinks it should and can change the world, it will be nothing more than a caucus in the Democratic or Republican parties. Christians want Jesus to be president. I thought Christianity was supposed to be the alternative to Caesar, so intent on its virtue that Caesar would not be able to withstand the intensity of its light. Christianity has become a wing of Caesar's Bureau of Propaganda.

In all the times I've spoken publicly, this is the first I've felt wholly myself, hiding nothing. I was nervous, though, appearing at a conference with such prominent theologians as Gregory Baum and Rubem Alves. I know so little. I have never read theology, and for most of the conference I didn't have the slightest idea what people were talking about. The morning I spoke, I prayed before leaving my room, telling God that it was His show, because what could I tell people who knew more than I did? When I got up to speak, however, words came that I do not recall ever saying even to myself. They came from somewhere within me that had never known words, and for the first time I was not ashamed to be one who hungers and thirsts for righteousness. There is only one reason to be alive and that is GOD ALONE. The human vocabulary should be reduced to those two words.

*August 4–6, Kansas City, Kansas.* I have not been here since we moved away, twenty years ago. I wanted to come, see no one, and walk the streets of my childhood. Unfortunately, I told my parents I was coming and they told friends, who arranged a public gathering, and in a moment of weakness, I consented to it.

I am a thing now to many who knew me as a child. They think I am famous and want to have their pictures taken with me. I refuse and they are hurt. I don't care. I am tired of people trying to impose their idea of me on me. I am not an idea, dammit! Whatever someone says about me is not true, and I refuse to be pinned by anyone's words, even my own.

*August 13–16, Abbey of Gethsemani.* I am in Room 215 of the guest house. Outside my window, the water tower, a tree and the sound of locusts. Silence overlays all and I am safe within it.

I came, not thinking about becoming a monk, but to better learn how to live the essence of monasticism in the world, to learn how to be a more fluent tongue of God's in dailiness. How much should I withdraw from the world? How much should I be involved? How do I shape my days so they will gleam like a silver bracelet?

Rule #1: Move slowly. If there is the urge to rush, exaggerate slowness.

I have to resist thinking that I am supposed to *feel* a particular something because I am in a monastery, so I laugh at myself when I feel only fatigue, sleepiness or annoyance at the inevitable noises and presences of others.

I am rereading *The Sign of Jonas*, perhaps my favorite book of Merton's:

> The inviolability of one's spiritual sanctuary, the center of the soul, depends on secrecy. Secrecy is the intellectual complement of a pure intention. Do not let your right hand see what your left hand is doing. Keep all good things secret even from yourself. If we would find God in the depths of our souls we have to leave everybody else outside, including ourselves.
>
> If we find God in our souls and want to stay there with Him, it is disastrous to think of trying to communicate Him to others as

we find Him there. We can preach Him later on with the grace He gives us in silence. We need not upset the silence with language.

Listening to Gregorian chants on records is an aesthetic experience. Hearing them in the chapel is experiencing Art at the service of God. The chants make even Bach cantatas seem secular. Listening to the pure, floating melodies of the chants at Gethsemani, I realize that Bach calls attention to his music. The chants direct my attention to God. They go beyond emotion to parts of the self which have been famished.

I wish I could pray, really pray, that is, lower my body and kneel, bow my head and fold my hands. I envy the Catholics who come in, bow to the cross, make the sign of the cross, kneel and pray. I can't do it.

I love the minor offices—None and Compline, particularly—but I don't like Mass. August 15 was the Feast of the Assumption of the Blessed Virgin and I sat through as much of the Mass as I could, but I could not believe what I was hearing. It all felt like church and church is boring.

> God makes us ask ourselves questions often when He intends to resolve them. He gives us needs that He alone can satisfy, and awakens capacities that He means to fulfill. Any perplexity is liable to spiritual gestation, leading to a new birth and mystical regeneration.

Rule #2: Begin each day listening to Gregorian chants for half an hour. Then read something—Merton. Then pray:

"O Lord, come to my assistance. Thank you for this life. May I live it well and according to Thy will.

"O Lord, it is good to be possessed by You. Make me worthy."

Then, eat a simple breakfast. Bread and butter, tea or coffee, cereal and fruit. Do it even when I don't want to, especially when I don't feel like it.

> Emotion does a man great injury in this monastic life. You have to be serious and detached and calm all the time. Faith is the antidote: Cleansing yourself of impressions and feelings and the

absurd movements of a half-blind understanding by a clear penetration into the heart of darkness where God is found.

On my last day at Gethsemani, a feeling of utter sweetness begins to permeate me midway through the afternoon. I sit in the monks' cemetery, then walk to the top of the hill across the highway from the entrance to the monastery and lie in the grass. It is as if I am rocking gently back and forth in the bottom of the sky.

I return to the monastery and stand before the statue of the Virgin Mary at the center of the quadrangle. I look up into her face and am transfixed, immobilized. I try to move and cannot. During Mass the day before I wasn't able to understand how grown men could be singing about Mary ascending into heaven. Suddenly, I know it is true! I look at her and think of the Immaculate Conception, and, awestruck, I whisper, "Why not? Why—*not?* If God *is* God, then, of course, He could and can do anything He so desires. Anything!"

I hug myself in delirious joy. I sit on the ground before her, my eyes never leaving her face, resting in the warmth of her embrace.

The next morning I leave, looking forward to returning to the world, because there is no separation between the monastery and the world. The monastery is simply the world without its façades and illusions. The monastery is pure Being, and that is the world, too, but I can't know that as long as I am of what is presented as the world, as long as I take seriously what the world decrees as real. I cannot know myself as long as I confuse me with who the world defines as me.

It will be enough if I become so real that I am ordinary, like prairie sagebrush. Maybe God will set me ablaze.

If He doesn't, it is of no moment. All is Well, now and evermore.

# *Part Two*

# 9

## Autumn 1975: Amherst, Massachusetts

At seven each morning the alarm clock buzzes like killer bees, stunning me into consciousness. If that is what it is.

I'm not sure anymore.

For six months now I haven't given myself to the pictures rising from the grave of night, the nocturnal messages from unknown parts of my soul which the ancients knew as visitations from the gods.

Beside the bed I keep a notepad and pen to write down what God is saying. I wish He would speak as directly to me as He did to Moses: "Hey, stupid! Go to Egypt and set My people free!" I would be content with Joseph's or Daniel's ability to interpret dreams. What am I to think of an elephant lumbering through one of my dreams with all the grace of a Himalayan avalanche? I doubt that Elijah dreamed about Kojak, Angie Dickinson or Cher, and if he did, he was too ashamed to put those dreams on a scroll.

I'm ashamed, too, but I am not God's prophet. I am thirty-six years old, the divorced father of a nine-year-old daughter and seven-year-old son, and I am afraid my life is an unclean thing.

Is that what God wants me to know? If so, then why doesn't He tell me how to cleanse this life He has given me? I listen to Gregorian chants each morning; I pray; I read Merton and learn only that I am not the person I could be and I do not know what to do.

Each morning while trying to gather the night pictures before they are scattered by the broom of day's light, I hear the sound of the toilet flushing. It is a sacred sound, a Bach prelude proclaiming that all is well: My son is alive.

A few minutes later I flush the toilet. Does he hear and record the fact that I, too, am alive? I doubt it. A father's existence is assumed, like air, water and McDonald's.

Five years after his mother and I divorced he has come to live with me. *We sit in a grimy luncheonette on a Brooklyn side street near where she and the children live. She asked me to come from Amherst for a conference with her and our son's second-grade teacher.*

*Malcolm's having problems in school.*

What do you mean?

*He's too competitive.*

What do you mean?

*All he likes is sports, doing something where he can run into someone and knock them down.*

He's testing himself against others. It's a way of learning who he is, what he can do. What's wrong with that?

*But he's so violent, which is possibly repressed anger at your having left. Every morning the other kids come in the classroom and they say good morning to me. Malcolm walks in and punches me.*

Sounds like he's angry at you, not me. Hit him back.

*I couldn't do that!*

Why? It's his way of saying good morning.

*He might hurt me!*

You're a grown woman!

*You don't know how strong he is!*

*I wonder if she knows it is not physical strength she fears but the power of the masculine. My son's burden is to grow up when feminism roams the streets with all the intelligence of a lynch mob. His teacher at the private, multiracial, nonsexist, "progressive" school to which I am paying three thousand nondeductible dollars a year does not love the ecstasy of leaping toward where clouds are born to glove a high line drive, the mesmerizing magic of the spinning spiral of a football arcing through an autumn afternoon as dazzling as a stained-glass window, the pride of ripped pants and grass-stained shirts, or the gleeful power in a tiny clenched fist.*

*There is nothing wrong with him, but there will be if he isn't respected and loved for who he is. And who he is, is male. Whether he lives that maleness in a John Wayne parody of the masculine, with the robust celibacy of a Thomas Merton, or the sensitivity of a Rod Carew depends on a lot of factors, but first and foremost, maleness must be a source of joy and delight for him.*

*He has my permission to defend himself in any way he can against feminist tyranny. If he doesn't, he'll find himself hanging from a nonsexist lamppost, crows pecking at his penis.*

*So his mother and I sit opposite each other on the ripped plastic seats of a booth, smoking and drinking bad coffee from thick white mugs. She says he still talks about wanting to live with me, as he has ever since I left. She has told me this many times, always, I thought, to raise another welt of guilt on my already flayed skin. This time I wonder if I had been hearing condemnation when a plea was being uttered, for when she asks, "How would you feel about him coming to live with you?," I respond with a vehemence that stuns us both: "I want him!" I want him, I repeat to myself. And I do.*

In the afternoons I sit in my rocking chair by the living-room window and watch him and his friends play football. I cringe as their little-boy bodies strike the ground with the force of falling worlds, and my son disappears beneath a writhing mass of shirts and jeans. I wait, involuntarily holding my breath, until he emerges unhurt and calls someone an obscenity I'm grateful I cannot hear through the thick glass of the picture window. I smile and give myself over to body's memory, which is older than mine, and I can almost feel again the heat burning my face like a torch in the chill dusk-autumn darknesses when it was my body at the bottom of the heap.

My son is returning part of my childhood to me. I remind myself that he is not a precocious genius simply because he knows the batting averages of every player in both leagues. I did, too—once. I remind myself that such a prodigious memory does not encompass remembering to pick up his clothes or turn out lights. I was no different.

I have to admit, also, that I always had to be right, and pouted when I did not get my way. These aspects of him enrage me. They shouldn't. He is being his age. What I cannot accept is my own uncleanness. I am thirty-six years old and childish. How can I tend his growing without completing the task of my own?

I am entering middle age without having left childhood. How can that be?

Sometimes I look at my son and wonder, from whence came this life? I had nothing to do with the creation of such a marvel, did I? How did that pasty liquid which spurted from my penis create this miracle of bone and flesh which I try to understand by calling it "my son"? The night he was conceived should glow in my soul like an eternal flame. It doesn't, and I am ashamed at how casually his life was conceived. I have given more thought to what brand of canned peas to buy. But Nature is intent only on its own renewal and doesn't notice or care about me. Hallelujah!

When he goes out to wait for the school bus each morning, I sit in the rocking chair sipping my second cup of coffee. I watch him and the other boys throw piles of leaves onto one another. I cannot hear their laughter but I see it fluttering like autumn.

After the bus leaves, I read mythology. I want to decipher the night pictures, uncover the symbols I live, and those that live me. What does it mean that more than two years ago I said, "I want to be a tree!" I read myths, looking for my own, and wonder who the people were who believed in Isis, winged snakes and devouring dragons, and why we do no longer.

As a child I disdained coloring books, but I have several "adult" ones now. For many hours a day I color Quetzalcoatl, Horus and Pegasus with Magic Markers, my intensity as feverish as van Gogh's when he painted the exploding sky of *Starry Night*. I do not understand what I am doing. Maybe I am learning to live without nailing concepts into wonder. When I colored falcon-headed Horus, I could not think about him because people don't have the heads of hawks. And what can I say about (or to) the goddess Isis, her wings broader than any bird's? Once, however, Isis and Horus shook the soul and directed it toward Being.

Daddy and I used to do jigsaw puzzles. Now I am the father and it is my son who sits at the card table with me, staring at the puzzle pieces, searching for the exact one to fill an exact hole.

I love opening the box of a puzzle and laying out a thousand tiny pieces, one by one. I stare at the picture on the box, then at the pieces on the table. There is no resemblance between them. Reality has been fragmented into unrecognizable shards and I, with patience and perseverance, must put it back together.

My son taught me a new way to do this. I match pieces by color. He sees shapes. I am learning to see shapes.

I sit for a ridiculous number of hours, silent, before a jigsaw puzzle, like the coloring books, it is a release from thinking. You can't do a jigsaw puzzle if you think. You have to see, letting your eyes move back and forth from the space to be filled and the pieces scattered on the table until no words pass through the mind. It is a form of meditation.

I fit pieces into place but cannot see how they are creating the picture on the box. Only when I stand back do I see what I have been doing. The whole is more evident when we stand at the edge of ourselves and see the picture that we are.

I want to see my son that way, to see the man forming in the boy's soul. It is to that man I am responsible. The child is the thousand scattered pieces that must find their places to create the adult. But there is no picture on the box to show me what he will look like. This is the fearful part of being a parent. I cannot have preconceptions about who he is and who he should be. I must listen and interpret his symbols.

But what did he mean when he announced last week, "I set a new record today. I've had my shoes on for thirteen hours and thirty-five minutes." And why won't he ever remove his New York Mets baseball cap? Is he prematurely bald, or did his hair grow into a billed cap, complete with team emblem?

On the second day of school, he was in a fight. Now that he is living with me, he isn't supposed to do things like that, I thought self-righteously, but one fight does not a juvenile delinquent make. (Does it?) A kid pushed in front of him as they were lining up for the school bus, and he decked him. I smiled to myself. The boy has character. We went to school for a conference with his teacher during which I established very quickly that my son had the right to defend himself. The teacher agreed, "but not in my classroom." I turned to my son and said, "Next time wait until you get off the school bus. Then deck the son-of-a-bitch."

My son does not know it, but he demands that I live as a whole person because all I can give him is who I am. Yesterday he announced that when he grew up he was going to write a book. Tears came to my eyes as I fantasized becoming the patriarch of a dynasty of literary Lesters which would make the Huxleys look like writers of copy for spearmint gum commercials.

"Well, if you're going to be a writer, you'll have to work on your spelling,'' I said in my best patriarchal voice. (Endemic to being a parent is not knowing when to keep quiet.)

He looked at me quizzically. "Who said anything about being a writer?"

''You did,'' I responded plaintively.

''Uh-uh,'' he answered firmly. "I said I wanted to write a book. I don't want to spend *my life* being a writer."

I am afraid of what he knows about me without my having uttered a word.

One evening he asks suddenly, "Dad? When you were a boy, were there any black kids in your class at school?"

I smile. "Malcolm,'' I say gently, "there were nothing but black kids in my class, the class across the hall, the whole school, and the neighborhood. I didn't speak to a white person until I was fourteen, except for a piano teacher I had when I was five or six.''

How can he imagine such a world? I was twenty before I lived among whites. His mother is white and he has never lived among blacks. I cannot imagine his world.

This difference creates problems. One afternoon we are working in the garden and he begins expounding on why Babe Ruth was a greater baseball player than Hank Aaron. Before I realize it, I am arguing with him as if he is a drunk in a bar. He refuses to relent until finally, I say, coldly, "Babe Ruth was a white man, and probably didn't like black people.''

I am immediately ashamed. How can I have said that to my son, whom I have trouble identifying when he's in a group of white boys.

I remember interviewing Muhammad Ali in the fall of 1968. This was during the years he was stripped of his championship and was persona non grata to the media. The blinds were closed in his room high in the New York Sheraton, and he sat on the edge of an unmade bed in darkness. He boxed an imaginary opponent for a moment, the speed and force of his hands and arms making ominous whistling sounds in the funereal gloom of the room. Then he asked me to loan him ten dollars, an honor I declined. Perhaps my refusal sabotaged the incisive interview I had fantasized, because he ignored my questions about boxing, the Vietnam War and how he spent his days. Or maybe it was because I was black that he felt compelled to recruit me for the Nation of Islam.

He talked nonstop for an hour about "the white man" and white women, making me wonder if he knew of my white wife in an apartment thirty blocks away. I began to fidget as his voice became like a pneumatic drill: "Why would any black man want a white woman? Ain't nothing beautiful about a white woman. They ain't got no color in they skin. Their hair is stringy like a wet mop that's been used too many times. They noses is shaped like a pickax. What's beautiful about that?" I thought about Raquel Welch and wondered if the champ needed an eye exam. Suddenly I was torn from my fantasy love affair by an index finger wavering in my face and I felt like a back-sliding Israelite being confronted by Ezra as a look of almost maniacal intensity came into Ali's eyes and he thundered, "No black man should marry a white woman, because a man wants his children to look like him!"

Is that why I was so cruel when my son said he preferred Babe Ruth to Hank Aaron? I see no memories of slavery in his flesh.

Every father wants to pass his life on to his children, particularly the son. That is not synonymous with imposing his life on the son. The quality of immortality the father seeks through the son is not motivated by what is unfulfilled in the father but by needing who you are as a man to be understood and continued into the next generation. The son redeems the father, not by imitation but by assimilating into his life the essence of the father.

I do not know how to describe the essence of me, but it cannot be separated from Sundays in church listening to Daddy preach as only black ministers can, from sitting on Grandmomma's porch at night and listening to her and Momma and Uncle Rudolph talk about the Old Ones, from collard greens, grits and cornbread, from that hurting in the heart this past April when Josephine Baker died and again in August when Cannonball Adderley and Haile Selassie died. Cannonball made wonderful music, and his "Mercy, Mercy, Mercy" got me through some bad nights during the Civil Rights Movement when I sat in bars listening to it on the jukebox. Jo Baker and Haile Selassie were two of the black faces I saw in *Ebony* magazine when I was a child—Baker in France with her adopted children from all over the world and Selassie in his palace in Ethiopia where lions stalked the grounds. Each was an image of freedom, and there weren't many of those in the Forties and Fifties for black children.

Maybe my son doesn't need such images, but he needs to know that I needed them, or we are cursed as strangers.

Yet he did not choose to have a white mother, to be born in New York City, or to live now in Masssachusetts where only three percent of the population is black, or in a county with only nine hundred blacks. I chose that he live as far as possible from everything that would tell him something of the essence of me.

The boys at school have given him a nickname, he told me last week. I ask what it is. "Milk Chocolate," he says calmly.

I manage a quiet "Oh? Why do they call you that?"

He shrugs.

"Do other kids have nicknames?" I ask.

They do. Charlie, Bob, Randy.

I nod slowly. "I wonder if your friends are trying to tell you that you aren't like them."

He wants to know what I mean and I explain how whites have always used names as weapons against us.

He denies this angrily.

"Is anyone nicknamed White Milk?" I ask gently after a long silence.

No, but there is nothing racial in his being called Milk Chocolate, he insists.

I shrug and admit that maybe I'm wrong.

He agrees eagerly, painfully, and I steer the conversation to what he thinks the Red Sox's chances are against Cincinnati in the World Series.

I hurt for him, yet for the first time our lives have met in the suffering place, which is the only place I can be known. A few more such meetings and who knows? I might tell him that I, too, think the Babe was the greater ballplayer.

I never wanted children. Neither did I not want them. I assumed they would appear out of the fog one day, situate themselves along the sides of the banquet-sized table at dinner and listen avidly while I discoursed with customary brilliance on literature, politics, art and music. That my son prefers The Fonz to Faulkner and the Beatles to Bach is an indignity I am not prepared to endure. But that is part of putting on the father hood.

Sometimes I think children cry out from the trunk of my penis to be born, and it angers me when I hear women say it is their right to do as they wish with their bodies. How came it to be *theirs?* That body was put into their keeping, but it is not their property.

Procreation has become politicized and Life is just another case on the legal docket. This past winter a black doctor in Boston was found guilty of manslaughter in an abortion case. The Right-to-Life groups are overjoyed, so certain are they of everybody's guilt in an abortion. The Pro-Choice groups are dismayed, so certain are they of everybody's innocence. The Right-to-Lifers care about the unborn and advocate more money for nuclear weapons. The Pro-Choicers want disarmament and seek to deny that a baby in the womb is life. They think they disagree with each other. They don't, because neither trembles before God.

Who are the real primitives—the Sioux who believe that prairie grass has a soul (*wakan*), or we who believe that something growing in the womb is not life? Abortion is not a woman's right, because the potential to create life is not exclusively hers. A man who claims his only role is to support a woman who wants an abortion abdicates his responsibility as a man, as co-creator of life. Once seed and egg unite, a man and a woman no longer have rights. They have desires; they have needs, and these must be respected and even heeded. But when abortion is reduced to a political right, my daughter and my son grow up without humility before the mystery of Life.

Being a father is a religious vocation, I am learning, because I am required to teach awe.

On Monday mornings I do the wash. I put the money in the washer, close the top and listen as the hot water begins filling the machine. When it is a quarter full, I add soap powder and bleach, and wait while the water mixes the cleaning ingredients. Then I put in the clothes, slowly, a piece at a time.

My son's clothes amaze me, particularly his underwear, for they are smaller versions of my clothes. They are not children's clothes, but child-sized men's clothes. As I drop them, piece by piece, into the washer, I remember that it was not so long ago that Momma did the same with mine.

Doing the laundry each Monday, I perform an act that is outside history, for on Mondays, I am sure, the worshipers of Isis and Quetzalcoatl did the wash, too. All our acts are the same, and in sweeping the kitchen floor, washing the dishes, making the bed, chopping wood or sitting in my rocking chair, I am inseparable from every person who has lived and is alive. Too often we see only what makes us different.

I fear that we are losing the ability to know light from darkness. We live more and more in the shadows and do not know that they are shadows. Thus we do the laundry and think we're only washing clothes.

It is this, too, that I want my son to know, but words are of little use. I am left, once again, with the burden and terror of my life and the hope that how I live with that burden and that terror will teach him that what we accomplish is not as important as who we are.

# 10

## Spring 1976

Spring. I was determined to catch it this year. Each morning since the first of April I look out the bedroom window for the first glimpse of forsythia. Every evening, washing dishes at the kitchen sink, I inspect the red maple tree for adumbrations of feathery buds. This year I was going to be as vigilant as a cat, waiting with silent tension to leap on spring, catch it, and tie it in a bow around my little finger.

Spring came, and it must have been during the night. Or maybe it was the afternoon I had the car inspected and would have missed the Second Coming of Malcolm X when I was told that I owed two dollars for the inspection sticker and ninety-eight for three new tires. But spring is like that, waiting until you blink your eyes, or blow your nose, and lo! it has arrived.

In New England the first sign of spring's advent is buckets hanging like fungus from the sides of sugar maple trees. The air is still chilled, but the sap is flowing through the limbs of the trees. Seeing the buckets renews my faith in the cycle of the seasons, a faith which February snows test and the winds of March almost destroy.

That is part of the cycle, though. Winter breaks our faith that any other season exists, or even could. Like the earth, we die and lie fallow, unaware that the new is preparing itself within our limbs, to be tapped for sweet juices, to spring forth in forsythia yellow.

I know. Yet I wish I could catch spring in a butterfly net, place it in a jar, and on a snow-encrusted January day, unscrew the cap and let it blow over me with all the wonder of love. Even now, when spring has convinced me that it will remain forever, it swells toward the dog days of August. Spring is not like me, wanting to stop life at a single lovely moment and hold it forever. Spring is always a-here-going-there.

No wonder I missed its birth cry. It does not pause for me to exclaim "Oh!" It does not even deign to compliment itself on producing, yet once again, blue-petaled periwinkles like the dust of fallen stars. Spring has no time to preen itself on its accomplishments, for it is preparing the earth for summer. The ground must be dried and warmed to receive the seeds the wind will scatter, that insects and birds will carry from one place to another, even those I lay in furrowed ground. Spring is not a prize won from the tight hands of winter. It is winter's child and summer's parent, and I try to find my place among the pine green that softens winter's white stare and the white-topped yarrow stalks of summer.

But I don't know where I belong on the rolling circle of the seasons. The definition by which I have known myself since I was eighteen died this winter, and now question marks pierce my heart like fish hooks.

The one constant has been writing. Now I owe books to publishers, books for which I've accepted advances, books I could write easily and quickly, but for five months not only have I been unable to write, I don't know why I should, or how I ever did.

Now my son lives with me. He is not a blank piece of white paper to be rolled into the typewriter. He is not a world to be created in my image.

I used to think I was a good father. I was generous with child-support payments and saw my children from Friday night to Sunday night twice a month. I took them ice skating, to the circus at Madison Square Garden, to see "The Nutcracker" at Lincoln Center and to the playground in Washington Square Park. Pity the divorced father who thinks activities make relationship.

I did my duty and thought I was a father. But on Sunday nights I returned my children to their mother and resumed my life, getting up each morning when I wanted to, going out when I wanted, eating when I wanted, and thought about no one but myself. That was not narcissism. There was simply no one else to think of.

In less than a year I have learned that you become a parent the day you stand before a human being barely four feet high, who weighs forty pounds, and realize that he has a power and control over your life that makes Stalin look like the leader of a Quaker meeting.

I no longer do anything when I want. I get up at seven, an evil hour for one accustomed to rising at noon. I cook breakfast, the most unnatural meal of the day. Not only do I have to be home by three o'clock to meet the school bus, but I must be prepared to answer questions ranging from "What's on TV tonight?" to "Why is knowledge spelled with a 'k' if you don't pronounce it?" to "Can I get a pool table for Christmas?" I am expected to hold a civilized conversation on the merits of Adidas sneakers as opposed to Pumas, a subject that doesn't lend itself to intellectual brilliance, especially when the person I'm talking to isn't smoking a cigarette and drinking coffee, the obvious prerequisites for civilized discourse. Then I have to get dinner on the table between five and six, though no moral person eats dinner before 9:00 P.M. I shop two, three times a week. My son insists that he really does drink that much milk. If I had the courage, I would go in his room because I know he pours it in his dresser drawers just so he can say to me at nine o'clock every other night, "Dad. There's no milk. Good night." I have tried to convince him that Coca-Cola has more nutritional value, and it's great over Wheaties, too. These demands are compounded by skiing lessons and hockey practices he must be driven to and picked up from, which reminds me that I must write the local hockey association and remind them that scheduling a hockey practice and game on Super Bowl Sunday is prohibited under the Constitution as "cruel and unusual punishment."

Then, there are the two thousand minute decisions to be made each day, any one of which, if I make the wrong one, can maim him for life, according to the psychologists. Will he grow up to be an ax murderer if I don't let him watch the first quarter of "Monday Night Football"? Will he become an exhibitionist because there is only one pair of his underpants in the laundry each week? (Is he eating them with milk?) If he keeps refusing to wear a hat in the winter, will that mean he's going to grow up to be like Jimmy Carter?

I never learned to care for myself; now I must think about and for him. God's revenge on a sinful humanity was to make us parents, because nothing makes you more aware of your total inadequacy.

I am weary of laughing at myself. I want to be able to provide a reasonably compassionate answer for his life, but I have nothing to offer except that I am a writer.

Now, I am unable to write.

I am going to make dandelion wine. With buckets in hand, my son and I pick the flowers from our and our neighbors' lawns. I've been picking for a while before I look at one. I stop, more still than dawn. I've never seen anything more beautiful. How many hundreds of tiny, perfect petals are on this one flower, each petal so intensely yellow that I almost have to shield my eyes. I look around and there are dandelion flowers everywhere, like a million tiny suns, and I laugh. How like God to make the most beautiful things the common ones. How human to see beauty only in the rare.

I listened to a bird sing today. Its song was rich and melodious, skipping from a high register to a low one with delightful improvisations in each and so loud and full that it seemed to come from everywhere at once. Finally I thought I had located it in a white pine tree. My eyes went slowly up the tree, searching each limb carefully. I passed over the robin perched on a limb midway up the tree and continued looking. The bird sang! Frantically I looked for it.

Then I wondered: Could that be the robin? The song came again and I looked at the robin in time to see its throat bulging and quivering with music. How could a bird so ordinary be the source of such beauty? Well, that's God for you.

Every evening I spend a couple of hours in my garden. I don't know what I am doing. I am of that generation of Southern blacks whose parents made the journey from the sweat of cotton fields and vegetable patches to the ease of city living, and although Daddy planted a garden in the backyard every spring, I was determined to prove (to myself? to white people?) that I was capable of more than tensing my muscles to grip a hoe. The mark of black success was hands as soft as rose petals.

Now here I am, fingers and palms blistered, my pants dirty from where I kneel to dislodge stones and pull weeds whose roots are like claws clinging to the innards of the earth. As I work, day after day, images of Daddy return to me. I see him go out the back door after supper, still dressed in a suit, his gray straw hat on his head, a seat cushion in his hand. He takes the hoe from the garage and walks behind it to the square patch of ground and works until it is too dark to see. When he comes in, he washes his hands, a smile as thin and beautiful as a half-moon on his face.

Neither Momma nor I worked in the garden with him, or ever asked, How does your garden grow? And he never asked for help or commented on our lack of interest.

I understand now that his garden was separate from us and his life with us. It was what remained of his life before, and each spring he renewed the covenant with his father and his father's father, whose lives were bounded by fields and haunted by train whistles calling them to futures they would never know. Daddy had ridden the train his father and grandfather and great-grandfather could only look at while leaning on their hoes. Now my life is acted out in worlds my father cannot imagine. When we see each other, he glows with pride as he tells me of meeting people and being asked, "Are you any kin to Julius Lester, the writer?" We laugh, and while the laughter brings us close, I feel a yearning within it, a hunger we have for the common ground that father and son are.

Every evening as I wash the dirt of the garden from my hands, I experience that ground; I have assumed responsibility for the covenant and my slave forebears rest a little more easily.

# 11

## Summer 1976

There is so much to atone for if I am to be worthy of my son. But I don't know how to beg forgiveness for the years with his mother when I lived as if all a marriage needed to be fragrant and many-petaled was my having said, "I do." I was young and did not know that other people are real, too. No one can avoid ignorance, or even be blamed for it. I could not have been other than who I was, done other than what I did. Nonetheless, I am guilty.

Sometimes I wonder if I do not need to atone for the sins of an entire generation. I do not know how to make my students understand that there is an evil arrogance in attempting to remake the world in your own image. That is what we tried to do, we who called ourselves revolutionaries. "We want the world and we want it now!" sang Jim Morrison and The Doors. But we never paused to ask, "What the hell does that mean?" We thought we knew what was best for the world. There is nothing wrong with wanting a world free of poverty, disease, war and prejudices. But in such a world will we know better how to love our children? Will we know any better how to love the ones we marry? Will we know, or even care to know, the name by which God calls us?

What if I had submitted to that irrational impulse to be a cantor when I was twenty-two? What if I had gone up to one of the Chasidim walking through Riverside Park in New York and said, "God wants me to be a cantor." Maybe I would have been laughed at. But what if the response had been "Come with me"? Then what would I have done? There is no greater terror than doing what you think God wants of you.

---

After a speaking engagement in Los Angeles, I rent a car and drive east to Arizona. From Phoenix I drive north toward the mountains.

It is not surprising that the whites who live here are among the most conservative in the country. I, too, have been bludgeoned by Nature's implacable and unsparing indifference. Nature is not a mother's breast, nourishing anyone who places the nipple in his mouth. Nature gives us a perfect reflection of who we are, without ever caring that we are.

The politics of fear is powerful here because the land is harsh and unyielding to those who do not love their finitude. This land tells me how inconsequential I am and either I smile, thanking it for allowing me to live with it for what is scarcely a second on its cosmic clock, or I clutch my life in utter desperation, hating the fact that the least particle of windblown desert was here ten million years before and waits patiently for the dust that I will be to join it.

I stop at the city being built by Paolo Soleri, the Italian architect. When completed, it will house two to three thousand people, and will be, it is claimed, a model of how a city can exist with Nature instead of against it.

Walking through it, I feel isolated from the expansive land surrounding it. The "city" feels more like a piece of live-in sculpture than a community. Yet, the guide tells me, it has been designed with complete attention to ecology. Ecology is not, however, a matter of technological design and efficiency. If I am ecologically balanced within, what I create without will be in ecological equilibrium. It is that simple and that difficult. No one can build a city. It is enough if each one builds his or her own house.

Dusk. There is a howling in the distance. It is a coyote. It is the sound my soul makes at dawn.

The wind is blowing, and from the porch of the reception area I hear music. I turn and see hundreds of wind bells hanging there. Soleri makes bells of all sizes and shapes and the sound of them in the wind is aural magic. I wonder if he knows that it is okay to be just a bell-maker.

### *Tuzigoot National Monument:*<br>*Montezuma Castle National Monument*

Tuzigoot is the ruin of a ninety-room pueblo in the Verde Valley. It was built in the twelfth century, when Héloïse was refusing to deny her passion for Abélard. What did they who lived here do with their passions? What was it like to live and love on this hilltop eight hundred years ago?

I look into the valley below and up at the surrounding mountains. Eight hundred years ago in the month of August, someone else stood here and what he saw was little different. But Cher did not appear in his dreams. He did not walk around with more knowledge about the world and events than he could ever use. He knew only what he needed to know: how to irrigate the fields, grind the corn, build a house with small stones, and praise his gods. I don't need to know more, do I?

Montezuma Castle is a few winding, mountainous miles southeast. It, too, was built between the twelfth and fifteenth centuries and has been abandoned for six hundred years. No one knows its real name, or whether it had one even. Montezuma Castle was attached to it by ignorant white people who thought it was the castle of the Aztec leader.

Tuzigoot stands on a hilltop as if growing there; this place was carved from the face of limestone cliffs. It is a nineteen-room apartment house, five stories high. It begins seventy feet from the ground and rises one hundred fifty feet up the face of the cliff.

That Indians created such an edifice without modern machinery amazes white people. I don't know why. In the thousands of years of human history, machines have been commonplace for little more than a hundred, and then only in the West. We are the oddities of humanity, wholly dependent on machines and technology, and damning those who aren't as underdeveloped.

Some of the ruins are open to the public, and I walk up the dirt path and crawl into one of the narrow, low-ceilinged rooms. I do not think anyone could have lived in it. It is dark and so low, even a child could not stand. No, these rooms were only for sleeping. Living was done in the valley. No one knows why they did not build their dwellings in the valley. The National Park Service booklet speculates that living high up on the cliff, the people were immune to attack from enemies. How American. As I crawl out into the light and squat on the cliff ledge, I see that it is only here that one does not intrude on the land. Here, tucked into the cliff, I sit as dusk descends as relentlessly as a hawk and know that my rightful place in the world is a low dark room in the face of a cliff.

### *Hopiland*

The Hopi communities are scattered over the tops of three mesas, each standing above the horizon like a Mayan temple. From the mesas I see all the way to the San Francisco mountains where the kachinas live. From these mesas the Hopi saw the Spanish coming and fought them, century after century, never incurring defeat. For eight hundred years they have been here.

The Hopis are known for two things to outsiders: draft resistance during World War II (Hopi means "peaceful people"), and the Snake Dance, which is among the lesser Hopi rituals. But the spectacle of people dancing with poisonous snakes in their mouths always attracts a lot of tourists.

It's ironic that what is permitted when done by Hopis is condemned when done by poor whites in the mountains of Georgia, Tennessee and Virginia. More startling is that Hopis and poor whites share the same form of religious expression.

The Christian Church regards snake handlers as beyond the lunatic fringe. I wonder if it isn't these outcasts from the Christian establishment who keep the faith vital. I read an interview with one who, when asked if he was afraid of being bitten, responded that he wasn't. He said he knew he wouldn't be when a particular feeling came over him. The only time he was bitten was the Sunday morning he *thought* about handling a snake. After that, he said, he didn't do any thinking, but waited until the urge to handle was so strong that it was *the only way* to give witness to his joy in knowing God.

The Hopi and Christian snake handlers know the Living God. No sitting in pews in proper dress to praise their God. When the spirit fills you, grab a water moccasin and shout HALLELUJAH! Wrap a rattler around your neck and yell GLORY! Put a sidewinder in your teeth and DANCE!

The snake is symbolic of many things, I learned from my reading this past winter. First and foremost, it represents sexuality, that energy and power which is life itself. The Snake Dance reconciles earth and sky, passion and reason, cathedral and kiva, and the monk becomes a lover.

The power of God has not so filled me that I am impelled to worship Him by dancing with a rattler in my mouth. I wish it were not so.

*Santo Domingo Pueblo, New Mexico*

It is the feast day of Saint Dominic and I am here at this pueblo named for him. This is no traditional feast day, however, for it is also the day of the Corn Dance. I arrive early, but already the Indians have attended Mass and removed the statue of Saint Dominic from the church, carried it through the streets to the accompaniment of guns firing and placed it in a bower of cottonwood branches which stands beside the kiva. (Ah, Saint Dominic! It must be a pleasure to get out of the church for a while.)

The dancing and chanting have already begun. Hundreds of men, women and children stand in rows, dancing in place, while to one side a chorus of old men chants. I understand nothing I see or hear, and it doesn't matter. Later I can refer to books and learn the symbolism of the women's headdresses, the painted bodies of the men dancing in and out of the ranks, the pine boughs on the shoulders of each dancer. It is enough to know that corn is the universal symbol of life and fertility, and the corn I planted in June was growing tall when I left. I, too, have cause to celebrate this life and the good harvest I want my life to be.

It is hot. Already, perspiration wets the faces of many dancers, but they seem not to notice. They are renewing their covenant, not only with their ancestors but with the Corn God. This is strenuous worship. I could not dance through the morning into the afternoon and the evening. Such endurance requires an active faith, one which knows it is necessary to dance and chant if the cycle of the seasons is to continue. This is faith beyond reason because the Indians know that the seasons will come and go, each in its time, without their dancing. But their knowledge does not make them passive spectators to the year's continuing line. They do not relax and put their faith in God. They remember what we have forgotten: God has put His faith in us.

What I am seeing is only the public part of a ceremony that has been going on for three days. They would be dancing even if tourists were not here. This is not a performance; it is holy communion.

*Taos*

I am sitting on the hood of my car in front of the hotel when a drunken Indian walks up. In slurred tones, he gives me a capsule of his life before asking for a ride to the pueblo a few miles from here. I tell him no. He can't believe I have refused him. Neither can I. But I don't like drunks. He is a useful reminder not to glorify or romanticize Indians. They do not carry the answers for my life: I do. I can watch a Corn Dance, but the drunken Indian is reality, also. Those who live in the continuous miracle are few. Most of us are drunkards looking for a ride home and being turned down by people like me.

*Taos Pueblo*

The Taos Indians say this is the spiritual center of the world. The Hopis claim the same for their land. I believe them both. In a world so multifarious, there must be more than one center.

A young Indian comes up to me. He gives me what I know as the Black Solidarity handshake, and I almost laugh aloud. He then proceeds to tell me that he and I are brothers and must come together to fight the white man. Even here, at the center of the world, I am defined by my skin color.

*San Cristobal, New Mexico*

The road goes up, up, up into the mountains for miles. I begin worrying that I have taken the wrong one, but just then there is a sign with an arrow pointing: "D. H. Lawrence Ranch."

I park the car at a white house and find the path leading up the mountain to the mausoleum where Lawrence's ashes reside. It is a small whitewashed building crowned by a stone eagle. Inside, a railing separates me from the urn which holds his ashes. In the corners, on each side of the urn, are large pine boughs. I smile. It is properly pagan.

It is important for me to pay homage to this man who tried to find the way to live—with integrity—in right relationship to the demands of the blood. Blood! It was one of his favorite metaphors to describe that part of us which is instinctual. Until I learn to live with what is pagan in me I will not be truly civilized and truly religious.

# 12

## Winter 1977

When my son is at school I go to his room and look at his stuffed animals—bears, dogs, cats and furry, floppy things of all shapes and colors. He has names for each, and when he was younger, he had them talk to me in high-pitched voices that set my teeth on edge. I did not know I was supposed to listen with the piety of the priest who receives the Pope's confession.

When I was a child there were only teddy bears and dolls, and if you remained attached to them beyond the age of six, your parents worried about your future. My teddy bear and doll disappeared one day and I was told it was time to grow up.

If you were a black child in the 1940s, childhood was a luxury that could get you killed. Education in those all-black schools was a process of being trained—intellectually and emotionally—to survive and persevere. We were not allowed to think that the white world could defeat us. It would discriminate against us, deny us jobs, force us to live where it wanted us to, lynch us, but defeat us? Never. If we didn't succeed in becoming doctors, lawyers, teachers, ministers or writers to serve our people, we were to keep the dream alive and pass it on to the next generation—the dream and the toughness to endure when dreams do not come true.

I am jealous of my son and his stuffed animals. How does he find room in the bed for himself at night? I am also suspicious, angry and afraid that his white mother and relatives are undermining him with their cuddly gifts, that stuffed monkeys as soft as love will render him weak and defenseless when it is his time to traverse the valley of the shadow of death. There will be nothing to cuddle then. He will need strength to believe in himself when he has no reason to. I demand perfection of him now so he will demand perfection of himself later because white people do not care if he lives or dies, do not care even that he is.

I know that I am too harsh with him, too strict, just as I am too harsh and strict with myself. But I did not know what it is to have a childhood. I lay awake nights staring through the window at a moon like a luminous skull, knowing it shone on a world waiting like a lynch mob and wondering if I would be strong enough and bright enough not only to endure but to make my forebears proud and the way a little easier for my descendants.

I am merely one in the generations of black intellectuals and professionals who were required to sacrifice their childhoods, personal dreams and desires because our task was to prepare the way. No other alternative existed.

I have wondered often who I would be if I were not black. But I cannot imagine what it is to live without my life dangling in space, stretched and broken by the noose of race. I cannot imagine what it is to have choices.

I went to Tanglewood one Saturday last summer. While walking around the grounds, I saw a young black kid hurrying by, a violin case beneath his arm. I stopped and stared until he disappeared behind a fence. He couldn't have been more than sixteen and I hated him for having opportunities I did not. I suffer in the shadows of the unrealized and unfulfilled parts of my soul, parts which will be forever stillborn. I could have been a classical musician, but as a black child growing up in the Forties and Fifties, such was not even in the realm of the imaginal. But there is still a part of me that wishes he could have studied harpsichord with Wanda Landowska, that fantasizes being guest conductor of the Boston Symphony Orchestra in its summer home at Tanglewood and lead them in playing one of the Bach Brandenburg concerti with such delicate sweetness that the stars would fall from the sky to belong to such perfect beauty existing on earth.

It will never be, and grief and rage bubble inside me like molten iron. Even now, at age thirty-seven, I ask myself, What do you want? and do not understand the question. It's a white folks' question, the rage and grief respond contemptuously.

That is not so, I respond weakly. If I do not know what I want, how can I live? To have done what history considered necessary has not been sufficient.

What do you want? I ask myself again, and, enraged, I shout back: I want not to live with the spirits of my slave ancestors needing me to sing the song they couldn't sing. I want not to have the spirits of all the black unborn telling me that I will be their ancestor and that the stone I hew from the mountain and carve into a step will enable them to move on up just a little bit higher.

When rage subsides I realize that I have stated what I *don't* want.

What do I want?

A Mercedes, to have Peggy Fleming be in love with me, to be rich, to win the Nobel Prize for literature.

What do I want?

I honestly don't know.

My son is at school and I cry. Every morning when I hear the school bus pull away, I lie across my bed and the tears come. I cry for the childhood I could not have. I cry because I will never know what it is to sleep surrounded from head to toe by stuffed animals. I cry because I will never know who I could have been. I cry because if I don't I will hate those who, from evil and ignorance and indifference, determined the parameters of my existence before I could claim it for myself. I cry because I hurt so damned much.

The ground is covered with snow and I am planning the garden. How odd. But I calculated how many canning jars I needed before the first tomato was red.

Gardening is teaching me that the seasons do not come in orderly succession. They are intertwined and interdependent, threads of different colors wrapping around one another. I missed spring last year because I was looking for it. But when the forsythia blooms, spring is over.

One morning soon I will trudge through the snow to the forsythia bush, and taking one of its thin, cold limbs in my hands, I will hold it quietly for a moment. If I am as still as a snowflake, I will eventually sense a tiny twitch from within the limb. With a satisfied smile I will come inside, uncork the first bottle of dandelion wine and drink to the birth of spring.

# 13

## Spring 1978

My time of depression is over. I do not know how it ended or even when. There was no revelatory moment in which I beheld the truth of my life with seven heads, each wearing a bejeweled crown around which danced an angelic host singing praises to God. There was only a moment in which I noticed that I was not in pain and I had not been for several days.

Something has changed within me. I don't know what, but the tears of others are my own now. S. is a beautiful blond girl who was in my "Contemporary Afro-American Novel" course last spring. Throughout the semester I marveled at how she managed to appear in class at nine-thirty each Tuesday and Thursday morning with mascara, a soft green eye shadow, lipstick and facial blush perfectly applied. She dressed with a subtle sophistication, and if she had applied her above-average intelligence as diligently to my class as she so obviously did to *Vogue*, she could have replaced me as teacher. She always sat in the front row, her perfect legs crossed to reveal the beginning of a thigh, the top buttons of her blouse undone to show the lacy border of her bra. I wanted to give her an "A" for the sheer pleasure her presence brought me and the enrichment of my fantasy life.

She came into my office at the beginning of this school year, gave me a big smile, then sat in the chair next to my desk and looked down at the floor. Something told me to be silent. Minutes passed. She would look up at me and then back at the floor.

Finally she said, "I had an abortion this summer." She lapsed into silence. "My parents don't know. They'd kill me if they ever found out."

"It must've been hard going through that by yourself," I offered quietly.

Her eyelashes were suddenly moist with tears. "And the father of the baby, he wasn't any help either."

"So you didn't have anybody?" I asked.

She shook her head. "But you know what's really hard?"

I didn't.

She smiled weakly. "You hear so much about abortion now. So I thought I'd just go and have it and that would be it." She looked up at me. "I didn't know I would *feel* anything! I mean, I knew that I couldn't have the baby. I'm still a baby myself. But nobody told me that I would wish I could've had the baby. Nobody told me I would feel like I'd killed my own baby!"

She sobbed. I closed the door of my office and held her for a long time.

I could not have done that before.

There is another difference, one which began at the Holloways' that summer of 1973: The family is a monastery and holiness lives in time, I learned, but how, how to live it? I still don't know, but for a moment or two each day now, I am still and listen to my heartbeat and I am awed that it is sustaining me in life as it brings me closer to death. The paradox is that this attentive awareness of and to my evanescence brings me into reverence for all that is and I want to live as if I am a song of praise composed by God, and not care if I am off-key or even tone-deaf when I sing myself.

I do not know if I will ever sing in unison with God. But how do you measure success with Him? He doesn't give promotions and raises; He doesn't invite your friends to a banquet in your honor. If you want a banquet you have to give it for yourself.

I do not know how to do that. I am not certain that I deserve one yet.

My daughter and her mother have moved to Amherst. I do not know this firstborn child of mine, though there has seldom been an interval of two weeks since the divorce that I haven't seen her. But the differences between her mother and me are most evident in how we raise our children. My daughter is accustomed to a kind of freedom that is alien to me. To travel the few blocks from her mother's house to mine must seem like a journey through space to a cube-shaped planet. She and her mother make decisions together. I give orders, and if asked why, I say, "Because I said so."

It is not surprising that my daughter said to me, "You don't treat me as an equal."

No, I am not her friend. I am her father and my friendship will have to be earned. I am not friends with my parents; I will never be. Our only common experience is that they are my parents and I am their child. I hope for more with my daughter and son, but perhaps when they grow up they will not like me as a person. I want to raise my children in such a way that they will be able to choose not to like me.

"We're not equals," I told my daughter. "How can we be? I was once twelve, and believe it or not, I remember what it is like to be twelve. You haven't been thirty-nine."

If I had spoken in Urdu I might have communicated more effectively. She argued with me about her "rights." I wanted to give her a lecture on *The Federalist* papers because she is growing up at a time when the concept of rights has been perverted until it is synonymous with desires. Even a cursory reading of the Bill of Rights makes it clear that rights are guaranteed to the individual as protection from the power of government and that is all. People talk as if rights were handed down by God at Sinai and sanction anything their hearts desire. I knew better than to say to my daughter that abortion per se is not a woman's right, that people who are gay have rights because they are citizens but whether that includes the right to be gay is something the society is still working out. She would not have understood and neither would I at age twelve.

But what I finally said was worse, because finally, in exasperation, I heard my mother's voice say: "You want to be treated like an equal? Pay next month's mortgage!"

I had spoken like the oppressor my daughter had always known I was. Unlike my mother, I regretted saying it.

It is the regret which is new. When I was young I wanted to live so that I would regret nothing at my moment of death. That is possible only if I will myself not to know that sometimes (more often than not?) I am the agent for the suffering of others.

To suffer and inflict suffering are as much a part of God as love. I hear my words, but I am not confident I know what I am saying. For my soul to live them I must sail into that uncharted region designated on ancient maps with the words "Here Be Dragons."

To say is not to know. To know is not to live. Not to mistake words for knowledge and knowledge for life is to be responsible for myself and God.

---

Last year I met a woman who knows that the night pictures are the soul's mirror, and who wants to live holiness in family. In fear and trembling, we have married. She, her five-year-old daughter, two cats, my son, I and our two cats have moved into a large house.

I know how to live holiness in family, how to imbue our children with reverence for their lives. By the way we live the ordinary. Yet I watch the news on television during supper each evening, which angers my wife. The house is filled with the smoke of the pack and a half of cigarettes I smoke each day, and when she and the children ask me to quit, I tell them angrily to mind their own business.

I betray holiness while wanting so much to be holy, to make my marriage holy, to make my new family holy. I do not need anyone to tell me what a contradiction I am. Some might call me a hypocrite even.

I am not. But something is missing and I don't know what it is. It should be easy to make the ordinary sacred. For some reason it isn't. At least not for me.

Every Sunday morning the university radio station plays Jewish music for two hours. I don't know why but I listen every week. I don't understand the words of the songs or what they are about, not even after the announcer explains. What is Purim? What is Pesach?

Yet there is something in Jewish music that makes me feel loved. I listen and that loneliness lying within me like a black hole threatening to suck the entire universe into its nothingness is destroyed and stars shine with a white heat and I become infinity.

Every week when I listen to the show "Zamir," I pretend that I am a Jew and the Hebrew words are my language and the melodies are my songs. But I am not a Jew and there is a pain in my soul so deep that it must have begun before I was born.

# 14

## Spring 1979

I am going to be a father again. At forty I am the same age as my father when I was born. Did he feel prepared, finally, to be a father? I do. I am ready to receive this child when he or she is born in August.

When I talked with Tillie Olsen about parenthood once, she remarked, "We should be allowed one child to make all our mistakes on. Then, that child would disappear and we would have our first one." We laughed, but it is true.

I wish I could begin again with Jody and Malcolm, begin again from that first moment when I saw them, begin again now, at age forty when I am not obsessed by the need to plant a flag with my name emblazoned on it at the peak of some summit only I see. I have been more authoritarian than I needed to be; I have not loved with the clarity their souls deserved. But the past cannot be changed. It can be repaired and God calls me to begin again as I am now.

Who I am now, however, is tired. I noticed today that the forsythia bush in the front yard is heavy and warm with yellow. How many days had its color been flinging itself at me?

My wife's body doesn't understand that morning sickness is supposed to stop at noon. It thinks morning sickness is a culture. Throughout the day, I hear her retching in the bathroom off our bedroom upstairs. She has been in bed since January. Fortunately I am on sabbatical this semester.

No one ever told me that being a parent required the physical constitution of a decathlete. There is always something to do, but when I finish I don't remember what I did. Whatever it was, it was important—I think. How many times a day do I put the twist tie around the loaf of bread which was left open? Or maybe the bread wrapper opens itself when I turn my back, making sure to fling the twist tie into the most distant and unlikely corner of the kitchen, or once, into the cat's water dish. And I know, without a doubt, that the dishes and silverware I washed and dried a half hour before come out of the cabinets when I leave the room, open the refrigerator door and smear butter, jelly, tuna fish and orange juice all over each other, and at the sound of my footsteps, they hastily arrange themselves over the kitchen counter, where I find them smiling innocently. They are not as malevolent as the cats, however, who have little buckets hidden somewhere (probably inside the toilet), and while I'm taking a nap, spread kitty litter in a neat path from their box in the downstairs bathroom, across the family-room floor to their food dishes in the kitchen. Unlike dishes and silverware, however, cats do not smile innocently. They look me directly in the eye and say, "Yeah, we did it. And if you mess with us, we'll call the ASPCA and tell 'em you're a cat racist."

---

I had planned to use my sabbatical reading recent novels by blacks and revising my "Contemporary Afro-American Novel" course. One evening in January, however, I happened to pick up Raul Hilberg's *The Destruction of the European Jews* from the pile of unread books stacked beside my rocking chair.

Since the anti-Semitic poem incident ten years ago, I've wanted to study the Holocaust. My reasons were personal and selfish. I wanted to understand the historical conditions which led to the Holocaust so I could recognize them if they ever appeared in this country and would know when to head for the wilds of Labrador. Of course, that is a naïve view of history. If America were going to destroy blacks, the scenario would be so different that I, like the Jews of Europe, could not recognize what was before my eyes. Nonetheless, I figured it couldn't hurt to know more about the Holocaust.

Each evening after the kids are in bed, I read. The more I read, the more depressed I am. However, this depression is unlike the one of a few years ago when I beheld my uncleanness and my childishness. I will not awake one morning to find this depression replaced by flowers budding from my soul.

A depression is also a hollow in the land. Its root meaning is "to strike." That is how I feel. I have been struck so fearfully that I have fallen into a hollow in the land, and I lie gazing upward, not caring if I am "to be crushed by the falling pieces of the broken sky," in the words of Seneca. I have been struck by grief and mourning for the six million murdered Jews. I did not expect this. I did not expect this mourning for my innocence.

I grieve for my childhood. I see myself kneeling in the dirt of the backyard at the parsonage. I stare intently at marbles inside a circle drawn in the dirt. I bite my lower lip and my eyes narrow, as if I am sighting along a rifle barrel. Between my thumb and bent forefinger is a large marble, a "toy" we called it. I release it toward the marbles inside the circle. It is summer 1944. I am five years old. I do not know that at that same moment in Poland, Austria, Czechoslovakia, Hungary, five-year-old boys and girls are being killed because they are Jews.

I am holding Momma's hand. We are walking up the long path to the public library in Kansas City, Kansas. How many times a week did she have to take me there? Two? Three? Four? Regardless of how many books she checked out for me, I read them within a day or two. How secure and whole I felt holding her hand, excited by all the books awaiting me inside. On those days other children were holding the hands of their mothers, naked, afraid, their bodies sensing death coming on like morning.

On January 27, 1939, Jewish children were born across Europe as I was born in St. Louis, Missouri. I am alive. So many are not who should be. If I had been a Jewish child born that day, I would not, in all probability, be alive now. How can I dare have had a childhood when one million Jewish children were murdered in theirs?

I am struck by guilt. But I was a child. I am not personally responsible for the death of a Jew. How am I guilty? What is this uneasiness forcing me to read book after book, horror after horror?

Is it that after Auschwitz, after Hiroshima, it is not possible to be innocent? I am alive and so many are not who should be. Innocence can be no more.

To be innocent is to believe that I am too moral, too good, too decent to do to another what was done to the Jews. To be innocent is to deceive myself about what it means to be human.

*The tombstone of my great-grandfather, Adolph Altschul, in the old section of the Jewish cemetery in Pine Bluff, Arkansas.*

*One of Adolph Altschul's daughters, my maternal grandmother, Emma Smith. Beside her is one of my cousins, Joseph Green.*

*My grandmother Emma on the porch of the house Adolph Altschul built in Pine Bluff. The house burned in the mid-1960s.*

*My mother, Julia Beatrice Smith, at her graduation from Normal School.*

*My father, Reverend W. D. Lester, on his graduation from Philander Smith College in Little Rock, Arkansas.*

*My mother in 1980 at our home in Amherst.*

*My father in 1980 at our home in Amherst.*

OPPOSITE: *I am on the porch of the parsonage in Kansas City at the age of four or five.*

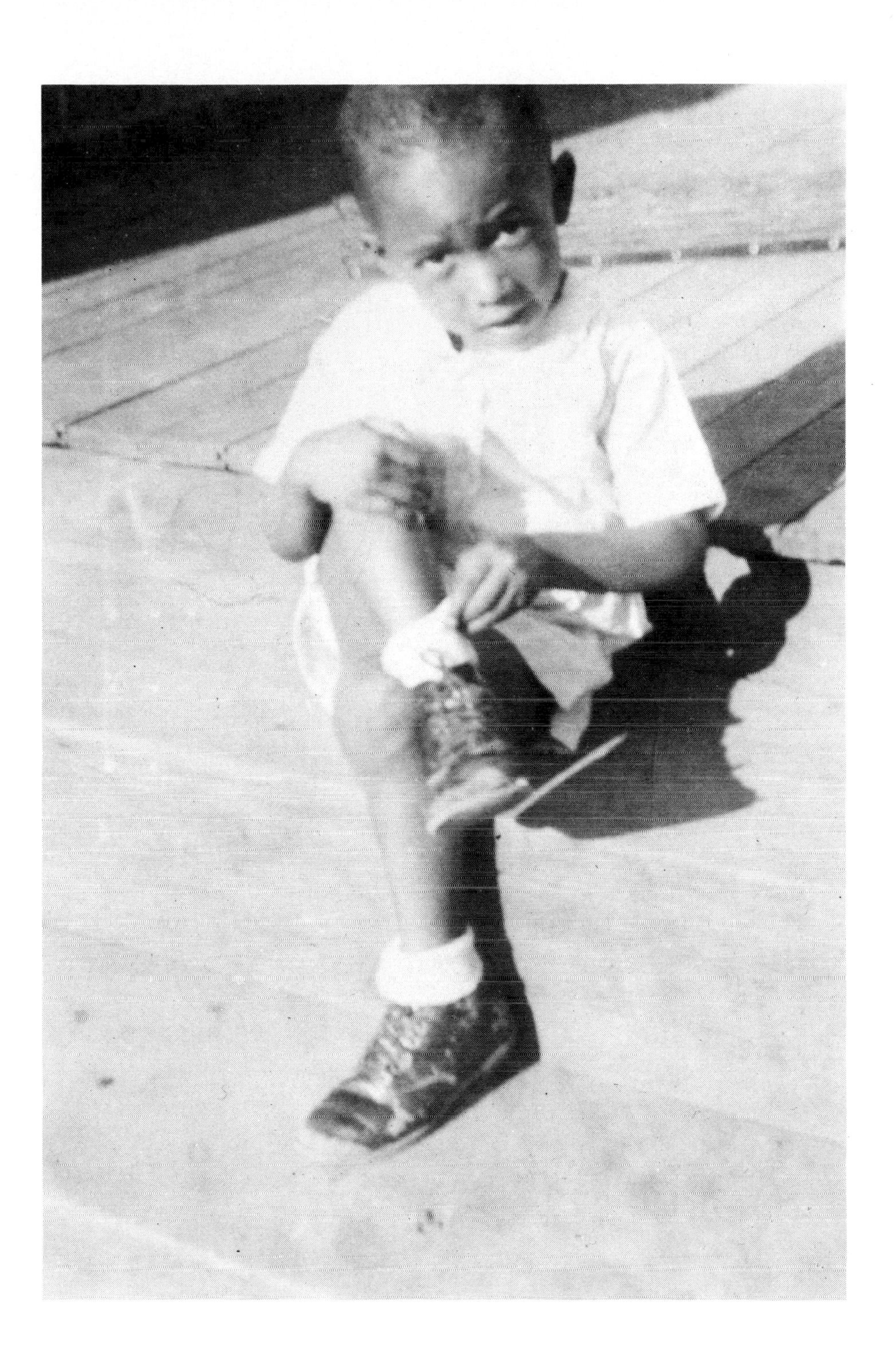

*My first round challah, one that I baked for Shavuot in 1982.*

DAVID GAHR

*I am wearing my prayer shawl (1987).*

Adolph Altschul

In the name of God Amen, I Adolph Altschul living on my place near Pine Bluff in the County of Jefferson and State of Arkansas. of the age of forty seven years and three months being of sound mind and memory. and Considering the uncertainty of this frail and transitory life. do therefore make, ordain, publish and declare this to be my last Will and testament: That is to say, first after all my lawfull debts are payd. and discharged, the residue of my estate Real & Personal, I give bequeath and dispose of as follows to wit:
To my Children Rena Altschul, Emma Altschul, Florence Altschul, Ada Altschul, Charley Altschul, and Rudolph Altschul. The West half of the South West quarter of the South West quarter Section Thirty six (36) Township five (5) South Range ten (10) West, Containing Twenty acres of Land and the North half of the North East quarter of the North East quarter Section Thirty four (34) Township four (4) South Range Nine (9) West Containing Eighteen or nineteen acres of Land. Also I give and bequeath and devise all my personal property and all the rest of residue and remainder of my real and personal estate to my Children now living or their heirs who may be living at the time of my decease to be divided equally between them Share and Share a like at the time here after Stated. To my brother Joe Altschul, my brother Morris Altschul, and my Sister Jeanette Altschul, I give and bequeath One Dollar each. To my wife Maggie Altschul (also not Considered under the law of this State my lawfull wife) which I have love and affection and Consider my true and honest wife I bequeath and devise all my real estate and personal property herebefore Stated as long she be a widow as soon she marry or die the Children of age have a right to take their Share those not of age Shall have the right to name their Executor, likewise I make Constitute [illegible] wife Maggie Altschul to be Executor [illegible] Will and Testament without giving [illegible] Court.
[illegible] whereof I have hereunto Subscribed my [illegible] my Seal the fourth 4th day of [illegible] the year of Our Lord One Thousand Eight [illegible] sixty Eight 1881

Adolph Altschul

My great-grandfather's will, the only item my family has that belonged to my grandfather.

DEATH RECORD

Mr. Adolph Altschul, aged about seventy-five years, died at his country home near this city Tuesday afternoon, after a lingering illness. The deceased was a brother of Mrs. Joseph S. Altschul and F. M. Altschul, of this city, and Mr. Joe Altschul, of Chicago. The remains will be interred in the Jewish cemetery this afternoon, the funeral taking place from the residence at 2 o'clock. Rev. J. S. Kornfeld will officiate.

*Notice of my great-grandfather's death in the* Pine Bluff Commercial Appeal.

Days pass. They are as heavy and silent as stones. I cook and nag the children about their chores. I shop; I watch hockey games on television with my son. I take my wife to the doctor.

There are no words inside me. Only images:

I am five or six years old and come downstairs one morning and notice that the clock has stopped. Momma tells me there was a "blackout" during the night. I know it has something to do with the war but cannot imagine what.

I sit on the top step of the front porch of my aunt's house in Little Rock, Arkansas. I sit all day, watching army trucks and Jeeps and tanks and soldiers go past. I know there is a war somewhere, what a war is and what a tank does.

I remember ration books. I remember buying orange stamps in school and pasting them in a book and when the book is filled, I am given a war bond. I remember sitting in the kitchen, a plastic tube in my hands filled with margarine. It is white, but at the center is a yellow globule and I press the tube until the yellow globule breaks and I squeeze the tube until the yellow color spreads through the whiteness and the margarine becomes yellow like forsythia.

The war was funerals of young men in khaki-colored uniforms and a bronze bulletin board in the church vestibule onto which were etched the names of those killed, and little children at church on Father's Day, white flowers pinned to the lapels of their jackets or on the right shoulders of their dresses. Their fathers had died in the war and on that Sunday we were afraid of them.

I remember, also, my red tricycle, my doll with her blue pajamas, the pear tree in the yard whose green fruit gave me one of the worst stomachaches of my life. I remember gathering eggs in the mornings and the bantam rooster who beat me so thoroughly and so consistently that Daddy finally had to sell the chickens. But before that I remember Daddy going into the chicken house on Saturday evenings, catching a chicken, bringing it to the yard and grabbing its head, twirling his arm around and around, faster and faster until the chicken's body flies through space until it lands in the dust where it flops and runs with drunken steps, blood spurting from the hole where its head had been until it topples over, twitching and flopping in the dust until death stills its body. Daddy gives me the chicken's head and after Momma scalds the feathers off and cuts the chicken up, she gives me the feet, and I take them and sit in the dark, narrow alleyway between the parsonage and the church and, staring, stroking gently, try to imagine what it is like to be a chicken and now be dead. Such ruminations do not affect my appetite, however, when the chicken, fried the color of burnished gold, appears on the table the next day after church.

I cannot reconcile these images with children inhaling gas at Auschwitz, children shot dead before pits at Babi Yar, a child grabbed by the ankles by an SS officer and swung through the air in a swift arc against the side of a railroad car or tree trunk, the child's head and life shattering like a falling star.

Why am I alive?

Why are they dead?

---

I do not understand:

Chaim Kaplan, the Warsaw Ghetto: "It is almost a *mitzvah** to dance. Every dance is a protest against our oppressors."

An anonymous Jew as he is being pushed into a cattle car, the Warsaw Ghetto: "Jews, don't despair! Don't you realize that we are going to meet the Messiah? If I had some liquor, I'd drink a toast."

Words written on the wall of a cellar in Cologne, Germany, where Jews hid: "I believe in the sun when it is not shining. I believe in love even when feeling it not. I believe in God even when He is silent."

I do not understand.

The more I read, the greater my numbness at the horror, the greater my numbness as I read of Jews affirming God in the midst of their own negation.

Elie Wiesel: "They were pressed together so that they could hardly move or breathe. Suddenly an old rabbi exclaimed, 'Today is Simchat Torah. Have we forgotten what Jews are ordered to do on Simchat Torah?' Somebody had managed to smuggle a small *Sefer Torah** aboard the train. He handed it to the rabbi. And they began to sing, to sway, since they could not dance. And they went on singing and celebrating the Torah, all the while knowing that every motion of the train was bringing them closer to the end."

Hermann Graebe, eyewitness to a massacre of Jews in the Ukraine, 1942: "I watched a family of about eight persons, a man and woman, both about fifty, with their children of one, eight, and ten, and two grown-up daughters of about twenty to twenty-four. An old woman with snow-white hair was holding the one-year-old child in her arms and singing to it and tickling it. The child was cooing with delight. The couple were looking on with tears in their eyes. The father was holding the hand of a boy about ten years old and speaking to him softly; the boy was fighting his tears. The father pointed toward the sky, stroked his head and seemed to explain something to him. At that moment the SS man at the pit shouted something to his comrade. The latter counted off about twenty persons. Among them was the family I have mentioned."

Would I be able to hold Malcolm's hand and talk to him of life, direct his eyes to the clear blue sky so that he would not see the soldiers raise their rifles, so he would not see his own death? I do not know.

Elie Wiesel, from a story by Leib Langfuss, a member of the Sonder Kommando: "Two Jews turned to a member of our Kommando and asked if they should recite the *viddui*, the last confession before dying. And my comrade said yes. So they took a bottle of brandy and drank from it while shouting *l'chaim*, to life, to one another with true joy. And they insisted that my comrade drink, too, but he felt too embarrassed, and ashamed. And he said no, but they refused to let him go. They pressed him to drink, to drink and to say *l'chaim*."

I awake each morning, tired. In the night I have wandered among naked bodies piled atop one another; I shovel bodies into ovens and I am the Jew closing the oven door and the Jew inside; I am smoke and flame spewing from smokestacks; I am particles of ash and soul seeking my burying place in cloud and sky.

One morning I awake and, with my eyes still closed, say to my wife, "Even God does not understand the Holocaust."

Another morning I awake and my lips are moving. I listen. I am trying to say "*Sh'ma Yisrael Adonai Elohenu Adonai Ehad*." At night those words resound in me and when I awake, they are the first words I hear from my lips.

"Hear O Israel. The Lord our God the Lord is One." So many Jews went to their deaths singing those words.

I do not understand. I do not understand what the words mean, why they are the ultimate affirmation for a Jew. I do not understand what it is about Judaism, what it is about being Jewish that so many died proclaiming their Jewishness.

I do not understand why I awaken trying to say "*Sh'ma Yisrael*," not even sure that I am pronouncing the words correctly.

Am I trying to be something I could never be?

# 15

## Summer 1979

The dog days of August. I don't know why they're called that. It has something to do with the position of Sirius, the Dog Star. Well, whatever Sirius is doing, I wish he, she or it would stop because the heat is like the vengeance of God.

My wife and I wait in sullen silence for the heat and her pregnancy to end. We know that August will be replaced soon by crisp September mornings foreshadowing cold and snow. With the passing of her second due date, we are no longer convinced she will give birth. The obstetrician swears a child is in there. I'm convinced that my wife is going to be pregnant until she's eighty-four and then give birth to a basketball.

There is much to endure this August because the world out there is pulling at me with cold and bony fingers. Andrew Young, the ambassador to the United Nations, has resigned, and Jesse Jackson, Joseph Lowrey and other black leaders have accused Jews of pressuring President Carter into forcing Young to resign.

Each morning I go to town and get *The New York Times.* Each evening I watch Walter Cronkite and listen to interviews with black and Jewish leaders. Maybe there is something I do not understand.

The facts seem simple: Young met secretly with the Palestine Liberation Organization's representative to the U.N. Official U.S. policy is, however, that there be no contacts between the U.S. and the P.L.O. When Secretary of State Cyrus Vance asked Young about it, Young denied having had such a meeting. When the media continued to insist that a meeting had taken place, Young finally admitted that it had. At that point, Young had no alternative but to resign. A Cabinet-level member of the government cannot be *caught* in a lie. Despite this, both President Carter and the Israeli government urged Young not to resign. Young said he chose to resign so he could speak freely on foreign policy and not because Jews demanded his resignation.

Why, then, are blacks blaming Jews? Why are blacks responding as if an injustice has been done the entire race? I want to think that I don't understand. Then I could watch dispassionately. But that would be insisting on innocence. That is what blacks indulge in with these attacks on Jews.

Since the Sixties a profound transformation has occurred in the souls of black folks and I fear we have become unworthy of our foreparents. I am beginning to realize that I am part of the last generation of blacks to grow up with a morality which demands that we recognize and acknowledge the humanity of white people, especially because they made the denial of ours a creed by which they lived. "You have to be better than them," teacher after teacher in those segregated schools told us. "We got to save them po' people from theyselves," the old ones would say. What I understood was that I protected my soul only to the extent that I did not give my soul over to hating those who had earned my hatred.

It was a paradox. I was educated to live with an unbearable tension between the real and the ideal, recognizing the real but acting, always, in relationship to the ideal. By believing in the humanity of whites, we of the generations before the Sixties avoided becoming victims or executioners, to use Camus's formulation.

With the coming of Black Power, blacks chose to resolve the tension by becoming victims, that is, they allowed their souls to be identified and synonymous with their political condition. They chose blackness, which did not permit whites to be other than white. The humanity of whites was denied by blacks as the humanity of blacks had been denied by whites. I suppose this could be considered integration.

By resolving the tension through canonizing themselves as victims, blacks relinquished the courage to suffer. They began singing songs of sorrow to one another instead of to God. Now they languish in the sentimental and self-righteous security of being victims. But a victim is merely an executioner too cowardly to sharpen his or her sword.

By attacking Jews blacks are thinking with damaged emotions.

They no longer perceive their pain. If one does not know he hurts, he cannot cry. And if he cannot cry, there is no salvation.

I know that I am going to have to write something and I don't want to. I don't need to be the center of controversy again, but sentences form in my mind against my will. I erase them. However, I cannot expunge the thought of my next-door neighbor, Alice Greenberg. She is a Jew. We are not friends, but once every six months or so, I'll be getting my mail from the box at the same time Alice is getting hers and we'll chat about our children with warmth and affection, not only for them but for each other as parents.

If I remain silent, how can I speak to Alice? But why do I care? She does not have the power to bestow absolution on my soul. Yet I would not have the need for absolution if I were not guilty.

*The Village Voice* has published two long articles on blacks and Jews and the Andy Young affair. Neither said what I needed to hear. I am reminded of what Mickey Spillane said when asked why he wrote the Mike Hammer novels. He said all he did was write what he wanted to read.

Reluctantly, I call David Schneiderman, editor of the *Voice*. Our conversation is brief. I ask him if he wants another piece on the Andy Young affair. He says yes, gives me a length and deadline, and we hang up.

I go to my study in the basement, take the cover from my typewriter, insert a sheet of paper and become a typist. It is as if I am taking dictation because the sentences rush into life with an eagerness I wish my unborn child would emulate. Quickly the article is done.

I reread what I have written. I am disturbed. I have written as if I am a Jew.

## THE USES OF SUFFERING

And so, Jews are being used as scapegoats again.

I cannot interpret otherwise the recent position taken by Black leaders on the Mideast and Black-Jewish relations. And I am angered by how self-righteous and arrogant Black leaders sounded: "Jews must show more sensitivity and be prepared for more consultation before taking positions contrary to the best interests of the Black community."

While I understand that such a statement comes from years of anger at active Jewish opposition to affirmative action, and how deeply Blacks were hurt by this opposition to what was in our "best interests," Black leadership still seems to be ignorant of the fact that Jews have been hurt by Black indifference to the fate of Israel.

I don't recall angry pronouncements from Black leadership when 18 Jews were killed at Qiryat Shemona by Palestinian terrorists. I don't remember Black hands held out in sympathy when 20 Jewish children were killed at Ma'alot, where Palestinians held a school of children hostage. When 31 Jews were killed in a Palestinian attack on a bus, Black leadership did not gather before the television cameras and microphones to say, "No! No! Not another Jew can be murdered on this earth."

Because Blacks have been silent while Jews continued to be murdered, I am appalled that they dare come forward now to self-righteously lecture Jews to "show more sensitivity" when Black leadership is guilty of ethnocentric insensitivity. Arrogance is, however, a common fault of oppressed people when they believe their own status as victims gives them the advantage of moral superiority. But morality is not found in lecturing others on morality. Morality is painfully earned by constant awareness of one's own limitations, mistakes, and fragile humanity. Morality comes by constantly adjuring yourself and not others to "show more sensitivity."

It is the absence of sensitivity to point the finger at Israel's relations with South Africa when Black leadership has failed to exemplify the least concern about the oppression of Soviet Jewry. How dare Black leadership thrust itself into foreign affairs on the issue of Palestinian rights after failing to take an interest when Jews were fighting against the expiration of the statute of limitations on Nazi war crimes in West Germany! The lack of Black sensitivity on matters of deep and abiding concern to Jews has wounded Jews as much as Jewish opposition to affirmative action has wounded us.

However, Black leadership not only wraps itself in a cloak of moral excellence; it goes further and chooses sides in the Mideast conflict. I shouldn't have been surprised by this, because, as Reverend Wyatt Tee Walker expressed it, "The Palestinians are the niggers of the Middle East." Such a statement is sickeningly obscene. Any pro-Palestinian sympathies I might have had died in Munich when 11 members of the Israeli Olympic team were murdered. But maybe Blacks have become so Western that we don't think it is "in the best interests of the Black community" to care that there are still people in the world who want to kill Jews because they are Jews. But who in the course of Western civilization has ever cared when Jews were killed? Why, then, should Blacks be different?

Not being different, Black leadership takes its stand for "human rights and self-determination for Palestinians." This sounds reasonable, but something deep within me says that it is wrong to talk about Palestinian human rights as long as Israeli children live with the prospect of death at Palestinian hands. How can Black leadership even think about self-determination for people who attack children? To do so implicitly condones the murder of children.

Black leadership should know about the murder of children, or have we forgotten the four children murdered in that Birmingham church in 1963? And surely we've forgotten that at the memorial services and rallies after the bombing, it was Jews, more so than other Americans, who stood beside us and shared our pain. Black leadership insults this very real part of Black history, not to mention insulting Jews, when it says that Jewish support for the Black struggle was given when it was "in their [the Jews'] best interest to do so." No, that is not true, because those Jews who supported, worked, and died in the Civil Rights Movement remembered in their souls the *pogroms* of Russia, the Holocaust, the dying that is so constant in Israel, and because they remembered, they made our struggle a part of their lives.

That Jews have not supported affirmative action does nothing to negate this. But this does not seem good enough for Black leadership, which takes the position that the support Jews gave in the past is denigrated now. I cannot understand why Black leadership lacks the simple humanity to express gratitude for past support, as well as the anger we feel now in the face of Jewish conservatism. Instead, Black leadership has acted as if Jews were responsible for Andy Young's resignation. I thought Andy was responsible for that, and, with great dignity, he explained that he needed to speak as he wished. But, as Western history amply demonstrates, whenever something goes wrong, it is easy to blame the Jews.

By doing so, Black leadership has shown itself to be morally barren. By its support of the Palestinians, it exemplifies a callousness of spirit to the meaning of the Holocaust, because when six million Jews are killed while the world is indifferent, the right of Israel to exist is unassailable. That is the only reasonable position I think one can have on the Middle East. Is Black leadership unable to perceive that the world is indifferent to Black lives? Are we unable to see the position of Jews in the world has not changed significantly since World War II? And what I hear in the self-righteousness of Black leaders, is, very simply, we don't give a damn.

The irony is that this new expression of anti-Semitism was spearheaded by the organization founded by Martin Luther King, Jr.—the Southern Christian Leadership Conference. Dr. King has been dead only 11 years, but when I listen to his SCLC successors, it is hard to believe that Dr. King ever lived.

I missed him these past few weeks, because, for all my political disagreements with him, he helped me understand that though I suffer by virtue of my race, I cannot indulge that suffering. Neither can I use suffering to crown myself with a tiara of moral superiority. I must learn to carry that suffering as if it were a long-stemmed rose I offer to humanity. I do that by living with my suffering so intimately as to never forget that, having suffered evil, I must be careful not to do something that will, as Dr. King put it, "intensify the existence of evil in the universe." Because I have suffered as a Black person I do not succumb to the thrill of making others suffer. I look at my own suffering and say, let this inhuman suffering end here.

How quickly, how effortlessly, those who knew and worked with Dr. King have forgotten that he taught that "all life is interrelated," that "all humanity is involved in a single process, and to the degree that I harm my brother, to that extent I am harming myself," and that "creation is so designed that my personality can only be fulfilled in the context of community."

I am deeply sorry that Black leadership spoke as it did, because my humanity as a Black person was diminished. The differences and tensions between Blacks and Jews are real, but the positions espoused recently by Black leaders were not "our Declaration of Independence," as Kenneth Clark put it. They merely show that Blacks, too, can be Germans.

• • •

I walk up to our bedroom on the second floor and, without a word, hand the typed pages to my wife, who is sitting up, reading. She lays her book facedown on the bed. I sit next to her and stare through the window across the field to a row of pine trees.

"It's very personal," she says when she finishes. "I've never read anything quite like it by you."

I nod. "It surprised me, too." Much of my writing has a tone of calm detachment, reflecting the fact that, regardless of how angry my words have been sometimes, my anger lacked personal conviction. I wrote as an observer, not a believer. This time, however, something opened within me that I did not know existed.

"How do you feel?" she asks.

"Scared. I wish someone else had written this. God knows I didn't want to."

She reaches for my hand and holds it tightly.

David Schneiderman called today. He likes the essay and it will appear in the September 10 issue. The deed is done. Now, I wait.

It is night and the house is quiet. I sit on the couch in the living room and suddenly my hands are shaking. It is not cold in the room. I feel no inner chill portending illness. Why are my hands trembling as if I have palsy? I hold one with the other. The shaking does not stop but spreads through my body until I tremble uncontrollably.

Two hours pass. Slowly, the trembling diminishes. Finally, it stops.

I go to the basement and read the article again. My body gives an involuntary shudder. It is frightened. So am I. What do we fear? Receiving a letter bomb in the mail? An assassin's bullet? No. Sometimes I think that if I were dead, at least I'd be able to catch up on my sleep. My body and I fear that we no longer have a sanctuary in time and space.

All my life I have tried to be who Daddy, Momma and the blacks of Kansas City and Nashville needed me to be—a servant of and to my people. Now I am attacking them, and a multitude of black voices ask, "Why do you attack your own people in public when there are so many white people, and that includes Jews, willing and eager to do it? We need you to be our advocate, not our judge.

Our enemies will take great pride in your words and use them against us. We hope you're proud of yourself."

I cannot respond. I have lived these past nine months amidst the ashes in the crypt of heaven. Auschwitz and Treblinka are part of my daily pain. The spirits of murdered Jewish children shoot marbles with me in the dirt of a parsonage yard. I had to write as I did or be guilty of murdering those children again.

Proud of myself? I say to the voices finally. Yes. Yes, I am.

## September 12, 1979

Maybe our child did not want to be born during the dog days, because he waited three weeks to be born as summer withdraws with clear skies and cool winds.

We name him David. It is my favorite name, the one I would have liked. It is important to me, also, that this child have a Jewish name. Maybe he will be the Jew I cannot be, a rabbi even. My son, the rabbi!

The article appeared in last Friday's *Voice.* I have scarcely had time to do more than note its appearance. My sabbatical is over and the semester has begun. Between teaching, David's birth, cooking and caring for the other children, I am fortunate to remember where I live.

Daily an editor from the *Voice* calls and asks my permission for the article to be reprinted in various Jewish newspapers around the country. Given my reputation among Jews, I am surprised. They are welcoming my words with an enthusiasm that is embarrassing. A man named Norman Gourse wants to buy space to reprint the article in the "News of the Week in Review" section of the Sunday *Times.* He is retired, with a sick wife, and is not wealthy, but is willing to spend however many thousands of dollars to reprint the article. I give permission.

I am thinking of developing a course that would explore how and where Jewish and black histories converge and diverge. Jews believe they have much in common with blacks. Many blacks are insulted by the idea. Probably both are right.

• • •

I am walking down the hall to my office on the third floor of New Africa House. I come in early on Tuesdays and Thursdays, the days I teach, to sit at my desk and stare out the window at the mountains. It is the only time I get to be alone, as alone as one can be in an office with people walking along the hallway and students coming to see me.

I pass the open door of A.B.'s office. "What's happening?" I greet him.

"You got a minute?" he calls back.

"What's up?" I ask, leaning in the doorway of his office.

"I wanted to know if you had lost your mind."

"What are you talking about?" I ask, genuinely confused.

"I'm talking about that shit you wrote in the *Voice*. Brothers have been calling me from all over the country asking me who the fuck you think you are and what the fuck you think you're doing."

I shrug. "You've known me almost fifteen years. You know I don't bite my tongue."

He laughs sarcastically. "Oh, I know, and a lot of off-the-wall shit you've written in the past I gave you the benefit of the doubt on, but you tore your ass this time."

The muscles in his face are twitching and, for the first time, I see that he is enraged.

"Depends on your point of view," I reply, still calm.

"You must not care what black people think of you."

"That's not the only value."

"What the fuck does that mean?" he yells.

"What're you so upset about?" I ask softly. "This is not the first time I've written something that has upset black folks. And I think blacks need to understand Jewish reality."

"Don't talk that shit to me!" he screams. He is out of his chair and charges across the room to where I stand in the doorway. "The Holocaust! I'm sick and tired of hearing about the Holocaust! You don't know Jews like I do! I went to school with the motherfuckers! I'd see them go from school to Hebrew school. I'd see them make the highest scores on tests! You don't know the motherfuckers like I do! Down South you didn't grow up with Jews. Up here I did, goddammit!"

I walk away and he follows me down the hall, yelling. "You're ignorant, Julius! You don't know shit! You don't know a goddamned thing about Jews! You think I haven't studied the Holocaust? Well, I have, goddammit! I don't see a damned thing about it that's unique. I think black folks have been through more hell than a Jew in Auschwitz could imagine."

I am trembling with anger as I stop and turn to look at him. "Don't ever speak to me again," I say quietly.

We glare at each other, our fists clenched. If he says another word about Jews, I will do my damnedest to kill him.

His face softens. "I apologize, man. I'm sorry. I meant what I said, understand, but I didn't have to say it the way I did."

I nod once. "I accept your apology. But don't ever speak to me again."

My hands shake as I fit the key into the lock of my office door. Everybody on the floor is standing in the hallway, staring at me. I turn and look at them. They avert their eyes and follow A.B. into his office.

---

I feel like a Mennonite who has questioned the existence of the Holy Trinity. Most of the people in the Afro-Am Department are not speaking to me. I was naïve enough to think that friendship was stronger than political differences. Did people like me merely because they thought I confirmed their picture of reality? If that is so, I was mistaken in thinking they were ever friends.

Norman Gourse actually did it. The article appeared in this Sunday's *Times.* I read it again. I like it. I do not know how to think about its being published on the day which will see the beginning of *Kol Nidre* at sundown.

Daniel Hillel, an Israeli friend who teaches soil science at the university, calls. "As a Jew I have felt very alone since this whole business with Young started. Your article restores my faith."

I do not know what to say and can only mutter a polite and embarrassed "Thank you."

He invites me to be his guest at *Kol Nidre* services with the Jewish Community of Amherst. Though I tell him that I will come, I am afraid to go, afraid I will be betraying my people again. But something in me needs to go, needs to be with—how odd. I almost said, needs to be with other Jews.

. . .

The synagogue of the Jewish Community of Amherst used to be a Congregational church and it looks like the stereotypical New England church, complete with white, pointed steeple. In 1977 I remember reading in the local paper about the purchase of the building by the Jews of Amherst. I remember wishing I could belong to it.

I've been to services here once when Daniel and his wife, Rachel, invited us to the bat mitzvah of their daughter, who is a close friend of my daughter. Sitting in the rear of the sanctuary that Saturday morning was like being in a land not even a diligent tour guide could have made me understand. The Hebrew words in the prayerbook bore no resemblance to anything I thought of as language. Reading the translations of the prayers, I was disturbed that so many referred to Egypt and Egyptians. There could never be peace in the Middle East as long as Jews kept alive what had happened in Egypt thousands of years before. At some point in the service, the Torah scrolls were taken from the ark and carried around the sanctuary. I was shocked to see people crowding the aisles and, with fervor, reaching out with prayerbooks and prayer shawls to touch the covered scrolls and then put the books or shawls to their lips. On some of their faces there was a look of rapture I found incomprehensible and repulsive. But when the scroll was laid on a table on the pulpit and someone began singing its words, I thought, "The Bible is a song!" and as I listened to the rapid chanting I felt as ancient as the first star.

I liked the rabbi. A soft-spoken man with a white beard, he talked gently, lovingly about what bat mitzvah meant, to accept the covenant of being a Jew. I felt as if he were speaking directly to me, as if he were making a special effort to welcome me.

I also liked his daughter, who acted as cantor that morning. As her lovely soprano voice sang the prayers, I found myself grieving that I would never sing those prayers.

I remember evenings in other years driving past this building and having my car stopped by a policeman so the crowds of people could cross. I always knew it was Rosh HaShana or Yom Kippur, but I could not imagine why they were so important to Jews.

I still can't but tonight I cross the street before the policeman's extended arms. I cannot see faces in the stopped cars. Are there any blacks behind the night-darkened windshields, who with shock, surprise and anger recognize and watch me walk toward the synagogue? I hurry across the street.

People I do not know stop me to shake my hand, to thank me for the article. Some embrace me. Someone tells me that I am a *mensch.** I don't know what that is but it doesn't sound like anything good.

I sit in the rear of the synagogue and when the cantor begins singing "*Kol Nidre,*" I think of my great-grandfather. I see him sitting in a synagogue somewhere in Germany on this night, listening to these words and this melody. Tears fill my eyes as the cantor's voice breaks with emotion, and something in me does not feel alien sitting here on this eve of the Day of Atonement.

I look around. There is not an empty space in the synagogue. Even the balcony is filled. I see many faces I recognize from the university, people I did not know were Jews.

Suddenly I see myself as if I am looking down from the balcony. I am the only dark face here. I look alien. The yarmulke perched flimsily on my head looks silly. I want to run out. I do not belong here.

# 16

## Autumn 1979

I receive letters from rabbis telling me they read "The Uses of Suffering" in synagogue on Yom Kippur. Other Jews write merely to say thank you. Some of the letters are from people who thought of me as an anti-Semite. Some say they are amazed at how I've changed. Others apologize for having thought I was anti-Semitic.

I am grateful for each letter because I did not know if Jews would believe my words. Some letters begin with a half-apology, saying that I must have received hundreds of letters thanking me. I write back and say that regardless of how many letters I receive, no one can ever hear "thank you" enough.

That is especially so now that most of the Afro-Am faculty has stopped speaking to me. I sit in my office and it is as if a scarlet letter "A" has been sewn to the front of my shirt. Adultery no longer merits shunning in our society but apostasy does. I did not know how many of my friendships with blacks would not withstand difference. It hurts. I miss swapping jokes with this one, gossiping with that one, and talking about the latest books on black history with another. And there is one very close friend from my days in The Movement whose love I will always ache for.

Beneath the pain, though, there is rage at my friends who are angry at me, angry at the existence of Israel, angry at Jews, but they have no anger for Idi Amin of Uganda or Pol Pot of Cambodia, who have murdered millions. I refuse to understand a morality that is selectively indignant.

Every day or so I am asked to appear on some radio or television show. Blacks and Jews are the "hot" topic now. (Next week it'll probably be Coke and Pepsi.) I was offered eight hundred dollars just to be in the audience of William Buckley's "Firing Line" when he had Jesse Jackson on. "You wouldn't have to comment or even ask a question," I was told. We could have used the money, but being known as the "black defender of Jews" would be the same as having been thought a "black anti-Semite." I am neither.

Now if someone from Buckley's show wanted me to sit in the audience while he interviewed Peggy Fleming . . .

Alice came over recently with a present for David.

I am going to offer the course next semester on blacks and Jews. I draft an outline and give it to Haim Gunner, who teaches in the Environmental Science Department at the university and is one of the leaders of the Jewish Community of Amherst. We met when we appeared on a panel last year as part of a day-long conference about anti-Semitism and racism on campus.

He and his wife, Yaffa, invite me to their house for lunch to talk about the course. We have been chatting casually for a while when the doorbell rings. Haim returns with a man whose mournful face is ringed by a white beard. It is the rabbi who conducted the bat mitzvah. He is introduced to me as Yechiael Lander, the Hillel rabbi at Smith College and Amherst College, and part-time rabbi of the Jewish Community of Amherst.

Why is he here? Is there something so offensive in my course outline that Haim and Yaffa thought it better for the rabbi to tell me?

I am nervous and uncommunicative during lunch. Finally, when the dishes are cleared and coffee is served, Haim says, "I took the liberty, Julius, of making a copy of your course outline and showing it to Yechiael. I hope you don't mind."

"Not at all," I lie.

"I like what you want to do," the rabbi says. "I like the way you explore definitions of oppression and the various forms it takes—political, economic, cultural, etcetera—and then see in what ways the histories of Jews and blacks converge and diverge. However, you must include something in the course about Judaism."

"I wouldn't be comfortable doing that," I say nervously.

"Well, you must."

"Are you sure it would be all right?" I ask timidly.

He looks at me as if I am ridiculous. "Well, of course."

What I am asking is, Does he trust me to teach Judaism? I know nothing. And I am black. Would Jews trust a black person talking about their religion? I look at him. I think he trusts me more than I trust myself.

"I read your article as part of my sermon at services at Amherst College on Yom Kippur," he says. "Thank you for writing it. It meant a lot to me and to a lot of the students. I know that I'll be able to fill your class with students from Smith and Amherst alone."

"Well, before you do that, I have to put together a whole new course."

I ask him, Yaffa and Haim what books they would recommend I read. When I leave, I have a two-page reading list.

---

Paul Puryear, the chairman of the Afro-Am Department, calls me into his office. Paul, who chain-smokes, is a heavyset, dark-skinned man with a beard. He is one of those in the department who has not stopped speaking to me. A blunt, outspoken man, he, too, is a Southerner bred in the creed that morality was the standard applied to one's own behavior first and only reluctantly to that of others.

"Close the door and sit down," he says, chuckling.

I do so.

"Did you hear about the departmental faculty meeting Friday?" he asks, lighting a cigarette.

"No. I didn't know there was one."

He laughs. "You weren't supposed to. I thought maybe somebody had told you about it."

I shake my head. "Nobody's talking to me."

"They still mad at you? Well, wait until I tell you what they tried to pull."

"I'm not sure I want to know."

"Oh, you'll enjoy this. They called a special meeting. I'm the chairman of the department and I didn't know a thing about the meeting. I happened to be here in the building and somebody who wasn't in on the plot asked me what the meeting was about. I said, 'What meeting?' He said, 'There's a faculty meeting at three. You didn't call it?' I said, 'Uh-uh." To myself I said, I'd better go to the meeting and see what's up. I mean, they don't come to the scheduled meetings. Something heavy must be going down for them to call a meeting on their own. So I go to the meeting. It was obvious they didn't want me there, but what could they do? Well, the subject under discussion was your new course, the one on blacks and Jews."

"What?" I exclaim.

"They were planning to take a vote to ban you from teaching the course."

"Who was there?" I want to know.

He shakes his head. "I'm not going to tell you that."

"I just want to know who my enemies are, Paul."

He shakes his head. "Think about it. You can figure out who all was involved."

"Well, they can vote until they're dead but they can't stop me from teaching that course."

"That's what I told them. I said, 'Ain't you fools ever heard of academic freedom?' I told 'em that if you wanted to teach the course, there wasn't a thing they could do about it and if they wanted to make an issue of it, I'd fight them all the way to the chancellor."

"What reasons did they give for not wanting me to teach the course?"

He chuckles. "They said you wouldn't teach it from the quote correct political point of view unquote. They said you were too pro-Israel."

"How did things end up?"

"When they saw I wasn't going to let them get away with it, they decided that A.B. should teach a course on blacks and Jews that would be politically correct, quote, unquote."

"Paul, you're kidding!"

He laughs. "Next semester we're going to have two courses on blacks and Jews. Wasn't nothing I could do. If I wouldn't let them stop your course, not that they could have, I couldn't turn around and stop A.B. from doing one."

"No. I understand that."

"But you ain't heard the best part."

"You mean there's more?"

"He's teaching his blacks and Jews course at the same time and same days as yours." He laughs loudly. "How many courses you scheduled to teach next semester?"

"Two."

"Well, drop the other one. I expect you're going to have a large enrollment for the blacks and Jews one and I don't have the money to assign you a T.A." He chuckles.

I thank him. He has done more than I would have expected, especially since he probably doesn't agree with a word I wrote.

I leave his office and walk down the hall to mine and call Saul Perlmutter, the university Hillel rabbi.

"I need to talk with you as soon as possible," I tell him.

I met Saul when he invited me to speak at a Hillel Sunday brunch several years ago. He invited me back another year and has been helpful in recommending books on Judaism and Jewish history for my course.

I go to his office in the Student Union Building and tell him of my almost violent encounter with A.B., of the departmental effort to sabotage my course, and ask him to recommend my course to any Jewish students who ask. He agrees and suggests I also contact Leonard Ehrlich, chairman of the Judaic Studies Program, to see if it will cross-list my course.

I present the revised course outline to the chairman of Judaic Studies. A few days later he calls. The Judaic Studies Program's curriculum committee has voted to include the course as one of its departmental offerings.

---

I did not know how integral anti-Semitism is to Western civilization. I was taught that Columbus discovered America in 1492. I was not taught that Jews were expelled from Spain a few days before he sailed. I learned about the Crusades but no teacher mentioned that the Crusaders massacred Jews as they made their holy way across Europe. Voltaire's *Candide* was presented to me as a classic of Western literature. Now that I have learned of Voltaire's anti-Semitism, I'm glad I found it boring.

I read book after book—Abram Sachar's history of the Jews, Chaim Potok's *Wanderings*, Father Edward Flannery's *The Anguish of the Jews*, Rabbi Leo Trepp's *History of the Jewish Experience* and *The Complete Book of Jewish Observance*, Samuel Sandmel's books on Jesus and Paul, his *A Jewish Understanding of the New Testament*. Most of what I read is new, but some isn't. I forgot that I had read many books about Judaism and Jews since hearing Dr. Poole talk about Anne Frank—Elie Wiesel, Chaim Potok, Isaac Bashevis Singer, not to mention Harry Kemelman's mystery novels featuring Rabbi Small. Still, my ignorance shames me. I was so ignorant I did not know I was ignorant. I had always assumed that the ascendancy of Christianity had made Judaism an historical relic. I remember looking once at the mezuzah* on the doorpost of Daniel and Rachel's house and wondering why they had it there. Surely they didn't believe it, whatever it meant.

Now I realize that the so-called Old Testament is the historical and religious record of a people, that it has an integrity of its own separate from the messianic gloss applied by Christianity. That Christianity took the sacred books of Judaism, claimed them as its own and then tried to obliterate Judaism and Jews makes me feel betrayed by my own civilization and my parents.

I imagine telling Daddy that his Old Testament is not the story of a people who lacked something because they did not know Jesus but is the story of a people who lacked nothing and therefore did not need Jesus. I imagine telling him that Jesus was a Jew who lived and died a Jew, who never addressed his aphorisms and parables to non-Jews. Jesus belongs to Jewish history, although in a minor and aberrant role. I imagine saying such things to Daddy and the entire universe crumbles, which tells me how much of a child, his child, I remain.

What enabled this minuscule group of people to believe in one God at a time in history when everyone else worshiped many? Even more astounding is that they believed in, worshiped and sang praises to a God they could not see, a God their religion forbade them to visualize or concretize, while Greeks and Romans offered gifts and poured libations to statues they deemed representations of deities. How did Jews maintain their belief in an unseen God, a God for whom they had no empirical proof? Obviously, they experienced something about transcendent reality others had not, because rational belief does not sustain a people, or a person, in being different.

I hope no student asks me what Judaism is, because I won't know what to say. It cannot be summarized into a system of beliefs. It is a way of living in the world through small actions. It is what I have been wanting to do all these years—make holy the ordinary, find the mystical in the mundane.

In Judaism studying a sacred text is an act of prayer. Resting on the Sabbath does not mean doing nothing. The Sabbath is another dimension of time and space into which a Jew goes to be renewed. For Jews the synagogue is not the center of religious life. The home and family are, and most Jewish holidays are celebrated in the home.

As much as I enjoy cooking, how can I not love a religion in which the enjoyment of food and wine is an act of holiness and the dinner table an altar? Suddenly I understand the camps I worked at in the Catskills and the bagels, lox, herring, whitefish, brisket and pastries parents brought on visiting days. I feel like I understand New York now! When I worked at WBAI, my production assistant, Nancy Allen, took me often, when we got off the air, to Ratner's, a Jewish restaurant on Second Avenue. I loved the food, and I still yearn for scrambled eggs and onions like those. But I was uncomfortable with how seriously Jews regarded food. Such yelling at waiters and waiters yelling at customers I'd never heard. But holiness is not piety, I am beginning to understand. Holiness is caring, and if the bagel tastes like it's a day old, yell!

I can't believe how little there is in Judaism about sin. You mean I can live without worry that my alternate-week fantasies about Raquel Welch and Peggy Fleming will not condemn me to hell? Jews don't even believe in heaven and hell, it seems. Maybe they exist, maybe they don't, seems to be the Jewish attitude. The only thing that's for sure is this life here on earth.

I don't know what to think, either, about how Judaism encourages one to question, to argue, to disagree, even with God. There was a rabbi who, after a pogrom, not only put God on trial but found Him guilty! But Judaism, if I understand what I am reading, insists that the Jew has the sacred responsibility to make a personal relationship to God and true relationships involve disagreements, arguments and even estrangements.

Fortunately, Judaism is not a missionary religion or an exclusive one. It says that you don't have to be a Jew to be a righteous person. I am relieved, because I can't imagine not watching "Dallas" on Friday nights and sports on Saturday afternoons. I cannot imagine preparing a festive meal on Fridays at the end of a long and tiring week. In our house Friday night is leftovers and please don't talk to me.

But I can study Judaism, learn from it and adapt what I love. I have a Jewish Bible now and each week read a few chapters and study the notes which comprise excerpts from various Jewish commentators—Rashi, Nachmanides, Abarbanel, Maimonides and others.

But being a Jew is more than loving Judaism; it is also belonging to a people. I cannot conceive how a person not born Jewish could belong to the Jewish people. I do not even know what that means—to belong to the Jewish people.

Part of me is glad I can never be a Jew. Part of me is angry with God for not having me born a Jew, and I would convert tomorrow if I were not black.

## Winter 1980

A.B. has three students in his "Blacks and Jews" course; there are eighty in mine. The price of such vindication, however, is reading eighty papers, and since I will be assigning four papers, that's three hundred twenty papers, which will amount to between fifteen hundred and two thousand pages.

The students are disappointed that there are only ten blacks in the class. In the ten years I've taught here, I've never had many black students in my classes, though. A black student told me once it was because my wife is white. On such reasoning and humanity the future of blacks may depend.

It's a good class, ninety percent Jewish, ranging from one very outspoken Orthodox young man to Reform Jews to anti-Zionists to Jews whose only relationship to anything Jewish is that they were born from a Jewish mother. There is also a German exchange student.

The students are bewildered by the joy with which I lecture about Judaism, the passion in my lectures on Jewish history. Some have come during office hours to tell me that my enthusiasm is making them look anew at the Judaism they had all but rejected.

I cannot rid myself of the desire to convert. Would I want to if I were not so isolated from blacks now? I don't know. But I do feel lonely and abandoned by my people. If I converted now, I'm afraid I would be doing so only because I am angry at my own people. I know that if Jews did not accept me, I would be devastated. I can only become a Jew when I know that is what God wants of me, when I know that being a Jew is right for me, even if no Jew in the world accepts me.

I doubt that Jews would accept me in my complexity any more than blacks have. When Hannah Arendt published *Eichmann in Jerusalem*, she became a nonperson among Jews as I have among blacks. Would Jews have responded any differently to a Jew who defended the black response to Young's resignation than blacks have to me? I don't think so.

I must accept that this loneliness is how God wants me to live.

# 17

## Summer 1980

I watch the passengers come along the wide airport corridor toward the double doors leading into the terminal. There is an old black man, walking slowly, leaning on a wooden cane. A gray summer suit hangs loosely, shabbily from his body. Age has shrunken and tightened his skin until it is taut around his skull and his thick lips and broad nose protrude from the skull as if they are features on an African mask. He reminds me of old black men I have seen on dusty back roads in Mississippi and Alabama, men whose bodies and faces have attained the quality of eternity at the edge of mortality, men at whom I looked and wondered what troubles they had seen, what troubles they had overcome to have acquired the quality of stones.

Behind the old black man an airline employee pushes a woman in a wheelchair. It is Momma, looking like a disgruntled dowager queen. Shocked, I look back to the old black man. It is Daddy.

His face becomes animated as the double doors open automatically and he sees me. His handshake is firm as he gives me his traditional greeting: "Well, what you saying about yourself?"

I put my arms around him and hug him. He chuckles nervously, pleased, and pats me on the back. We are not accustomed to touching, he and I, she and I, he and she. It is as if their bodies are forbidden to them, as if their bodies have been sanctioned only for work, as were the bodies of their parents and slave grandparents, and if their bodies were to know joy it could only be through the smooth wood of a hoe handle, the upraised ends of a plow, in arms extending above the head to pin damp clothes to a line. I want to hold him closely enough so I can feel the clods of earth in a cotton field, his grief for those boys of his youth whose souls went to God with the burn marks of a lyncher's rope. But I dare not. I want to hold her thin body and touch apple blossoms and the fuzz of the peaches she pulled from the trees in the orchard, the loneliness and fear in long, waist-length black hair and skin as luminous as the new moon being hated by black folk and white. But I dare not.

"Not much," I respond. "What you saying about yourself?"

"I'm percolating like weak coffee." He laughs.

Two summers ago he had a stroke and I was told to come immediately. I did not. He and I are bound to each other in ways my brother and even Momma do not know. I am his Joseph and he has given his God into my keeping. I knew his time to die had not come. I called him in the hospital and told him that I couldn't come for a week and that he wasn't going to die.

My wife and I went after he was brought home from the hospital. I was not prepared to look down at my father lying in bed. I did not come expecting to shave him each morning, this man who used to cut my hair, this man who put sugar in milk to induce me to drink it, this man who brought me soup and soft-boiled eggs when I was sick and sat on the edge of my bed looking frightened even though it was only chicken pox or mumps, this man whose warmth and laughter and clumsy tenderness taught me love. Now he needed my warmth and laughter and clumsy tenderness. He did not need me to be a son and neither of us knew how I was to be the father.

My wife and I coaxed him back toward life. He would never be in life again, however, and I understood. Ol' Death had breathed into his face with a foul-smelling breath, but my wife massaged his hard and calloused feet and he purred like a street-toughened cat taken in by a child. She got him talking about his youth, though he was never young (how could he be with both parents dead by the time he was fifteen, leaving him with two young brothers to raise and a farm to work).

One afternoon he got out of bed and took me into his study, the middle bedroom that was mine once, sat down at his desk and took a folder from the middle drawer. In it were the papers for his crypt at the mausoleum. I was not shocked or surprised. We have always been matter-of-fact about death—him, Momma, and me—talking of its inevitability with more ease than we talked about anything else. He handed me three sheets of paper. On one he had written the order of his funeral service, the passages from Scripture he wanted read, the hymns he wanted sung. On the other two sheets he had written his obituary. It was a listing of the facts of his life—where he was born, the honorary degrees he received, the churches he pastored, his accomplishments during his years at the Board of Evangelism. I nodded and handed it back. He knew and I knew that these facts were not his life. His funeral program should have on it his smile, and as the mourners enter the church they should be handed small envelopes, inside of which would be a small piece of his dignity—the way he looked in a suit and tie, the pride with which he carried himself in the days when his body moved through time and space as if fired by an inextinguishable sun.

During the five days of his and Momma's visit, I see that the sun has already slipped below the horizon, and the colors spreading over the evening sky are brilliant when he takes his nine-month-old grandson on his lap and plays with him as he used to with me. The colors intensify when I ask him what it was like to be him growing up in the South in the first decades of this century. I want to know all he knows, want to see all he saw, and though I thought I had heard all his stories, there are ones he had never told me—funny ones about possum hunts and train rides.

Father's Day. It is the only time I will sit at one end of the table and stare at my father at the other and along the sides, my children and his grandchildren. I will not see him alive again.

## Spring 1981

Daddy calls. There is pain in his forced "What you saying about yourself?"

A minister friend gave him a copy of an essay I wrote for *Katallagete,* he tells me. Silently, I curse the minister. In the essay is a section in which I describe sitting in church as a child and looking at the figure of Jesus on the cross and my rejection of him as the bearer of my sins.

> Why should I give my sins to Jesus? They were my sins. It was my task to mediate them. To give one's sins to Jesus felt like the effort to preserve innocence. "To put oneself under somebody else's

cross," Jung wrote, "which has already been carried by him, is certainly easier than to carry your own cross amid the mockery and contempt of the world."

To carry my cross. To lift my stone. To live with the suffering that comes to me, whether as a consequence of my actions or being born black.

To live with the suffering that comes to me because I was born.

How do you lift a stone that weeps?

You reach down and pick it up.

Daddy does not understand and, I realize now, has never understood. He has tried to accept but he cannot. How could he have spent most of his eighty-three years traveling and preaching, bringing the word of Jesus to thousands and thousands and having them accept Jesus into their hearts as Lord and Saviour, and yet neither of his sons goes to church, neither of his sons believes in that Jesus who is the center of his life.

I hear that eternal child in me wanting to plead, "But, Daddy. Just because I don't believe in Jesus doesn't mean I'm not religious." But I do not allow the child to speak, because Daddy cannot understand. To be religious is to be Christian, and Protestant Christian at that.

But I hear him say, "I wouldn't have minded if you had converted to Catholicism, you know. I knew that you were attracted to the Catholic Church. I would be happy if you went to somebody's church."

I do not know what to say. I want to remind him of the five days he spent in my house, of how we held hands and said grace at every meal, of the love in this house. How can he not know how insanely religious I am? How can he not know?

He doesn't and I will never be able to convince him. But I do not need to and I hear a smile in my voice as I say, "I'm sorry you don't know, Daddy, how religious I am. You didn't fail, Daddy. You didn't fail!"

There is silence in my ear. Finally he says, "I wish I could be sure of that."

"You can," I reply simply.

"Well, I'm going to send you some things I've written."

A few days later an envelope arrives. I scarcely recognize his handwriting on the front. Inside is a folder containing several of his sermons. I love them because they are my father, but I cannot read them.

## July 31, 1981

It is 5:00 A.M. when the phone rings. As I stumble across the bedroom in the early morning light, I know.

But he is not dead. He had a heart attack at 1:00 A.M. and is in the hospital. He is not expected to live.

I consider flying to Nashville but he will die before I arrive. I go back to bed and tell my wife that Daddy had a heart attack and is not expected to live. Then I go to sleep.

I awaken two hours later. The sun shines with summer's brilliance and I smile. Then I remember. My father is dying.

What do you do when you know your father is dying? I wash my face, dress and go downstairs where my wife is feeding the baby. We discuss the day's logistics. She has to shop; I have to take Jody to a doctor's appointment, pick up my check at the office, go to the bank. We arrange the day so that one of us will be here to answer the phone.

Five-thirty. I am sitting at the kitchen table watching Malcolm hitting a baseball across the yard. The phone rings. I do not need to answer it. I do.

Momma is direct. "He's dead." Her voice is steady and strong. There is no emotion in it. There is only the fact. He's dead.

I ask her how she's doing. She says she is all right. She wants to know when I am coming. I tell her I'll come Sunday. She asks me when I think the funeral should be. I tell her Monday. She agrees. I ask if she wants me to call my brother. She says that she spoke to him that morning and he is driving down from where he lives in Indiana. There is nothing more to say. We hang up.

I bang my fist into the wall and mutter damn, damn, damn, and then I gasp. I want to cry but no tears come. I go outside and tell Malcolm, "He's dead." Then I pick a Frisbee from off the grass and motion Malcolm to the far end of the yard and sail the Frisbee at him and memories, unwanted, unbidden, rush forward like a lover and there is Daddy my father pitching a ball to me, playing basketball with me before supper, Daddy Daddy Daddy teaching me how to sweep a floor without raising dust, Daddy oh Daddy laughing at jokes I would tell him, teaching me to play croquet, Daddy oh God my father and, as I leap to catch the spinning Frisbee, stretching my lean body and looking up to grab the Frisbee with the tips of my fingers, I wonder if my firstborn son knows how precious such moments are, and dear God, how quickly they pass and now, now, dear God, what am I supposed to do, now when all that warmth and all that love and all that tenderness is unmoving flesh.

# 18

## Autumn 1981

I sit in my office. I stare through the window at the Berkshires. They are mountains. They twinkle with yellows, oranges and reds. Once I exulted in the multicolored air of October. Now I cannot remember what exultation is like, or why I exulted.

I looked at my wife this morning. I looked at the children last night. Their faces are familiar, but who are they? My father is dead and I do not understand why.

I know he was old. I do not understand why he had to die.

"I feel he wouldn't have died if I hadn't done something wrong," I tell my wife one night, sitting at the kitchen table. And I sob. "I know that's silly, but I feel like there was something I didn't do, and that's why Daddy died."

I am forty-two years old. I am no longer a child, and yet my loss is a child's loss. My father is dead. How do I live? Who am I now that he is dead?

I was talking with Richard Noland, a friend who teaches in the English Department, and he quoted me Freud's statement that the death of the father is "the most important event, the most poignant loss, of a man's life."

That helped, because I did not know that Daddy was synonymous with existence. He talked so much about death and I have known so many who have died. I thought I was prepared.

When I walked into the airport terminal in Nashville, I expected to see him waiting for me, looking for me. For a moment I didn't know why he wasn't there. Then I remembered and I walked along the corridor, and down the escalator to the baggage claim area, alone.

Even when I saw him lying in the casket at the funeral home I cannot say I knew he was dead. I'm not sure that Jesus rose from the dead, but if any man could, it was my daddy! But as I watched his casket being slid into the vault at the mausoleum the next afternoon and heard my brother cry out and watched my father's youngest and surviving brother collapse, I knew, for an instant, that I would never see him again.

In the next instant, I thought, My father, dead? Ridiculous! So much life cannot have been removed from creation and creation continue. But it does and in a few moments I will walk down the hallway to my one o'clock class on the history of the Civil Rights Movement. I will talk about how voter registration campaigns were organized in Mississippi, as if it matters. I will respond to my students' comments and questions and at two-fifteen class will end. Then I return to absurdity.

I begin stacking my lecture notes and books.

Something is wrong.

Something is wrong with my left eye.

It doesn't seem to be blinking.

I go to the bathroom and look in the mirror over the sinks. I blink my eyes. The left eyelid does not move. I blink them again. The left eyelid does not move. I grin. The left side of my mouth does not move. I pull at the skin. I slap my face. I blink my eyes again. The left eyelid does not move. I twist my mouth. Only the right side responds.

The left side of my face is paralyzed! I open my mouth and begin saying the alphabet. If I talk slowly, the letters are distinct. I say my name. It sounds slightly slurred, but I can be understood.

I return to my office, pick up my lecture notes, and books, and walk into class. I tell my students that if I sound like I am drunk, I am not.

"I was sitting in my office just now and the left side of my face suddenly became paralyzed. My father died recently and this is not an easy time for me." Then I begin class.

The doctor says I have Bell's palsy and there is nothing that can be done except to wait for it to go away. He asks me if I have been sleeping beneath an open window. I wish it were that simple.

I wear a black eye patch because my left eye tears from being constantly open. My wife buys me straws so I can drink. I must look silly sipping coffee through a straw.

Rebecca Dobkins, a student in my Civil Rights Movement class, comes into my office one afternoon and hands me a book. "When you mentioned in class that your face was paralyzed, it sounded familiar to me. It took me awhile, but I eventually found this book in the library. I put a little piece of paper at the page I thought you might find interesting."

It is a book about Apache Indians. The page she has marked is the beginning of a chapter on the "ghost disease." The symptoms of the "ghost disease" are simple—paralysis of the facial muscles on one side. The cause? The spirit of a dead person is inhabiting one's body. The cure is a complex dance and ritual whose purpose is letting go, and sending the ghost to the realm of the dead where it properly belongs.

I do not want to let my father go. I do not want him confined to the world of spirits.

I am alone in the house. My wife has taken the two older children out for the evening. David is asleep upstairs.

I sit on the couch in the family room and the tears come. Four months after he died, I cry with a child's helplessness and write in my journal:

> Daddy died! My father died and I feel so abandoned and so terribly alone. How could he do that to me? How could he? Didn't he know that the memory of him is not the same as him? I'm so so sorry he died. So so sorry. He was such an alive person. That's what I'll remember the most—the aliveness, the vitality of the man who was my father.
>
> My father is dead and that's not right. Why did Daddy have to die? I want him to be there—like the sun and air and grass. Just be there. Be Daddy.
>
> For so long I didn't feel much. I was afraid to feel, because I was afraid the feelings of loss and abandonment would kill me. I knew that he wasn't alive anymore, but dead? That's different.
>
> Dead is a big huge empty space, a void.
>
> It is hard to accept that, or even believe it. My daddy isn't dead. He just isn't alive, because if he's dead, then what's to become of me? Who am I supposed to be now? What am I supposed to do? Am I

supposed to walk around and act like everything is the same as it always was when I know that nothing is as it was? Just what the hell am I supposed to do? Who am I supposed to be now?

I don't understand why my daddy died. My daddy loved me so much and now all that love is gone. That's what the void is. All that love has been withdrawn and I don't know what to do because there's no replacement. There's no replacement for a father's love. It was there for forty-two years, then whack! All gone! No more! No substitute, no replacement! When the sun goes out, the solar system is destroyed.

I loved my father so much. So much of who I am is because of him. So many of my strengths are because of who he was and what he taught me and who he raised me to be. And so much of what I have done with my life was for him, too—thinking about him, wanting my life to compensate him for the disappointments in my brother. How can I let him die? How can I accept him being dead? What am I supposed to do with my life now that it can't be an offering to him, regardless of what else my life is?

He was father and mother to me. Not only did he give me a sense of right and wrong, an introduction to faith, but he gave me the encouragement to be an individual; he gave me warmth and let his pride in me show. That's why his dying is so devastating. He was damned near everything in making me who I am, in forming so many of the essentials of my character.

I am so much like him. I talk like him. I look like him. I speak publicly, as he did. I use humor like he did. My interest in folklore comes from him telling jokes and stories. My interest in history comes from him talking about the past. My feelings as a Southerner and my connection to slavery come through him. My religiosity comes from him. My faith comes through him. I have his quick temper and sternness, too.

I miss you, Daddy! I don't want you to die; I don't want all that joy and goodness and dignity not to be in the world, not to be there for me. I want to always be able to hear you pick up the phone and say, "What you saying about yourself?" And I'll say, "Oh, nothing much."

I don't want you to be dead. I don't want you to not be. I had no idea it would be so lonely without you, so incredibly and awfully lonely without you there like some pillar on which I stood and out of which I grew. You were my roots—personal, religious, racial. You were the foundation.

We never talked with each other like I would've liked, but that was okay. You had a way of letting me know you were there. I remember the times you would come and stand in the doorway of my bedroom. I'd look up from the book I was reading and you wouldn't know what to say and I wouldn't know what to say and that was all right. Sometimes I had the feeling that there was nothing you wanted to say but that you just wanted to look at me. It was enough for you that I was there and it was enough for me that you were there. All the differences between us didn't get in the way of that. And I guess that was what was so incredible about you—it was the mere presence of you that could make a difference. It was your presence, and the knowing where you'd come from and what you'd made of your life.

I've got a new book coming out and this will be the first one you won't read and I wish you could. I'll miss the act of making an offering to you, of paying you homage.

Don't sons exist to make whole the father? To take who the father is and carry it into the future, recast and made anew? That's what I did for you and I guess I need to know that it's okay to keep doing it. Because that's what I've always done. I don't know as I know any other way to live.

I admired you so much.

We understood a lot of things about each other, you and I. We understood a lot of things without agreeing on most and that's pretty amazing.

Maybe our relationship doesn't have to end because you're dead. I accept that you were tired, that it was hard for you to see your body failing, your mind dimming. And I accept that you decided to quit while you still had some say in the matter. That's why I experienced a certain joy in your dying, because I knew you wanted it, knew it was right, and knew that you had done it with your exceptional dignity. I love you for that. I accept all that.

But I don't see how I can accept that our relationship is dead, too.

I've wanted to ask you how it was for you when your father died.

Oh, my father, my father.

Daddy.

Daddy.

# *Part Three*

# 19

## December 18, 1981

Movement has returned to the left side of my face. It came during the past month in twitches of pain like electrical shocks in my cheeks and beneath my eye. Several times a day, though, I stand before the mirror and wink my left eye and exercise the left corner of my mouth. The shadow of the ghost remains, however. A permanent crease cuts my face from the end of my left nostril to my mouth, and the skin on that side of my face is loose. It is a mark of death—mine and my father's.

I am no longer a son. A week from today we will be in Nashville with Momma for Christmas, her first without Daddy. I will not be there as her son because it will be my task to put up the Christmas tree this time; I will sit at the head of the table on Christmas Day and carve the turkey. Each Sunday since Daddy died, I talk with Momma; I was stunned to learn she has never been in a bank. Now, I must answer her questions about taxes and plumbing and why she must make a will and why Daddy's will must be probated. And one day I must tell her she cannot live in that house alone just as she had to tell her mother.

I am no longer a son but do not know what else there is to be. With sadness, the thought comes—I can be me. Is that what Freud meant, that a son cannot be himself truly until the father is dead, until the son stands in that void the father leaves and knows that the only other human being who can fill that space is himself?

I go to the office to turn in my final grades and get my mail.

"When does Chanukah* begin?" the secretary, Jean, asks me.

"Sunday night," I respond, without thinking.

"Well, you have a happy Chanukah."

"And a merry Christmas to you."

I am walking out of the building before I wonder why she wished me happy Chanukah. And why did I receive it? And how did I know when the first night of Chanukah is? I chuckle to myself as I think: She must think I'm Jewish.

Since I began teaching the "Blacks and Jews" course, I cancel classes if they come on Rosh HaShana, Yom Kippur or the first day of Passover. It's funny she thinks I would have to be Jewish to do that.

Night. I am lying in bed. My eyes are closed, but I am not asleep. Suddenly, I see myself dancing in the middle of a brick-laid street. A brown yarmulke is on my head and I am dancing around and around in a circle, my arms extended like the wings of an eagle. I am a Chasid and I am grinning and laughing, dancing, around and around and around.

The joy of the vision permeates my body and I smile. I want to laugh aloud, to get out of bed and dance. I want to shout: I am a Jew! I am a Jew! I am a Jew dancing the joy of God!

The next morning I awake and joy swirls around and within me like dandelion flowers dazzling the sun.

I am a Jew!

I want to run downstairs and tell my wife. But I am afraid. What will she say? What will she think? I am afraid of my joy. I will wait and say nothing. This joy may dissipate in tonight's sleep.

Two weeks pass. Joy is no longer an emotion I feel; it is who I am. I am so happy each day that I have to force myself not to burst out giggling for no reason.

When the children are in bed, I tell my wife. "I think I'm going to convert to Judaism."

"I'm not surprised," she says.

Shocked, I ask, "What do you mean?"

"I don't know. I'm just not surprised."

Having said the words aloud, having heard her matter-of-fact response, I am afraid again. What am I talking about? Why do I want to be a Jew?

The answer is simple: I am tired of feeling guilty for not being in synagogue on Rosh HaShana and Yom Kippur. I am tired of feeling lost on the first night of Passover. I am tired of being jealous when I see Jews going to or coming from synagogue. I want my eyes to shine like sky as do those of my Jewish students when they return to class after having gone home for the first night of Passover.

I am a Jew. I wonder if I have been always and if playing "*Kol Nidre*" on the piano when I was seven was a tiny act of affirmation which I am able only now to embody. I will not be converting to Judaism. I am becoming, at long last, who I always have been. I am a Jew. I'm only sorry it has taken me forty-two years to accept that.

Two more weeks go by. I must be sure that this is what I want to do, what I need to do. But why do I doubt? The joy is there each morning when I awake. I not only see it smiling at me like a lover when I open my eyes, but it takes me in its arms and strokes my body.

I call Rabbi Lander.

The joy is not with me as I drive from Amherst to Rabbi Lander's office at Smith College in Northampton. There is only fear. What am I doing? Julius the Jew? Ju! Ju! That's what kids used to taunt me with when I was in elementary school and I never understood why they thought saying that would hurt my feelings. Ju! Ju! Jew. Jew.

For the rest of my life, do I want to hear people say, "Gee, you don't look Jewish," thinking they are being clever and witty? Do I want to be an object of curiosity, a sideshow freak: Julius Lester, former black militant, former anti-Semite, becomes a Jew? I would be less odd if I grew another head.

I keep hoping the car will skid on a patch of ice so I won't be able to keep my appointment with Rabbi Lander. But I drive safely into the parking lot behind the white chapel. I sit in the car for a moment. I can back out and go home. If I do, I will hate myself.

When I enter Rabbi Lander's office in the basement of Helen Hills Chapel, I look at the books on the shelves. The joy returns. Or maybe it is that I return to the joy. I look at the books with Hebrew lettered on the spines and the letters dance as I danced in my vision. I see the volumes in red binding and the gold-colored letters on the spine which read THE TALMUD* and I want to cry. There is another set of books with the simple word MIDRASH* on the spine. And I know: What is within those books is who I am.

Rabbi Lander and I chat for a few moments about our children and then he asks, "What can I do for you?"

I remember the only other time I sat here with him. It was in the fall of 1979 as I was preparing my first lecture for the "Blacks and Jews" course. I had decided to begin the course with a lecture on slavery as the womb from which Jewish history and American black history are born.

I began reading the Book of Exodus, but was immediately baffled: Why was the man who was to liberate the Jews raised by Pharaoh's daughter? And who was Pharaoh's daughter that she defied her father's edict that all newborn Hebrew male babies be killed?

I began writing, imagining myself into the questions. The daughter of Pharaoh comes down to bathe in the Nile. Did she need to cleanse something more than her body? Did she need to wash away her identity as the daughter of Pharaoh? I see her walking beside the banks of the Nile and seeing the basket floating by the bank. It must have looked like a tiny coffin. How could she not think that the body of a Jewish boy was inside? Yet she sends one of her slaves to get the basket. Then, most remarkably, instead of ordering the slave to open the casket, she opens it herself. What a courageous young woman! To perform such an act, she had to open to something within herself first.

I stopped writing. What was I doing? Was I violating Jewish history and Judaism by imagining myself into a sacred text in this way? I needed Rabbi Lander to read what I had written.

"This is a *midrash,*" he said.

"What's that?"

"Well, it's a Jewish way of exploring a text, a way of encountering oneself in a text without violating the text. What you've written is quite good."

A year has passed. I sit in Rabbi Lander's office again and wait until he finishes lighting his pipe. "I think I want to become a Jew."

He smiles. "I had a feeling that's what you wanted to talk to me about." He chuckles. "I'm not intuitive at all, but when you called me, something told me that you wanted to talk about conversion."

My wife had not been surprised. Rabbi Lander is not surprised. Was I the last to know?

# 20

## Winter 1982

*Alef. Bet. Gimel. Dalet. Hay.* Each time I look at a Hebrew letter and translate it into sound, I feel like a magician with the powers to transform moonlight into ribbons of gold and water into a shimmering sun. The letters themselves are magical and alive. They breathe and move with the litheness, grace and solemnity of ceremonial dancers. My dreams now are filled with *alefs* and *lameds* and *shins* swaying and undulating through a deep space which they light like stars.

One afternoon a week I learn the Hebrew alphabet with Aimee Tracey, a Smith College freshman whom Rabbi Lander asked to teach me. Though my wife is not converting, she is studying the alphabet with me. Even with her beside me, I feel like I'm seventeen again as I walk into a girls' dorm. When I open my Hebrew primer and begin to read haltingly, I am five. Aimee is yeshiva-trained and is very serious. Each week I expect her to rap my knuckles with a ruler or have me stand in a corner where I would pull at my imaginary *payess.** I am not good at languages. But I'm not sure Hebrew is a language even. The iconography of the letters is so compelling that the language becomes not mere words but a way of conceiving and experiencing reality. This is especially true because I am learning to read the printed, calligraphic script at the same time as I am learning to write and read cursive. It is like learning two languages.

Becoming a Jew is to learn a language, too, except this one is of the soul. Becoming a Jew is not memorizing a set of beliefs and principles. It is learning to feel as a Jew feels. If I were hearing that from someone, I would say he or she was crazy. But I am not.

One morning every other week, I meet with Rabbi Lander. A Reform rabbi, he is very traditional and it is the tradition that he is teaching me. "Whether you choose to observe and follow it is your decision, but you *must* know it."

He usually has a prospective convert begin by studying Jewish history, but since I already have, I start with Abraham Joshua Heschel's *The Sabbath.*

It is one of the most beautiful and poetic books I have ever read.

> The Sabbath is not for the sake of the weekdays; the weekdays are for the sake of the Sabbath. It is not an interlude but the climax of living.
>
> The seventh day is a *palace in time* which we build. It is made of soul, of joy and reticence.
>
> All our life should be a pilgrimage to the seventh day; the thought and appreciation of what this day may bring to us should be ever present in our minds. The Sabbath is . . . our awareness of God's presence in the world.
>
> What *we are* depends on what *the Sabbath is* to us.

To give one day to God does not seem like a lot. I have a feeling it will be. From sundown Fridays to sundown Saturdays I am used to eating leftovers and watching television, preparing for classes, grading papers, and on Saturdays watching television from the time the first pitch is thrown, football snapped, or basketball tipped until a "Hawaii Five-O" or "Kojak" rerun goes off at 1:00 A.M. Sunday. But from reading Heschel and the chapter on Shabbat in *The First Jewish Catalog,* it seems that Shabbat is a spiritual discipline. It is not relaxing and doing nothing; it is attentiveness to the holy and yet, as Heschel writes: "One must abstain from toil and strain on the seventh day, even from strain in the service of God." How can I be attentive to the holy without working at it? I am beginning to understand why the rabbis so diligently defined thirty-nine categories of work prohibited on Shabbat. You must empty yourself of the secular to make room for the holy.

But there are so many details to be mastered before I can begin observing Shabbat—how to light the candles, the blessings for candle-lighting, the wine and bread, the blessing of the children. It doesn't sound like a lot, but attention to detail is not one of my strong personality traits, and Judaism is a religion of details. But I love it! For example, after *ha-motzi,* the blessing over the bread, is sung, a corner of a loaf is broken off and that is broken into small pieces for each person at the table. The pieces are put on a plate and the plate passed around. The reason is quite profound: If I handed each person a piece of bread it would imply that I am the source of the bread. Putting the pieces on a plate indicates that I am the maker of the bread but not its creator.

I am learning songs—*z'mirot!* Shabbat begins with songs of welcome to the Sabbath Queen. (Judaism conceives of the Sabbath as feminine. In medieval Europe Jews walked to the edge of town at sunset on Fridays, dressed in white, to welcome the Sabbath Queen descending from heaven, and then escorted her into the town. I would like the Sabbath to be that real.)

My wife is excited about observing Shabbat on Friday evenings. One of Rabbi Lander's concerns was the effect of my conversion on the family. I am fortunate my wife is so open to something so new and so enveloping.

When I told the children I was converting, Jody and Malcolm were shocked. "I thought you couldn't be Jewish unless you were born Jewish," Jody said.

When I explained that that was not true, she wanted to know, "Does this make us Jewish now?"

"No," I said, smiling.

"Do we have to become Jewish?" Malcolm asked.

"No."

They were visibly relieved and had nothing more to say or ask.

I hope one of them writes a book about what it was like having me for a father. Not only can I not imagine it, I'm not sure I would want me as a father. Parents are supposed to be like the face of a mountain—solid, unchanging and always there. What is it like for them to have a father who is more like a bird, and you never know in which tree he is going to be roosting, or when he is going to fly off into the distance, sail in great circles overhead or swoop down, talons extended? It would not be easy for me to read the book they would write.

---

The Chosen People. Every time I see that phrase in a book I am uncomfortable. No, it is more than that. I don't like it! It sounds arrogant and superior. Why do Jews think they were chosen and no one else was? Am I to believe that God has favorites and Jews are it? "I have taken you as a people unto Myself," God says somewhere in Scripture. Then what about the rest of us, God?

As much as I love Judaism, as much as I want to be a Jew, I know already that unless I make peace with the concept of chosenness, my conversion will be stillborn. I'm afraid to discuss it with Rabbi Lander, afraid he will say I can't be a Jew. But I have to tell him.

Rabbi Lander explains that chosenness is not a mark of favor but of responsibility. Jews are responsible for living in the world in a certain way, i.e., with ethical values, with a sense of morality and divine purpose.

That makes sense, and yet Christians, Muslims and humanists live with ethical values, a sense of morality and purpose. There isn't anyone on earth who wouldn't claim that.

How do you belong to the Chosen People without thinking yourself better than everybody else? I understand the resentment of non-Jews in ancient times against this minority claiming it was chosen by God and everybody else wasn't. That's not exactly the way to ensure good relations with your neighbors.

Yet the words are there: "I have chosen you to be My people," God says. What do the words say about how Jews experienced themselves in relationship to the universe? Something happened to them, something very real and transforming happened inside these former slaves which gave them a special, unique and singular relationship to the Divine. And whatever it was was so powerful that it has been happening in every generation since, and Jews die rather than relinquish it. Babylonians, Greeks, Romans, Christians, Muslims and Nazis persecuted and murdered Jews because Jews insisted on their singularity.

But Jews have never glorified martyrdom. There is the story of the man in Auschwitz who raised his eyes to heaven and said, "If we are your Chosen People, then do us a favor? Choose somebody else." But I am sure that that man, if he survived, did not choose not to be chosen.

Why?

I understand now.

Judaism is not in the knowing; it is in the physicality of doing.

After reading Heschel, I thought I understood Shabbat, but the extraordinary beauty of his book is like lead next to entering Shabbat itself, which I now do each week. I understand what Rabbi Lander meant when he quoted the saying of an Israeli poet: "It is not that Israel has kept the Sabbath; the Sabbath has kept Israel."

Now the weekdays exist in relationship to sundown Friday. On Monday mornings my wife will say, "Five days to Shabbat," and each day thereafter, at some moment of weariness, one of us will look at the other and say, "How many days?" Shabbat is the sun around which the six days revolve, bringing light and life to them.

Friday mornings I get up early to bake two loaves of challah. My wife is usually out shopping. David plays quietly with the babysitter, Erica, who, it so happens, is Jewish, and after she puts David down for a nap, she sits on a stool on the other side of the kitchen counter and talks about watching her aunt, who lives in Israel, knead the dough for challah.

I mix the flour, water, oil, salt, sugar and yeast in a bowl and then knead it for ten or fifteen minutes on one of the countertops. I am using a recipe Rabbi Lander gave me, his mother's recipe. The challah rises for an hour or so, then I knead it again, flatten it, cut it into strips and roll them into ropes. Then I braid the two loaves. The first time I did it I had to ask Elena, my stepdaughter, to show me how to braid. I'm still not good at it, but slowly, laboriously, I get it done. Then the challah rises again, after which I brush the loaves with beaten egg yolk, sprinkle on sesame seeds to symbolize the manna God provided us in the wilderness, and bake!

I like it that David will grow up with the smell of baking challah in the house on Fridays. It will be his first Jewish memory.

When I take the loaves from the oven and stare at the mysterious beauty of their interwoven braids, they are like two songs of praise that are the color of earth, undulating like gentle hills covered with sparkling dew. I put them on bread racks to cool and then begin cooking.

Shabbat dinner is a banquet for God. If I have a hobby, it is collecting cookbooks, so I have not hesitated to buy every Jewish cookbook I can find. Cooking for Shabbat each week I am becoming a part of the Jewish people. Every dish I cook has been cooked and eaten on Shabbat for centuries. I especially like the Sephardic dishes like fassoulia, a simple but delicious stew of beef, green beans and pearl onions, or lamb tagine, a lamb stew with prunes and almonds.

When it is time for Shabbat to begin I am tired, having been on my feet for eight hours. But I take off my apron, look at the white tablecloth my wife has put on the table, the two pewter candlesticks, tall white candles extending from each, the challah resting on a plate and covered with a white cloth, the *kiddush** cup beside it, and the exhaustion drops from me as if it were a skin for which I have no use.

I go upstairs and put on a suit. Sometimes when we are all dressed, my wife and I sit and have a drink, staring with happiness at the beautiful table and the flowers she always remembers to place in the middle between the two candles.

We sit and my body tingles when my wife stands to light the candles and says, "Come. Let us welcome the Sabbath. May its radiance illumine our hearts as we light these candles."

We chant the blessing over the candles and I recite a psalm. Then we sing the traditional songs of welcome to the Sabbath—"*Lecha Dodi,*" "Come My Beloved," and "*Shalom Aleichem,*" "Peace to You." Then I read words of love to my wife and she to me after which I recite the *kohanic** blessing in Hebrew and bless my sons, admonishing them to be like Ephraim and Manasseh, the two sons of Joseph whom Jacob blessed and made into one of the tribes of Israel, and my wife blesses Elena, admonishing her to be like Sarah, Rebecca, Rachel and Leah.

Then I sing in Hebrew the words from Genesis describing God finishing His labors and resting on the seventh day. One of the children reads the words introducing the blessings over the wine and bread. The blessings over the wine and bread are sung and I rest within Shabbat.

Shabbat dinner is long. Not only because there are so many courses but because instead of gobbling down the food so we can turn on the TV, we sit and talk with the children about what they've been learning in school, the triumphs and disappointments of their week. I get the latest jokes, those they dare tell me, and sometimes they ask my wife and me about what school was like "in the old days."

After dinner the children may watch TV or go to their rooms.

I would like to forbid their watching television on Friday evenings, but do not feel that I can. They are not becoming Jews; I am. If I did not allow them to watch TV, they would experience Judaism as a restriction on their lives. I don't want that. But I long to experience the Sabbath as I know it can be—a day in which one is wholly removed from the world as it is for six days.

If my wife is not too tired, we study Torah together once David is asleep. We read aloud the portion for the week, stopping to ask questions and talk. We seldom get through more than a chapter or two. There is so much to say.

We are in the Book of Exodus and this week's *parashah** describes the building of the tabernacle. We talk for more than an hour about the twenty-first verse of the thirty-fifth chapter: "And they came, everyone whose heart stirred him up, and everyone whom his spirit made willing, and brought the Lord's offerings." What is the difference between the heart and the spirit? Can one's heart be stirred up but his or her spirit not be willing? And exactly what is it to have one's heart "stirred up"?

Then in verse twenty-six there are these words: "And all the women whose heart stirred them up in wisdom spun the goats' hair." "Stirred them up in wisdom" . . . what a wonderful phrase. I don't know what it means, but it is so evocative.

The import of the whole *parashah* is that we are to fashion ourselves into a tabernacle. How do I do this? How do I make myself into a dwelling where God would come and reside?

---

The Jewish Community of Amherst does not have Saturday services. There is a Conservative synagogue in Northampton but I would feel like I was breaking the Sabbath to drive there. Too, I know no one there, and my blackness burns my skin when I think of walking into a synagogue where I don't know anyone.

So, on Saturday mornings I read Jewish books—*Pirke Avot (Sayings of the Fathers)* and study *midrashim.* In the afternoons I watch sports on television. I'm not supposed to, but I will probably need a personal visit from God before I'll find a virtue in not watching the NCAA basketball tournament, and even then, I'm not so sure I wouldn't be able to convince God to pull up a chair and watch Patrick Ewing slam-dunk!

Saturday evening we have Havdalah, the ritual separating Shabbat from the rest of the week. We sit at the table and look through the window until we see three stars in the sky, which, the rabbis said, was the sign of the new day. I feel a deep sadness as I light the braided candle. At the end of the ritual, when I extinguish it in the cup of wine, there is a sharp pain. I have been expelled from Paradise. If I feel this way after a minimal Shabbat observance, what must it be like for one who is truly observant?

It hurts, sometimes, that I will never be able to experience Shabbat in its purity. But the children were watching cartoons on Saturday mornings long before I decided to become a Jew. My wife worked around the house on Saturdays long before I decided to become a Jew.

Nonetheless, it is painful. How I would love to cuddle with the Sabbath Queen.

---

Chosenness. I think about it historically, and I begin to understand that, yes, Jews are the Chosen People.

The revelation of God as One enters history through the Jews. I wish I knew in my flesh what that experience was. Its impact and force must have been the spiritual equivalent of a giant meteor striking the earth, because this tiny group of people separated themselves from everyone in their world and dared to be different, dared insist that there is only one God, invisible and indivisible. This is extraordinary, because it is the belief in the reality of the Spirit.

Judaism is a curious mixture of the rational and the mystical. I get lost very quickly when I try to read the Talmud. I cannot follow the incredibly involved reasoning of the rabbis. Even *midrashic* exegesis leaves me bewildered sometimes. But Judaism does not *believe* in reason; it uses it as a tool of worship but reason itself is without intrinsic value. Value is found in suffusing the daily with holiness, and that is the *via mistica.*

What is unique about the *via mistica* in Judaism is that it is not an experience for the few. It is not an experience of grace but is integral to practicing the religion. At Havdalah there is a line we say: "We who were called at Sinai to be a kingdom of priests are charged to make Havdalah." A kingdom of priests! What an absurd and marvelous notion.

I choose and I am chosen. I choose to accept responsibility for the Sabbath. I choose to accept responsibility for bringing God into the world once a week.

The unseen soul is as real as what is seen. That experience enters history with the Jews. To guard and embody that experience with attentiveness to the nuances and intricacies of holiness is the Jews' task. It is that for which God chose Jews.

Even saying it that way, it sounds arrogant and superior. But now that I am entering the covenant, I experience it as a blessing and a curse, a burden and a joy, but arrogant? Superior?

No.

# 21

## Passover 1982

Last year Rachel and Daniel Hillel invited us to their home for a seder. Because we were the only ones present who did not read Hebrew, much of the Haggadah* was read in English. Daniel explained anything he thought we might not understand. I nodded and smiled politely, understanding little and feeling nothing except a Puritan sense of waste at how much food was on the table.

This year I prepare a seder for my home and wonder if a Gentile can understand Judaism and Jewishness. The thought is as repugnant to me as when blacks tell whites they cannot know what it is to be black. It is a statement that negates literature, art and music, nullifies the realm of the imaginative and says it is impossible for human beings to reach out from one loneliness to another and assuage both. If that were true, I would not see aspects of myself in haiku and the poems of Sappho, the music of Bach and the watercolors of Winslow Homer.

But Jews are different. If I were converting to Catholicism or Buddhism, I would not be afraid to tell anyone. But an otherness clings to Jews like barnacles. My wife fears that I am becoming unfamiliar to her. I tell her that I am only becoming wholly myself. I know what the problem is, though. The word "convert" makes it sound as if I am dollars about to be turned into francs. That is not so. I am merely receiving who I have always been.

And yet, as I prepare for Passover, I understand her anxiety. Passover is a blending of history and religion, of celebration and commemoration, a drama of remembering, of transforming history into personal memory so that it is I who am emerging from bondage in Egypt.

Becoming Catholic or Buddhist does not require this personal immersion into a historical experience, which is also a transcendent, religious one. Joining other religions does not require becoming part of a people who are inseparable from that transcendent, historical experience. There is no entity called "the Catholic people" or "the Buddhist people."

But Jews are a people. They are of many nationalities and tongues—atheists, agnostics, and some who practice Zen meditation and chant Buddhist mantras and sing Hindu hymns. Yet they are Jews. That is what is so confusing to others about being Jewish. It is not a belief system or even subscribing to a particular religious practice. It is belonging to a people, not only those living but also those who are not.

During my New York years I had dinner one evening with Diane Wolkstein, who writes children's books based on folktales as I do, and is now New York City's official storyteller. I remember a comment she made about being Jewish. "When the shofar is blown on Rosh HaShana I think about the sound of the shofar being heard that day in synagogues all over the world, and I think about how many thousands of years the sound of the shofar has been heard in synagogues all over the world. I can't describe it, but it's the most incredible feeling in the world." I do not know if she is a "practicing" Jew, and it does not matter. What matters is that response to the sound of the shofar, that response to hearing it, not only as yourself but as every Jew who ever was.

Listening to her that evening, I thought I would die from the pain of not belonging to something so vast. Now I do! On Friday evenings when I raise the two loaves of challah and we sing the blessing, I think not only of Jews in Boston and New York and Philadelphia and Baltimore who are doing the same, but of all the Jews through the centuries who performed that simple act.

Is this the change my wife senses in me, despite my noble words that I am only becoming myself? Does she look into my eyes now, expecting to see a reflection of herself, to see my love giving her back to herself and instead see something called a Gentile?

I cannot admit it to her, but sometimes that is so. On Shabbat, I rise from my chair at the head of the table, hold the *kiddush* cup and say: "O God, You have chosen us and set us apart from all the peoples and in love and favor have given us the Sabbath day as sacred inheritance. Blessed is the Lord for the Sabbath and its holiness." Those words divide us. I am saying that I belong and she does not. And yet Friday after Friday she sits opposite me at the table and hears those words, is humiliated, even, by them. But if I need those words to be me, she is willing to extract more love from deep within the pain my becoming a Jew is causing her. I need that love, but as great as it is, my becoming a Jew is separating us more than her whiteness and my blackness ever could have.

Tonight when I begin the seder, I will join with all the Jews in the world. Jews are never foreigners to one another. That is inherent in Judaism and Jewishness. To be like everyone else is to cease to be a Jew. If Jews do not hold to separateness, Jews cease to exist.

It is not possible for Gentiles to experience this separateness as other than a rejection of them. Daniel and Rachel are close friends, and yet at their seder table I was an outsider, and there was nothing they could do to make it different. That is simply how it was. They were commemorating and celebrating an event in the history of the Jewish people; I was a spectator because I was not a Jew.

My wife is right; I am changing when I can think that she is a spectator to my life.

## Shavuot 1982

On this day we received the Torah at Sinai. Torah. Such a complex little word. It is usually translated as "law," which angers me. Certainly there are many laws in Torah, but the laws are not Torah; they are the means by which and through which one is led deeper and deeper into Torah.

In the fall of 1979 when I started studying Jewish history, I did not understand the stories about devout Jewish men who spent their lives studying Torah. Now I know: Everything is in Torah. There is no need ever to study anything else.

What do I understand Torah to be at this neonatal stage of Jewishness? On the simplest level it is the Five Books of Moses, though these are generally called the Pentateuch or Chumash. Torah can also mean the entire Hebrew Bible, though this can also be referred to as the Tanach. In its fullest sense, Torah means the Tanach, plus the *Mishnah,** *Gemara** and *midrashim.* Orthodox Jews believe that at Sinai God gave Jews not only the Tanach but all the commentaries that were to be written, i.e., the Talmud.

For me, studying Torah is an act of engaging God with my imagination, my reason and my feeling. On Shavuot we read the Book of Ruth, but reading Torah is not merely saying the words of the text. I imagine myself into the text. What does it mean that Naomi's husband and two sons die? My wife wanted to know if there was something wrong with the masculine principle in society at that time. And in the context of the story, what would be the masculine principle?

I love Judaism because of the questions I ask. The answers will change as I change and from each new answer will rise new questions as beautiful as lotuses. I wonder what questions I will ask of the Book of Ruth when I'm eighty.

It is Shavuot and as I walk through the tall, white double doors of the Jewish Community of Amherst, I hope the trembling in my stomach does not show in my hands or legs. As long as I keep my Jewishness at home or in Rabbi Lander's office, I am fine. But when I go into a synagogue my new identity is not strong enough to continue seeing myself with my eyes. I see myself with the eyes of those who have been Jews since time began who probably have grains of sand in their shoes from the forty years of wandering in the desert.

I enter quietly, unobtrusively, and sit in a back pew. I nod at Rabbi Lander, who is chatting with someone at the front. There are not many people present, and I doubt there will be enough for a *minyan.** A tall, middle-aged woman turns around to see at whom the rabbi was nodding. She gets up and comes back to me.

"My name is Sarah Berger. Please come sit with me."

I am grateful and move to the front to where she is sitting.

The service is short and very beautiful. I love that so much is in song, but there are no hymnbooks. Jewish worship is rooted in an oral tradition with songs of worship having been passed down for who knows how many hundreds or thousands of years. During the service we read silently and then, suddenly, the cantor starts singing.

Eagerly I look at the Hebrew text but I never find the words she is singing. I can recognize all the letters of the Hebrew alphabet now, but translating those letters into words feels as complicated as creating a human being from the dust of the earth. But as I listen to the music, that voice within that mocks me, that causes me to question why I want to be a Jew is not only stilled but is replaced by a wondrous love.

## Summer 1982

Each evening I watch Beirut being bombed by Israeli jets. I sit before the television set and see buildings crumble and people run through the streets, screaming. I listen to interviews with Israeli government officials, generals and soldiers who say that the presence of Israeli soldiers and war planes in Lebanon is to drive the Palestinian Liberation Organization out of the country and give the Jews of Israel physical security.

I do not know. I am not Israeli. I have not lived through five wars in twenty-four years. I do not board a bus wondering if a bomb has been planted beneath one of the seats. My dailiness does not include walking the streets seeing soldiers with rifles on their shoulders. My dailiness does not include memories of sons, fathers and brothers killed in one of those wars.

I am sitting in Judie's, a restaurant my wife and I like to go to for lunch once a week. We hear shouting and look to see a group of students marching down the street carrying signs. They are shouting: "Israel out of Lebanon!" Leading them is a young man who was in my "Blacks and Jews" course last semester.

"That son-of-a-bitch!" I exclaim to my wife. "Well, at least I didn't give him an 'A.' " How can a former student of mine so readily take sides, so easily feel that he knows who is right and who is wrong? Did he learn nothing in class about the responsibilities suffering imposes?

As the short line of marchers passes the restaurant, I recognize them as belonging to Amherst's radical left fringe. I look at the face of my former student and his eyes gleam with a dangerous righteousness, as if God had come down that morning and tied the cloak of truth around his shoulders. It is the same look I see in photographs of some Palestinians and some Israelis. It is undoubtedly the same look that burned my face during the Sixties.

As they march stolidly down the street, their chanting fades and I am left angered because their political posturing is a personal attack. But I am not Israeli. I am not responsible for what Israel does as a nation. I have not been to Israel and will probably not go for many years because I do not want to see Jews treating Arabs as blacks were treated in the South. I do not want to see how racist many Jews can be. I fear that if I go to Israel I will have to write a Hebrew version of *Look Out, Whitey!*

And yet when a non-Jew attacks Israel I feel threatened. Israel is mine. Don't non-Jews understand that after the Holocaust, Jews feel more alone and isolated in the world than ever? Jews no longer expect non-Jews to approve of them, accept them and certainly not love them as members of the human family. Jewish survival depends upon the willingness and ability of Jews to act in their own defense. That is the lesson of the Holocaust. That is why Israeli planes are bombing Beirut.

I can defend what Israel is doing. That does not mean I like it, or even that I approve. I want Israel to be "a light unto the nations." I want Israel to be better than other nations, to set a new standard for politics and international relations. It is not going to do that.

That saddens me. It hurts. But it doesn't hurt nearly as much as seeing a former student who is also not angry because Jewish life is threatened.

# 22

**Summer 1982**

I look at Momma. I will understand infinity before penetrating the mystery of how I was conceived in, nurtured by and born from her thin body. She was in bed the entire pregnancy because the doctor feared she might lose the baby. There was no machine to monitor the fetal heartbeat in 1938–39, no way to draw the amniotic fluid and test it to check the health of the fetus, no cameras to photograph the fetus. She lay in bed and waited. Twelve days after her forty-second birthday, I was born.

My students have remarked that I talk about my father often in classes but never Momma. Perhaps that is because we are so much alike. Daddy lives in my soul; Momma lives in my personality. We are private and silent. If Momma has ever spoken her pain to anyone, I cannot imagine to whom. I have spoken more to my wife than anyone, but even to her I do not speak from that place of silence in me as distant and hard as the farthest star.

Momma and I share, also, a suspicion of emotion. It makes us appear to be cold and unfeeling. We aren't, but sometimes we do not know how to show the emotion expected of us. Once, not having seen my parents for a year or so, I decided to surprise them and came home unexpectedly. I rang the doorbell and when Momma opened the door and saw me, her first words were "Don't you have a key?" For an instant, I was hurt. Then I laughed because I can imagine myself greeting a child of mine with those words.

Another time I showed up unexpectedly at the end of the summer and rang the bell. Momma opened the door, saw me, frowned, and her first words were "How did you get so dark?"

I laughed. "I was born that way, Momma."

She grunted. "You weren't born that black."

Mother is matter-of-fact and blunt. She hurts other people's feelings and if it is pointed out to her, she says, "What I said was true. If his feelings were hurt, that's not my fault." I can be matter-of-fact and blunt, too. Maybe that is why I am the only member of the family who is not intimidated by her and talks to her as an equal. Even Daddy was afraid of her.

In the spring of 1978 she was seriously ill and almost died. After she came home from the hospital, Daddy called me and said she had lost the will to live and he didn't know what to do. I flew down and he met me at the airport.

When I entered the house, Momma was sitting at the table in the breakfast room reading the paper and did not look up when I came in. I put my bag in the guest room and sat down at the table with her.

"Well, are you going to live or die?" I greeted her.

She laughed. "I'm still thinking about it."

"Well, it's your life, so I can't tell you what to do with it. But please make up your mind soon, because you're about to worry Daddy to death."

I walked out of the room, found Daddy sitting in his study and said, "She's going to live." I knew because she had laughed.

Each Sunday night since Daddy died I call her, and one Sunday night this spring I said, "Momma, you can't live in the house by yourself anymore. I'm going to come down and put the house up for sale."

---

Daddy saved everything! From early morning until late at night, Malcolm and I work in the basement, where magazines, old newspapers, boxes and junk are piled to the ceiling. I find the saxophone my brother played in high school forty years ago; I find my clarinet, which I put in its case for the final time in 1953. In a corner near the furnace is the round picture tube from the first TV set we owned—1948. There are cigar boxes filled with bars of soap from hotel bathrooms, albums of postcards from all the places the ministry took him, airline and railroad timetables, thirty-year-old issues of *Life* and *Look*, a scrapbook with matchbook covers pasted in its many pages. I didn't know Daddy collected them.

As I fill plastic bags for Malcolm to carry out to the alley for the garbagemen, it is as if I am throwing away my father. Each thing I touch is him; he gave it emotional meaning and who cares what emotion caused him to save tiny bars of soap, each one still in its wrapper. Was it fear of another depression? I do not know. I do not need to. It is my father and I miss him.

His life has not ended because his heart stopped. I am left with these extensions of him. Who am I to decide what of him will be thrown into the back of a garbage truck and what will remain for me to show to my children and say, "This was your grandfather's" and for them to show to their children and say, "This was your great-grandfather's." What do I do with his ministerial robes, especially the one with the red sash which I remember so vividly from childhood? What do I do with his honorary degrees, his plaque from United Airlines proclaiming him a member of the 100,000-Mile Club, the proclamation from the governor and legislature of the state of Tennessee honoring him on his retirement from the ministry? There is nothing I can do except put them into a Glad bag, hand it to Malcolm and hope Momma does not ask, "What's in there?"

But she does. A box or bag is not taken out that she does not open and look through, asking me sharply why I am throwing such-and-such out and then telling me when Daddy bought it, acquired it, was presented with it and how much it meant to him. She fondles it, whatever it is, and then sighs deeply before letting it drop from her hands or thrusting it into mine. "Go on," she says bitterly. "You might as well throw out everything in the house." Then her voice softens. "I guess there's nothing else you can do."

Some afternoons when I am trying to take a nap and rest from the morning's journey through my father's life, Momma comes into the bedroom, a suit, tie, shirt, belt, cuff links of Daddy's in her hands. "This would look nice on you," she says.

I take it and will carry it back to Amherst, knowing I will not be able to throw it out either. Not soon, at least. Maybe never. I think about a day when it will be Malcolm's time, if he is the one, to decide what of me to keep, what to take to the dump, and I want to go home and throw away everything I own. I do not want to impose on any of my children the terrible burden of burying me, object by object, memory by memory.

But I will only add more boxes to the ones now crammed in the garage and basement. What is in them? School yearbooks, adolescent manuscripts, photos of high school and college girlfriends, drawings? For all I know, the meaning of life could be in one.

I must not deprive my children of this bitter intimacy of knowing me in ways they could not when I was flesh. I will not take from them all the questions I will not be alive to answer.

("Daddy, why did you keep the tube from our first TV set? What did that set represent for you? Was it a sign that you were becoming more successful in the world? Or was it that each time you saw it down here in the basement you touched once again the magic of sitting in your living room and watching pictures that came from you knew not where or how? And Daddy, why have you kept Momma's old washing machine all these years, the one with the hand wringer? Seeing it, did you remember the day you bought it, and how proud you were that you had a church which paid you enough money that your wife would no longer have to wring the clothes by hand?")

I do not want to deprive them, either, of the surprise of themselves. There is a floor-to-ceiling cabinet in the corner of the basement by the outside door. Its shelves and the boxes and paper sacks within are so covered with silt and dirt that I am reluctant even to begin going through it. But I must. Cautiously I extend my hand into the darkness and the first object I bring into the light is a dipper.

I stare at it and my heart beats faster. It is the dipper that rested buoyantly in the pail of water on Grandmomma's back porch. Beside it was a white metal basin. I see myself standing on tiptoes. I grasp the dipper, turn it sideways until it fills with water. It is heavy and trembles in my hand as I take it out, but I manage to pour a dipperful of water into the basin without spilling any. I know the water is cold and, looking around to see if Momma or Grandmomma is watching, I drop my washcloth into the water, squeeze it tightly and quickly throw the water into the yard. It is morning.

In a paper sack I find two black flatirons and I see Grandmomma in the kitchen, the flatirons resting on a bed of coals in a tub. She picks one up, spits on it. The iron sizzles and she wipes the bottom with a white cloth and runs it quickly, expertly, over a dress.

Also in that cabinet are the ventriloquist's dummy with which I used to have boring and unfunny conversations, my childhood copy of *The Little Engine That Could,* my Hopalong Cassidy hand puppet, a hand-drill and plane I watched Daddy use with all the admiration a son has for a father. I show each item excitedly to Malcolm. He is unimpressed, and I want to put my arms around him and say, "In my boxes are memories of you like golden threads spun by fairies in the deepest night and left on my pillow and on some awful day you will hold those shining threads in your hands and present them as proofs of your existence as a child to your teenage child, who cannot imagine that you existed before his or her birth, who will resent that you existed before, but you will yearn for your child to receive these offerings of yourself because by offering them your memories, you are offering the child another birth, one through a canal of memory you will not know you have until you hold in your hand a golden thread gleaming like dandelions and you will despair if your child sees only dirt and grime and age on a teddy bear that kept you safe from night's dragons and does not see also (on that day when you bury me for the final time as you bend the last twist tie around a garbage bag) that you are taking the first step of your life as yourself and not as my son, that you are becoming yourself as you rediscover and reclaim all the objects that say you were my son." But he is only fifteen. He thinks he knows that I will not live forever. He can't know that until he knows that he will not live forever. He will not know that until he sees me sealed within the earth.

I open a box. Inside are envelopes. They are addressed to Daddy. The handwriting on the envelopes is Momma's. I pick up the top one, blow off the dust and look at the postmark. 1923. It is a letter she wrote Daddy before they were married. To open the flap, remove the letter, unfold it and read would be to confront my parents not as they who gave me life but as two human beings, young, in love, afraid and too human. Do I want to know? Or do I want them always to shine in the nave of my soul? To read and to know will be the final task in ceasing to be my father's son.

I put the box aside to take with me. One evening I will sit and I will read and I will make peace with my parents' humanity.

---

Momma is partially deaf, though she is loath to admit it, and does not hear me leave the house at 6:00 A.M. I am forty-three years old but sneak out like an adolescent. I am not ashamed. One does things in the way he is able to do them. Sometimes that means acting like a child even when you're forty-three.

I am going to the morning *minyan* at the Chasidic *shul** on West End Avenue. Why would Lubavitcher* Chasidim have a large synagogue in Nashville, Tennessee, of all places? Then again, why not? Ironically, it is led by Rabbi Posner, the father-in-law of Rabbi Israel Deren, who heads Chabad House on the University of Massachusetts campus in Amherst.

I have never been to daily services because neither the Jewish Community of Amherst nor the Conservative congregation in Northampton has them. I don't know why I'm sneaking out of the house at 6:00 A.M. to go to an ultra-Orthodox *shul.*

That is not wholly true. I am going because I am afraid. I am afraid more and more, so afraid that I fear to name the fear. This fear is not the one of how my blackness will be received, or the fear of leaving behind so much that is familiar without knowing what will replace it. It is not even the fear that I am a fool who will be laughed at by Jews and blacks. Those fears are familiar now, which makes them even more real.

This fear is existential, because I do not understand myself. I do not understand how I have lived, and how I have arrived at this place of so radically changing not only how I live but how I conceive of myself. The only answer I can offer is that I am following my soul, but what does that mean? What the hell is the soul, anyway? How do I know when I am hearing it and not some neurosis or complex? Is the language of the soul that swelling exaltation of tears and laughter? Is it the warmth of gratitude to God that I am blood and bone and flesh and anxiety and arrogance and sentimentality and exuberance and coldness and cruelty? Is it a silence as deep and eternal and incomprehensible as death? I don't know. I am only doing what I must do, not knowing what it is that I am doing.

I went to the mausoleum to see Daddy. I told him that I am becoming a Jew and I didn't want him to be hurt. I wasn't repudiating him but affirming all he gave me—the faith, the passion, the courage. I told him that I wanted him to be happy that God had led me to a place of joy and peace. I told him how much I missed him, but that if he had not died I did not know if I would have been able to become a Jew because only now, now that I am no longer his son, can I be me, and then I cried because my life needed his death.

Services have begun. The men are gathered in the library and I slip quietly into a seat in the back, take a prayerbook and begin reading. I do not understand what is going on. There is only this mumbling of Hebrew around me, each man reading in a low undertone at his own pace. The slowest reader is mumbling Hebrew faster than a speeding bullet. In the far corner two men are talking loudly about last night's game on "Monday Night Baseball."

Suddenly, an old man opens the doors of the ark on the opposite wall and everyone stands and their voices become louder as they bow and then the ark is closed and everyone sits down. Their voices wail for a moment or so, though no one is in unison with anyone else, and then the voices subside into the ominous drone of a beehive.

Someone catches my eye and nods his head in greeting. I return the nod. A few moments later, another man walks over, shakes my hand, and returns to his seat. I turn the pages in the prayerbook but my eyes are not really seeing the words, partly because I am half-involved in the conversation about the baseball game, which is becoming an argument over whether the manager should have taken out the starting pitcher in the seventh inning.

A large bearded man hurries in through a side door and starts mumbling even though he hasn't even opened a prayerbook. He has on a large prayer shawl, and because he looks like what I think a Chasidic rabbi should, he probably is. He stands before the ark and his body begins rocking back and forth as he mumbles away in Hebrew faster than anybody else in the room.

After a while, people close their prayerbooks, shake hands with each other, and start talking and laughing. I assume that the service is over, close my book, and before anyone can speak to me, I slip quietly out the front door.

I have no idea what I just experienced because it bore no resemblance to anything I've ever known as religion. Reform services are similar in style to Protestant worship. A service leader calls out page numbers in the prayerbook and tells people when to rise and when to sit; people recite prayers together, and above all, nobody is off in a corner arguing loudly over last night's baseball game.

For all I know, there might be some mornings when God is more interested in hearing about a baseball game.

---

It has been almost thirty years since I have been to Pine Bluff. Nothing I remember remains. When Momma says, "This is it," I do not know what she is talking about.

The mill is no longer here; the road has been paved. Where Grandmomma's house stood is thick woods. I slow the car trying to see what was. I cannot.

We are looking for the family cemetery but Momma does not know how to get to it.

"Your daddy always brought me down here. He knew right where it was. I just never thought about it. He knew. Why did I have to worry about knowing?" She sighs. "I guess I should've worried about it."

She tells me to turn left and I drive slowly for a few blocks. "Slow down, Julius." She looks around. "Turn left and go down that street. I think that's where it is."

The pavement turns into a dirt road. "Keep going," she says.

I continue until the dirt road ends. Momma looks around anxiously and then gestures to the left. "I think the cemetery is over there somewhere."

Malcolm and I get out of the car and walk across a clearing, past a pile of discarded furniture, bottles, cans and unidentifiable debris. I am saddened that the forty acres of land my great-grandfather purchased has become the neighborhood garbage dump.

Malcolm and I stumble through the woods but cannot find the cemetery.

"Can't find it, Momma."

She is standing beside my car, which was Daddy's car, leaning on her cane. "Well, it's back in there someplace."

A tall thin man with a tiny hat perched on his head comes walking down the road.

"How y'all today?" he says.

"Fine. And you?"

"Just fine, thank you." He stops and looks at the license plate. "Y'all sho come from a long ways."

"You wouldn't happen to know anything about an old cemetery someplace around here, would you?" I ask.

He smiles. "Sho! It's right over yonder on the other side of that pile of junk. Them is Altschuls what's buried in there."

"Well, we're Altschuls, too," I tell him.

"Sho 'nuf!" he exclaims. "Well, I carried one of them Altschuls back up in there my own self. Sho did."

"Which one?" I want to know.

"Never did know his name. He was a tall man, though. Taller than me. Must've been, oh, let me see." His eyes narrow. "Must've been twenty-some years ago now. I was young then. Still in my teens. I live right over there," he says, pointing to his right. "Born and raised there and ain't never left. I was coming along here one afternoon, just like I'm doing now, and seen the hearse parked right about where this car is here. And they didn't have enough folks to carry the casket and asked me if I would give 'em a hand. So I done it."

I look at Momma. "Uncle Rudolph?" I ask.

She nods.

"That was my great-uncle," I say to the man.

"Sho 'nuf," he says. "Well, I helped carry him in and lower him down."

We thank the man and he goes quickly on his way.

"Let's go, Momma."

She does not move but stares at the rocky ground. "You and Malcolm go on."

"Momma!" I exclaim. "We drove all the way down here from Nashville so you could visit the cemetery one last time."

"I know. But I'm afraid I might fall."

"Momma, I'll carry you."

She shakes her head. "You all go on."

I feel foolish for not having thought that the cemetery would be on the other side of the dump. What I can't figure out is whether people put their trash there as a bulwark against the dead, or whether they figured that dead objects belonged with dead people.

A rusty wrought-iron fence surrounds the cemetery. The gate is missing. Malcolm follows me inside. Two rows of tombstones lie flush with the earth.

I point to a grave. "That's your great-great-grandmother. Maggie Carson. She was a slave." The birth date on the tombstone reads 1846. She lies here with her children Julia; Rena; Rena's husband, Fate; Emma, my grandmother; Ada; Charles; and Rudolph. One is missing. Florence. She moved to Indiana and passed for white. Momma told me that she came back once, in the middle of the night, to see Maggie and was gone before sunrise. A few years later she sent a postcard and was never heard from again.

There is so much I want to tell my son about those who lie here because I fear that when I die, there will be no one to remember. Momma is the only one of her siblings who comes here. I am the only one who has visited Daddy since he died. Maybe there is one person in every family who assumes responsibility for the dead as a way of caring for the living.

I want my son to ask me questions so I can tell him about Grandmomma raising four children alone on these forty acres. I want to tell him about that thin woman and how she looked so much like a white woman and that whatever that did to her was passed to her oldest daughter and then to me and now it is his, though I do not know what it is. I want to raise her from this earth so my son can look into her piercing eyes, so he can see the absence of sentimentality in that face and maybe then he will understand why there are moments I answer his questions with a stare and it is her stare and it is a stare that says, "We survived the fire and the flood, the going in and the coming out. We survived to tell the tale and you are here because we were here and all the suffering we could not tend to is now yours to make sacred. Will you be worthy of our offering? Will you be strong enough to withstand the grief we bequeath you?"

Aunt Rena lived at the eastern edge of the property next to the railroad tracks. I could see her gray frame house from Grandmomma's porch. She was as white-looking as Grandmomma and her husband, Fate McGowan, looked white, too. "Your aunt Rena hated it when I married your mother," Daddy told me once. "Back in those days she and your uncle Fate had the finest horse and buggy in Pine Bluff. She didn't think I was good enough for your mother. 'That nigger is too black,' she told your mother. She didn't know she would end up stark raving mad, without a dime to her name, and this too-black nigger would be the one who paid the undertaker for her funeral."

A path led through the field from Grandmomma's to Aunt Rena's. I must have been fifteen or sixteen the last time I walked that path with Momma to make the obligatory visit to see her. We walked up to the house and stopped in horror as we stared at the screen door hanging loosely by a hinge, stared at the chickens running back and forth from the porch and through the house, stared through the screen door and into the house to see, standing in the kitchen, Aunt Rena, a torn dress hanging from her body like rags loosely knotted together, revealing dirty and withered white thighs, a breast hanging from her wrinkled chest like sorrow. Her white hair was loose and wild around her face. She stood there staring out the kitchen window, cursing something or someone only she saw.

I did not see Momma cry when Daddy died but she cried that day and I knew she cried not only for what was but for what had been and would never be again and I wanted to see her memories of Aunt Rena as a young and beautiful woman because I wanted to feel something more than repulsion and disgust and fear of that mad and ugly and dirty and old white woman who was my great-aunt.

But that is the sadness of memory. Momma did not have Grandmomma's memories of Rena as a child and teenager, and I did not have Momma's of Rena as a young woman, and Malcolm does not have mine of Rena old and mad. But that will not matter if he remembers to remember, if he remembers that, at one time, there were those who did remember, if he remembers that they lie here. I know he will not remember their names to tell his children and he certainly will not remember any fragments of the fragments of stories I have told him. But I do not care as long as he remembers to remember. If he does, he will know that the lives of his children did not begin with their births, or even his.

---

We return to the motel. I open the telephone book. There are four Altschuls listed. I stare at their names, hoping one will stand up on the page and say, "Call me."

I want to call each of them but do not know what I would say. "Hi. I'm your black cousin you don't know you have." They have lived in Pine Bluff for more than a century and I cannot imagine that they are not prejudiced. That is unfair. It is my own prejudice revealing itself. No, it is fear, the fear of being rejected by them as well as the fear and hatred I still carry from those summers of riding on the backs of buses in Pine Bluff, the fear I saw in Mother's compressed lips when we went to town. I cannot call them.

I write down their names and addresses on a piece of motel stationery and put it in my address book.

---

"Momma? Did Great-grandfather go to synagogue?"

"I believe he did," she says after a thoughtful pause. "I know that he used to get up on Saturday mornings and go into town and I believe Grandmother said he was going to synagogue."

I smile. "Do you remember any traces of anything Jewish in the family?"

She is thoughtful again before she answers. "After Grandfather died, Momma used to light a candle once a year. I don't know why she did it. Or maybe I just don't remember anymore. I know it had something to do with Judaism, though." She pronounces it "Ju-day-ism."

"Do you remember when she did it? What month?" I ask, excited.

"No. It was sometime in the spring, though."

It was a *Yahrzeit** candle, I am sure. Grandmomma remembered. I wonder how she knew to do it. Did Adolph ask her to do that for him as he lay dying? And if so, what was the link between him and her that he knew she was the one? Grandmomma remembered. And Momma remembered Grandmomma's remembering without knowing what she was remembering.

If I can ever find the date of Great-grandfather's death, I will remember that of which I have no memory.

---

It is finished. I hope Daddy is pleased at how I have disposed of his life. I am taking more back home than I'd planned, but I couldn't throw out all the color slides he'd taken over the years. He was not a good photographer, but he loved it so much. I know that I will never look at his slides, but I couldn't discard them. I didn't want to throw out his matchbook collection and regret that I did.

In his study are two Coca-Cola bottles of water. Taped to each is a piece of paper. On one, written in his hand, is "Water from the River Jordan." On the other, also in his handwriting, is "Water from the Dead Sea." I don't remember when he and Momma went to Israel, or the Holy Land as they call it. But I can see him kneeling on the shores of each and lovingly, carefully, filling these bottles. I suppose I should pour the water down the sink and throw the bottles out, but I can't. Neither can I take them with me. I associate them with Christianity and Jesus. They belong to Daddy's life, not mine.

In the bottom of a trunk I found a box filled with Daddy's letters to Momma from before their marriage through the first year when they lived apart because Daddy was teaching school in another town. I take them and tell Momma I am doing so.

"You can't have those!"

"Momma, you'll just throw them out one day."

"Those are my letters. I can do with them what I please."

"Not anymore. They're your life but they're also my past."

She looks at me with Grandmomma's face. "Boy, get out of my sight!"

I smile. "Thanks, Momma."

---

The night before I leave I take the two Coca-Cola bottles of water to the mausoleum and leave them on the marble bench before Daddy's crypt.

# 23

## Autumn 1982: Rosh HaShana

The High Holy Days. I don't like the term. It makes me think of Anglican cathedrals with stone floors as cold as sin. The more traditional Jewish term for the ten days from Rosh HaShana to Yom Kippur is Days of Awe. I don't know what it means because I have not experienced any awe. Quite the contrary. I am depressed and discouraged. The more I read and the harder I study, the more difficult becoming Jewish is.

I sat in synagogue on this first day of Rosh HaShana and knew myself once again to be an Outsider. The service seemed to be without order or reason. The cantor sang and then he mumbled more rapidly in Hebrew than I can think in English, then exploded into song again, after which he mumbled some more. This is worship? I thought. This is chaotic primitivism!

I think every Jew in Amherst was there today. Even the balcony was filled. Then there was me. If people didn't know anyone else was there, they knew I was, with my black self. How can I become a part of the Jewish people when I don't look like other Jews? Three-quarters of the way through the service I left and came home.

I sit on the couch now, silent, angry, disappointed in myself, glad no one knows I am studying for conversion. I can't do it! I can't be a Jew. What made me think I could? I wish I knew another convert, a black one, but I don't know Sammy Davis's phone number.

But if I do not become a Jew, who am I?

I cannot go back to who I was, and I do not know who I am becoming.

## Yom Kippur

Instead of sitting at the rear of the synagogue I sit at the front on the right side. I do not see all the people but only the service leader, the cantor and the ark.

The cantor is an Israeli, Gadi Elon. He is tall, handsome, with curly hair that is graying at the temples. His background is Chasidic, and with his rich baritone voice he brings a fervor and enthusiasm to his singing that is wonderful. Though I still cannot follow his rapid Hebrew, this time I do not try but give myself over to the sound, allowing it to beat at me, to flay at my self-consciousness, my sense of foreignness until they are like granules of pulverized stone and I am emptied of who I was.

Throughout the morning and into the early afternoon I stand with the rest of the congregation several times for the collective recitation of my/our sins.

> For the sin which we have committed before Thee under compulsion or of our own will,
> And for the sin which we have committed before Thee by hardening our hearts;
> For the sin which we have committed before Thee unknowingly. . . .

The list continues for pages and then with the cantor we sing, "*V'al coo-lam e-lo-ha sli-chot s'lach la-nu. M'chal la-nu. Ca-per la-nu.*" ("For all these, O God of forgiveness, forgive us, pardon us, grant us atonement.") Haltingly, clumsily, my lips find and sing the Hebrew words!

Part of the service was called Yizkor. It is the service of remembering the dead. Four times a year there is Yizkor—Yom Kippur, Shemini Atzeret,* the eighth day of Pesach, and the second day of Shavuot. It is a simple and deeply moving service. Today the names of the departed relatives of members of the congregation were read. I recognized many of the last names and knew them to be the father, mother, wife, husband or child of someone I knew. I wanted Daddy's name read but I am not officially a Jew yet. But I thought of him and was glad for this time to be with others and remember.

It is in the act of remembering the dead that I have no doubts about belonging to the Jewish people. There is nothing macabre about remembering the dead. Judaism knows that we carry our dead within us, and Yizkor helps us to carry them and our own mortality as a part of life. By remembering the dead we are reminded that life is deeds which caress and flay the souls of others. When I am a memory I hope my gentle caresses outnumber the stripes.

It is late afternoon now. I have been fasting since sundown yesterday and been in synagogue almost continuously since nine-thirty this morning. I am tired and I am hungry but I understand now what Rabbi Lander meant when he told me "Jewish worship is work." I understand now the genius of being in synagogue all day. The interminableness of it, the monotony of the repetition of confessing one's sins, the very length of the services combine to wear one down, and at the point of exhaustion, there is this quiet release into a mysterious peace and exhilaration. To be forgiven for my sins is not an intellectual contract between me and God. It is something that must take place within my body and it requires my effort, my active involvement.

As I stand for the last time and we begin singing "*Avinu Malkenu*" ("Our Father, Our King"), there is a fervor in my voice and in the voices of those around me. It is getting darker in the synagogue as the sun sets and for the last time the cantor sings the Kaddish, that incredible prayer of praise, and then, for a final time, all our voices come together in the *Sh'ma.* There is no fatigue on our faces now. I look around and people are smiling, and then the cantor raises the shofar to his lips and blows a *tekiah gadol,* one great, long blast. The sound brings tears to my eyes because I hear not only the sound of this shofar but the sounds of all the shofars that have been blown for thousands of years at this moment on the Day of Atonement. It is the sound my great-grandfather heard in a synagogue somewhere in Germany, and it is the sound Moses heard in the wilderness.

The cantor takes the shofar from his lips and with great exuberance begins singing: "*L'shana haba bi 'rushalayim*" ("Next year in Jerusalem"). We join his singing and suddenly I see myself as I saw myself in that vision on the first night of Chanukah last year and I want to dance, to spin around and around until I collapse in laughter and joy.

## January 3, 1983

It is *erev** *Shabbat.* I wait for Rabbi Lander to begin services. Tonight I publicly proclaim that I have chosen to become part of the Jewish people.

Last week I appeared before my *bet din**. Rather than be examined by Rabbi Lander and two other rabbis, I chose two members of the Jewish Community of Amherst whom I respect. This was unorthodox but allowable under Reform Judaism's rules of conversion.

One was Haim Gunner, whom I respect for his knowledge of Judaism and Jewish history, and his love of the Jewish people and Israel. The other was Monroe Rabin. I don't know Monroe, but I love to listen to him lead services and chant from the Torah scroll. He does not have a melodic voice but there is such love for Torah in it. I listen to him and see myself standing in the market of some village in Israel two thousand years ago on a Monday or Thursday morning when the Torah was read.

Haim and Monroe are serious about being Jews and I want to be taken seriously as a Jew. If my answers to their questions were not satisfactory, they would say I was not yet ready.

I expected to be examined on my knowledge. Their questions went deeper, however, to my motivations, my purpose in becoming a Jew, and what did I expect my life as a Jew to be, i.e., did I really understand what it was I was proposing to assume?

I wondered if Haim was remembering stories of converts in centuries past who betrayed the Jewish people in times of trouble. I wondered if either of them was battling doubts as to whether or not he could trust this black man, who, even though he had spoken out against black anti-Semitism, was nonetheless black.

I know there will always be a gap between me and Jews rooted in *Yiddishkeit,** but *Yiddishkeit* does not represent all of Jewry. Neither is it the only way to express Jewishness.

When they finished questioning me I was asked to leave the room. I was shocked. Was there some doubt in their minds? Were they going to call me back into Rabbi Lander's office and tell me that I needed to study for another year? I paced the hallway for what seemed like hours before the office door opened and I was asked to return.

I looked at Haim because, whatever the verdict, I knew I would see it on his face. He was smiling. He offered me his hand, grinned and said, "Well, I hope you know what you're doing."

"I do," I replied seriously.

Rabbi Lander is disappointed that I decided not to be circumcised. He talked about it at length, affirming that in Reform Judaism circumcision was not necessary, but his own feelings were different. I knew that if he insisted on circumcision I would not continue with the conversion process. I have done as much as I can, and it has been more difficult and painful than I would have imagined. I will keep my foreskin.

Near the end of the service, Rabbi Lander calls me to the *bimah*, and while four people hold over me a large *tallit*,* he recites the *kohanic* blessing:

> May the Lord bless you and keep you.
> May the Lord make his face shine upon you and be gracious unto you.
> May the Lord lift up his face upon you and give you peace.

A chill goes through me and I think of my great-grandfather and great-grandmother and it is not in my imagination but in my body that I feel them joined once more. I feel also a deep peace, for at long last my great-grandfather is at peace.

So am I.

Part Four

# 24

## September 1983

It is the day after Yom Kippur and the prayers still sing inside me, emptying me of myself and releasing me into an overwhelming love which has no name except *HaShem,* the Name.

Days of Awe. Yes. That is what they are. I have known myself as a dweller in eternity and I have stood where all is forever present and forever One.

I know it cannot be described but I must try, and that is so Jewish. I don't think I've ever met a quiet Jew. The Kotzker *rebbe** is the only one I've read about and no one knows what to make of his spending the last twenty years of his life in silence. I think Jews talk so much and write so many books about being Jewish because we can't believe that what we know cannot be put into words and that offends us. But being Jewish begins where words stop, where words can go no further. Yet there are all the volumes of Talmud whose sole purpose is to explore in infinite detail what it is to be a Jew. The rabbis of the Talmud disagree with one another, but even their disagreements are an expression of this awe that astounds, and awe is the sanctification of mystery and love for the unknown and unknowable.

The Days of Awe do not begin with Rosh HaShana for me but in Elul, the month preceding. That is when you begin preparing yourself to stand before God to be judged on Yom Kippur. Elul is a time of introspection, a time to remember who you have been and what you have done during the past year and bring to consciousness your sins. It is not an easy time, and in synagogues that have a daily *minyan,* the shofar is blown at each morning's services. It is a call to the heart to know itself in all ways and not to be afraid of laying itself open before God, for God is merciful. Because He is, how can you be otherwise? During Elul you ask forgiveness from those you have sinned against during the year.

I didn't. I wanted to, but was afraid. I was not strong enough to confront my pride and silence it, so I didn't ask my wife to forgive me for all the times I threw silence at her like stones as sharp as knives. Those times were many, more than I can bear to remember. I had lunch with a friend recently, and apropos of nothing he said, "You must be hell to live with."

"What makes you think that?" I asked.

"I look at you sometimes and you seem like fire under ice."

It reminded me of a Sunday during the winter of 1962. I spent a week on the islands around Charleston, South Carolina, with Guy Carawan, the folksinger and a mentor of my youth. One Sunday we attended church on one of the small islands, a church where the faces of the worshipers, their singing and praying, brought images of Africa to me, images I did not know were within me. Afterward, I was standing outside waiting for Guy and an old woman whose face and body looked as if it had been carved by the cold winds in the sails of a slave vessel walked up to me and stared intently into my face. She was not smiling, and I returned her gaze without smiling either.

"You look like you could change water to wine," she said.

Before I could respond or react she turned and walked away.

Her words frightened me, as did the words of my friend. What did they see in me that I was afraid to see for myself? My children fear me. I see it in their eyes sometimes. They do not have the security of knowing that I will always receive them with love. Many times I do, but there are an equal number of times when they are chilled by my silence which gleams with all the hardness of sunlight on a glacier. Then there are the times of fire when to approach me is like seizing lightning.

How do I explain how I must live to tend and nurture the images and words that continually rise within like fish coming from the depths of a river whose darkness only they have penetrated? How do I explain a passion for the holy so overwhelming that it threatens my sanity at times?

But they don't need to understand as much as they need to know that I am aware that the ice and the fire of me leave deep scars on them, scars which are not wholly healed by the soft and warm places alongside where I have touched them with my deep and abiding love. To ask their forgiveness is the only way to say, Yes, I know.

And if they were to ask my forgiveness I would know that they accept my humanness and the pain that being composed of fire and ice inflicts on me. Elul teaches that to be human is to be destructive as well as creative. As a Jew, I am called to accept responsibility for both.

I don't know how. I only know how to glorify myself for my goodness and indulge in self-flagellation for my evil. Both are sentimental responses, and my goodness brutalizes others with the same force as my evil.

Beginning with *S'lichot,* the midnight service on the Saturday preceding Rosh HaShana, there is a communal recitation and public acknowledgment of one's sins. For me this is the entrance into the Days of Awe. From then until the final blowing of the shofar at sundown on Yom Kippur, I am led more and more deeply into an unfathomable and infinite realm, and as I go, I am stripped, garment by garment, until naked, I stand before God, pleading for another year in which to repair my life and my loves.

Rebbe Nachman of Bratslav said: "If a man does not judge himself, all things judge him, and all things become messengers of God." If I do not accept responsibility for the evil I do, the very earth will rise up to judge and condemn me. The stars, the trees and the wind will pronounce sentence, and who will execute it? That does not matter. I need only know that the sentence will be executed if I do not judge myself.

In the *Pirke Avot* Simeon ben Zeman Duran says: "Sacrifices to God are a broken heart. That means that praying with a broken heart is more effective as atonement than offering animal sacrifices—for he who prays with a broken heart offers up his own fat and blood."

My heart did not break this year. I am still too proud and too stubborn. I know that next year I will be proud and stubborn still, but maybe less so.

## Winter 1984

I am in love!

What an odd thing to say about a religion, but it is true. I am in love with Judaism, with being a Jew. But this passion is not that blindness which transforms a woman of mere flesh into a goddess with the power of life and death. I am having a love affair with my soul!

I have begun my second semester of modern Hebrew. Three days a week I sit in class with undergraduates and they see just how dumb one of their professors really is. The teacher insists Hebrew is easy. What does she know? She's Israeli. Of course she thinks Hebrew is easy. I think it would be easier to figure out why Jell-O exists.

I am not good at languages and it doesn't help my ego when I walk into class and the teacher is sitting at her desk reading a novel in Italian, which, she explains, she has been teaching herself. Foreign language courses should be taught by people like me for whom the learning of one verb conjugation merits a plaque in the Baseball Hall of Fame, or somewhere. Hebrew is supposed to be easy because it's logical. That's wonderful, but *I* am not logical! I learn intuitively. When she told me that Hebrew is logical, I wanted to say to her: And if I were logical, do you think I would have become a Jew?

But I persevere. I study two, three hours a day, and on the weekends, six to eight. Knowing the *alef-bet* is not sufficient. I can't know what I want to know or do what I want to do unless I open my mouth and have Hebrew come out instead of English.

What do I want to know? What do I want to do? I don't know yet. I suppose I want to be equal as a Jew. Knowing Hebrew will give me the confidence to go anywhere among Jews. And Jews are the only ones with whom I can share my great love!

My religious practice is not what I would like it to be. I wonder why God didn't have me become a Jew during the thirteen years I lived in New York. There I was, living in the city with the largest concentration of Jews in the world. I mean, there are more Jews in New York than in all Israel. There are almost as many synagogues as bars in New York. Obviously God is not logical either, because only after I put down roots in a small town in western Massachusetts and had decided in which one of the lovely New England cemeteries I wanted to be buried did He come along and say, "Go be Jewish!" Every time I ask God how I'm supposed to be Jewish in Emily Dickinson's hometown, He says, "Don't ask me!"

I want to keep kosher but I can't impose that discipline on my family. I want to observe the Sabbath strictly, but my son has hockey games on Friday nights and I must choose between him and not driving on the Sabbath. I have chosen the Sabbath and feel awful for having done so. Malcolm says it doesn't matter if I come to his games or not, but it does.

I am sorry my family is outside my joy. I am sorry that I do not know how to bring them into it. The separation between me and them is like a flaming sword.

I need to share my joy, my love, and there is no one. I am on the religion committee at synagogue, but involvement in the mundane details of synagogue life does not satisfy my need to be joined with others in my passion.

I am reading *Sparks of Light*, a book on Chasidism and psychology by Edward Hoffman. In it are some wonderful and illuminating quotes.

Rabbi Dov Baer of Lubavitch said: "Each soul can only ascend to the root of the Source whence she was hewn by means of song." Is this why I respond viscerally to Jewish music? It is a music of praise. It is not an aesthetic experience, which is why it goes beyond the senses to the soul.

Rebbe Nachman of Bratslav: "Consider what you are doing, and ponder whether it is worthy that you devote your life to it." Is being a Jew worthy of whatever pain, whatever sacrifices are required? Is devoting my life to being a Jew worth this gulf between me and my family? God forgive me, but yes.

Rabbi Schneur Zalman of Liady: "All we can do is accept the facts as they are and do so in love and generosity." I do not know how. I do not know how to be generous to my failings, to my inadequacies.

In *Sparks of Light* I was surprised and relieved to read the descriptions of the crowded living conditions in the ghettos and that one of the problems Chasidim frequently brought to the *rebbe* was how difficult it was to study while being surrounded constantly by the noise and demands of the family.

In this week's *parashah, Yitro,* three verses were important to me: "And if you make for Me an altar of stones, do not build it of hewn stones; for by wielding your tool upon them you have profaned them."

Why "And if?" Rashi* translates the Hebrew, *im,* as "When." I don't understand why. *Im* means "if." Who am I to argue with Rashi? However, the literal translation would seem to imply that God is not commanding us to build an altar of stones but giving us the choice. If we choose to do so, then God wants the altar built in a particular way. Why are the stones to be uncut? Is it that they are to be left as God made them and not shaped according to our sense of aesthetic proportion and rightness? The altar is the place on which sacrifices are to be laid. Thus to render ourselves holy, which is the purpose of sacrifices, it must be done on that place which is as God created it and not as we would make it. What place is that? The soul?

Then there is this verse: "You shall be men holy to Me: you must not eat flesh torn by beasts in the field; you shall cast it to the dogs."

What a curious conjunction of imperatives: Holiness = not eating torn flesh = casting it to the dogs. Rashi's commentary is illuminating: "If you will be holy and keep yourselves aloof from the loathsomeness of carrion and trefa you are Mine, if not you are not Mine." It is a reiteration of what is so central to Judaism—separating the sacred from the profane in every way, on every level, being a people apart in order to be holy, to belong only to God.

One final verse: "They shall not remain in your land, lest they cause you to sin against Me; for you will serve their gods and it will prove a snare to you."

This is a remarkable admission by God. He is saying that the holy is fragile, and if it is placed next to the profane, the profane will have greater appeal. The holy is difficult; it requires effort. The profane is easy and requires only sloth, for which we have genius. God does not want pagans to remain in the land because, regardless of how much effort might be exerted in holiness, holiness will not survive. We must be a people apart or we will not survive.

I am used to thinking of holiness as powerful, but it isn't, which is why Judaism is so much work, why it is so concrete, why it demands so much. Holiness cannot be taken for granted. It must be fought for and won each day.

Now that I am officially a Jew I have a new problem. Where do I belong in the Jewish world? Though I was converted by a Reform rabbi, I never assumed I would be a Reform Jew. Reform Judaism has provided my entrance into Judaism, but is it my Jewish home? I don't think so. I am very traditional, conservative even. (Despite the fact that I wear a cowboy hat and used to wear an earring.)

The Jewish Community of Amherst is divided between Reform and Conservative Jews and thus does both kinds of services. Even though I am not fluent in Hebrew, I prefer Conservative services. Through the use of Hebrew the link with Jews throughout history is reaffirmed. The very sound of the language evokes images of Jerusalem and Sinai for me. But I don't know enough about Conservative Judaism to know if that is where I belong. My impression is that it exists in a kind of nether world between Reform and Orthodox, trying to be a little of both without being anything in itself. If I lived in a Jewish community, I would want to be Orthodox, but I could never accept sitting at worship while the women were forced to sit behind a barrier, prohibited from being called for *aliyot** or participating fully in the service. Wouldn't it be ironic if now, having become a Jew, I won't find a place in the Jewish world?

But the question is irrelevant. As long as I remain uncircumcised, I am a Reform Jew. Even though I've studied the rabbinic commentaries on the meaning of the covenant of circumcision, I do not understand why it is so important. Despite the Reform movement's attempts to make it unimportant, Jewish tradition and custom are so strong that most Reform Jews have their sons circumcised eight days after birth.

If somebody would promise me that circumcision would not affect my enjoyment of sex adversely, I would do it. But the medical books I read talk about the sensitivity of the foreskin and what it adds to sexual pleasure. Some maintain that circumcision diminishes not only sexual pleasure but sexual desire.

Well, if I have to choose between being a circumcised Jew and sexual desire, forget it! I have this fantasy of being in the bathroom at a synagogue somewhere and the man at the next urinal notices that I'm not circumcised and suddenly the entire congregation rises up and chases me out of the *shul* and down the street, yelling, "He has a foreskin!"

But when I began studying with Rabbi Lander, my one rule was not to do something simply because it was Jewish. I do only that which makes sense to my heart. For that reason I have not observed the holiday of Succoth, the Festival of Booths. Sitting outside in a wooden structure and eating my meals for eight days is not something my heart gives any indication of understanding, desiring or needing.

However, Judaism does not reveal itself in words, as I keep learning. Chanukah was incomprehensible when I read about it, but my heart had no objection and we observed it. What a revelation to sit at the table after dinner each night, each of us with a menorah, lighting the tiny candles and watching the light increase night after night as we added candles until the final night when eight candles were lighted and we turned out the lights and the entire room was ablaze at the time of year when there is the greatest darkness!

Judaism is a doing which can be grasped only by the heart.

Maybe it's that way with circumcision, too. But what if it isn't? Krazy Glue is strong, but could it keep my foreskin on?

---

I am in print as a Jew. Last summer I got a letter from Bill Novak, whom I've never met, though I know his work, about a magazine he is editing for the National Havurah Committee called *New Traditions*. He wondered if I knew any Jewish writers in the area who might be interested in contributing. He didn't know that I am Jewish now, so I wrote back offering to write an essay about my journey to Judaism.

Copies of *New Traditions* arrived today. It is a good magazine. I like the layout and typeface. There are good people writing for it, too. Susannah Heschel, Danny Siegel, Art Waskow are the names familiar to me. And there's a good interview with Zalman Shachter.

I haven't read my essay yet. I'm afraid to. That is always how it is when I publish something deeply personal. Why, then, do I write autobiographically, almost confessionally?

I don't know. I write but don't reflect on it afterward. I read interviews with writers and am amazed and embarrassed that they know so much about the whats and whys of their work. I write instinctually. It was something given me to do and I do it. I know a lot about how to ply my craft, but when I'm asked, "What did you mean when you described such-and-such a character as such-and-such?," I go blank. I would love to be able to give Faulkner's classic answer to such questions: "Hell, I don't know. I was drunk when I wrote that." I don't drink. Well, that's not true, but I've never gotten drunk from Sprite. I'm not a literary person like Philip Roth, Updike and so many others. I write, but I'm not a writer. Writing is the means by which I seek to render myself holy.

That is the only way I can understand why someone as intensely private as I am reveals so much of my life in print. It is not my life I write about so much as it is the lives of everyone. Through myself I seek to understand God and humanity.

Since my journey to Judaism began I'd wondered if I would write about it. How could I not? But seeing my name on the cover of *New Traditions*, I am not certain that I have not written prematurely.

What do I know about being Jewish? The more I read, the more ignorant I know myself to be. I am forty-five years old and am so far behind. Regardless of how many hours I study Hebrew each day, fluency does not come. I am deficient in Jewish religious experience: I have never attended a Jewish wedding, a Jewish funeral, a *bris.** I have never attended a weekday service except for that morning in Nashville.

There is so much to know and so much to do. I do not have forty-five more years. My past is greater than my future. How can that be when I was just born?

## Spring 1984

I read an entire page of Torah in Hebrew today and understood it!

I knew it would happen. When Jesse Jackson announced his candidacy for the presidency late last year, I was not excited. I knew his Achilles' heel was his attitude toward Jews, and I waited for him to nick himself with his poisonous arrow and he did.

He referred to Jews as "Hymies" in what he thought was an off-the-record conversation with a black reporter for *The Washington Post.* How disrespectful of him not to treat a black reporter as he would any other professional journalist. Fortunately, the reporter knew his obligation was to his craft and not his race.

As a black I am demeaned by Jackson's assumption that a black journalist could be used and manipulated. As a Jew I am angry. How would Jackson feel if it were reported that Gary Hart or Walter Mondale had referred to a black in an off-the-record conversation as "Mose"? He would be quite justified in calling that candidate unworthy of the presidency. The NAACP, the Urban League and every other black organization would be demanding that he withdraw from the race. If Jackson had any integrity he would withdraw voluntarily, thereby proving himself worthy of the presidency.

But I have expressed these opinions only to my wife. This is one issue I will not go public on. I can't. Anything I say will be dismissed by blacks. As word of my conversion has filtered through the black community here, there are some who do not know how to talk to me anymore. One person can't greet me without bringing up something Jewish, or without putting into the conversation the one or two Yiddish phrases he knows. I want to grab him by the shoulders and say, "Because I'm a Jew does not make me an alien species of humanity. I still speak the Southern black English I've spoken all my life."

Photocopies of articles critical of Israel appear mysteriously in my mailbox at the office. I don't know who puts them there. Whoever it is is having problems understanding how it is possible to be black and Jewish and assumes that I am no longer black. I suppose I'm not, if blackness is synonymous with black nationalism warmed over once too often. If blackness is synonymous with unthinking and blind loyalty to the race, regardless of what any of its members do, then I am not black.

It doesn't matter because, once again, blacks aren't speaking to me. This time, however, I haven't published anything or made any public statements. But I know why.

James Baldwin is teaching on campus this academic year. I have spent a lot of time with him. We know each other as only writers can and we have talked and argued almost until sunrise many nights about our definitions of ourselves as writers, about blacks, about Israel; we've swapped stories and gossip about other writers and our misadventures in the world of publishing. He has been at the house often, almost every Shabbat evening, in fact. He has sat at our Shabbat table and read the words from Psalms that are part of our Sabbath evening ritual. He has seen me hold the kiddush cup as we chanted the blessing, raise the loaves of challah as we chanted *ha-motzi*. And we have certainly discussed my being Jewish, to which his initial response was "Well, I'm not surprised." (Is there some conspiracy of people who have known for years I should have been Jewish but wouldn't tell me?) The personal bond between me and Jimmy is quite deep because we know the penalties writing extracts, how its demands diminish our human capacities even as what we write seeks to expand the capacity for being human in us.

So why am I surprised? Why do I feel betrayed? Why do I feel he dishonored the love and caring my wife has shown him? Why am I sorry that my children shared their purity with him?

One of the courses he teaches is my "History of the Civil Rights Movement." Every Tuesday he lectures in a large auditorium and on Thursday the class of some three hundred or so meets in sections taught by individual faculty members. Last Tuesday Jimmy devoted his lecture to the Jesse Jackson affair.

He began with a diatribe, albeit an eloquent one, blaming the media for reporting it. I was sitting in my customary seat in the back of the auditorium and my mouth dropped. No one put words in Jesse's mouth, did they? After denying he said it, Jesse finally admitted he had. But Jimmy's view was that Mondale and Hart say things like that about blacks but the media won't report it. His sense of history is supposed to be better than that. When former vice-president Spiro Agnew referred to someone as a "Fat Jap" it was reported widely, to Agnew's embarrassment. Nixon's Secretary of Agriculture, Earl Butz, had to resign for telling an anti-black joke in a setting similar to the one in which Jackson made his "Hymie" reference. Jimmy insisted on blaming the messenger, however.

He then went on to hold Jews responsible. Exactly how Jews were to blame escaped me. Maybe because we were so ungracious as to say that we were insulted by being referred to as "Hymies." But I was shocked when Jimmy referred to Jews as being nothing more than "white Christians who go to something called a synagogue on a Saturday rather than church on Sunday."

I love Jimmy. It was reading *Notes of a Native Son* my sophomore year at Fisk that told me that I, too, could be a writer, because Jimmy wrote with a lyricism and love closer to me than the anger of Richard Wright. I know he is not an anti-Semite, but his remarks in class were anti-Semitic, and he does not realize it.

At the conclusion of his lecture, he called for questions or responses. Then the real horror began. His words had given black students permission to stand up and mouth every anti-Semitic cliché they knew and they did so, castigating Jewish landlords and Jews in general. Jimmy listened and said nothing. I was grateful when an Afro-Am faculty member stood up to say that Jewish involvement in the Civil Rights Movement should not be denigrated, minimized or castigated as paternalism.

When class ended, I was scarcely out of my seat before I found myself surrounded by Jewish students, most of whom I did not know, most of whom had tears in their eyes. One young woman from Smith College seemed to speak for all of them when she asked, fearfully, "Do you think what he said is true?"

I responded with characteristic eloquence: "Jimmy was full of shit this morning!"

In my section of the class on Thursday, my students were so disturbed that we spent the entire class discussing Tuesday's lecture. The Jewish students were hurt and angry; the white students were bewildered, and the black students were silent. I suppose I could have been more diplomatic and circumspect. But then I wouldn't be me. I told them I thought Jesse Jackson was really auditioning for a role as one of "Charlie's Angels," that Baldwin was wrong in his analysis of the Jackson affair because his outrage was misdirected. Why weren't he and other blacks angry at Jesse?

I did not expect what I said to remain in class. Neither did I expect people in the Afro-Am Department not only to stop speaking to me, yet again, but also this time to include a hostility in their silence which frightens me. The hostility was open when one department member stuck his head in my office and said, "I thought Jimmy's lecture Tuesday was quite good. I thought he handled the discussion very well." The look of cold defiance in his face was chilling.

I wish they would sit *shivah** and be done with me.

I had lunch with Jimmy to talk about his Jackson lecture. He was surprised and distressed to hear how I and the Jewish students felt about his remarks.

"You know I'm not anti-Semitic."

"I know, Jimmy, but I know you. In your lecture you didn't speak as someone who understands Jewish suffering and Jewish fears."

He admitted I was right and said that next Tuesday he will apologize to the Jewish students.

There was a sale of Jewish ritual objects at B'nai Israel, the Conservative synagogue in Northampton. My wife and I went seeking a Havdalah candleholder and ended up spending two hundred forty-five dollars for a beautiful Seder plate, Elijah's cup and mezuzah. I wouldn't have done it, but my wife not only urged me; she insisted.

I've wanted a mezuzah for years and especially since I converted, but my wife wasn't comfortable about it. I don't know what caused her to insist that I buy one now. I wouldn't have otherwise.

I love it so much. It is on the doorpost entering my study-library. Each time I enter I touch it and kiss my fingertips. It is a tactile prayer, reminding me physically that I am to render myself holy for God.

The semester has ended. I had lunch with Jimmy before he returned to France. We had not spoken since our previous lunch.

He never apologized to the Jewish students.

# 25

## Summer 1984

I blinked my eyes and nine years passed. An instant ago he was eight years old, lying on the living room floor, studying the large pages of *The New York Times* sports section with the reverence of a yeshiva student. Today he strides through the house, shirt off, like a magnificent conqueror who has slain dragons, rescued fair maidens and forced the three-eyed giant to reveal the secret of why white milk makes yellow butter.

Ah, my son! I call him my son, but that word reveals only his relationship to me. I call him my son but I do not know who he is or how he came to be him. One afternoon eight years ago he looked at me and said, "Dad, do you know why I like to play hockey?" Along with the meaning of life, that was a mystery I had given up trying to penetrate so I was eager for his answer. "Because I like to hit people," he answered solemnly. At that moment I knew this son of mine was forever beyond my comprehension and my task was simple—to love him as he was.

Each evening I listen to the sounds of him lifting weights in the basement. He is male in ways as foreign to me as quantum physics and blond hair. Whereas I have always been a solitary, a monk in the rain without an umbrella, as Chairman Mao said once, he knows the camaraderie of team sports. His teammates hug him when he scores a goal in hockey and he hugs them when they score. Girls cheer and call his name when he knocks an opposing player on the ice. During lacrosse games, the coach and his teammates slap him on the butt when he runs on and off the field. No one would dare slap me on my butt.

He walks through the family room wearing only a pair of shorts and I see what the male body is supposed to look like. He undulates with muscles and pulsates with strength. His body is so beautiful he should be posing for a sculpture to be placed in the Parthenon. He is taller than me now and I do not mind raising my eyes to look into his face. I had thought I would. But just as my father had to raise his eyes to look into mine and those of my brother, it is only proper that I look up. Those generations which began in the terrible darkness of some unknown slave shack are reaching, inch by inch, closer to the sun.

This time next year he will be preparing to leave for an as-yet-unknown college. Already, though, home is just the place where his bed is located. I do not know where he goes or what he does. He does not say and I do not ask. We have entered, he and I, that space in adolescence when the values I have presented to him are to be tested and evaluated as to whether they are the ones he needs for his life. It is frightening for both of us, but we do not acknowledge that to each other. One evening he knocks at the entrance to my study and comes in.

"How would you feel about my playing football next year?" he blurts.

I look at him. He knows how I feel. As avid a football fan as I am, I have not been able to bear the thought of seeing my son lying beneath a pile of boys wearing equipment that weighs more than I do.

"Well, it's your last year. You're bigger now. You keep yourself in good condition. I don't want you going through life regretting not having played football in high school."

He is visibly surprised. "I can play?"

"Sure. Why not? Do you think you can handle playing football, hockey and lacrosse? That's a lot."

He shrugs. "I think I can do it."

I know he wants something else, but requesting permission to play football may have depleted his supply of courage for a while. Whenever he does, I will say, Yes, I will break the Sabbath and come to your football games on Saturdays. And next winter I'll be at your hockey games on Friday nights.

It is not enough to simply love another; I must learn to love as that other needs to be loved. If I do not, my love is merely an emotional generalization, suitable for all and mattering to none.

A few evenings later, there is the sound of his familiar knock at my door.

"Do you want to know, or would you like to be surprised?" he asks.

Should I reach for the checkbook, head for the Canadian border or call an ambulance? "Tell me," I say guardedly.

"Well, I'll give you a hint. You're going to be getting a letter from the senior class." He smiles proudly.

I keep my face expressionless, but I am terrified. Is his graduating class inviting me to be their commencement speaker?

A few days later, the letter comes. I read it several times and the desire to say "NO!" swells like a tsunami with each reading. What would I say? What if I make a fool of myself and embarrass him? But beneath the terror is also the tender recognition that maybe, just maybe, I have become worthy of my firstborn son.

---

After Abraham was circumcised, he was sitting in the shade in front of his tent one hot day when three strangers, who were really angels, came along. Abraham invited them to stop awhile and, eager to be hospitable, ran to kill a calf.

I believe everything in Torah is true in some way, everything, that is, except this story. Its first flaw is that Abraham saw only three angels. I have seen the whole heavenly host, and more than once. Second, Abraham did not run to catch a calf. Abraham did not run ever again. I think Abraham is probably still sitting there under that tree wondering if he will ever walk. I know my ambulatory days are over.

I sit here in my pajamas watching the Olympics. I look at the riders on horses jumping barriers, the water polo players swimming up and down the pool, the archers and pistol shooters, the gymnasts and marathon runners, but I do not know who is winning or losing because I can't keep my eyes off the men's crotches. Who has his foreskin and who doesn't?

This was my first operation and I was terrified. Dr. Miller, the surgeon who was going to hold my future in his hands, asked if I wanted just a local anesthetic or a general. I said, "Knock me out!" I said the *Sh'ma** over and over as the anesthesia dripped into my forearm. An hour later I awoke in the recovery room and the first thing I did was to peek and see if my penis was still there.

When the children are out of the house, I untie my pajama bottoms and stare at my shriveled penis, its head swathed in bulky bandages. It looks like it is sulking, baffled as to why I did this to it. "I have served you magnificently over the years," it says. "I never failed you, not even when I was taking a well-deserved nap and you said, 'Wake up! It's joy time!!' I have always risen to the occasion. If I had ever dreamed that you would cut me, mutilate me . . . What if that doctor's fingers had slipped? Did you think about the fact that you could have become a boy soprano at age forty-five? But you didn't think at all. And now, look at me."

My penis is right. No rational thought process led to the decision to be circumcised. More and more I felt incomplete as a Jew.

In studying what is written in Torah about circumcision, I was haunted by God's injunction that no uncircumcised man can participate in the rites of Passover. On the first day of Passover we read the section from Joshua where he orders all the men circumcised immediately after crossing the Jordan and entering the Promised Land, because it is Passover. The place where the circumcisions occur is called Gibeath-ha-aralot, hill of the foreskins. (Torah is not for the faint of heart or weak of stomach.) It is a disgusting image, but one I could not rid myself of. (How high is a hill of foreskins?)

After the circumcisions, the men "abode in their places in the camp, till they were whole." How curious. It is not "till they were healed," but "whole."

That is how I feel. Now I am whole. My foreskin lies atop the hill. I stare at my penis. Only a small bit of skin was removed but it is as if something within me has been set free.

Well, I may be free, but I hear my penis plotting to get back at me. It is planning on not becoming erect for the rest of my life. I watched rhythmic gymnastics today and my penis, which has been known to get erect at the sound of a Hebrew feminine noun, lay between my legs like a piece of seaweed left by high tide. I know its weakness for Danskin tights. It has been known to raise itself from deep slumber when I've passed stores with Danskin-dressed mannequins in the windows. When I told it that the gymnasts were wearing Danskins, it opened one eye, looked at me, stuck out its tongue and went back to sleep.

I received a letter from a Rabbi Allen Maller of Culver City, California. He read my essay in *New Traditions* on my conversion and wrote to say that I am a "perfect example of a *gilgul.*" Enclosed were some extracts from his book, *God, Sex, and Kabbalah:*

> . . . the resurgence of interest in reincarnation . . . makes it worthwhile to take another, closer look at *gilgul.*
>
> I myself did not believe in the concept of *gilgul* until very recently.
>
> Then, in my studies of Kabbalah, I came across a fourteenth-century text, *Sefer Ha'pliya,* the Book of Marvels, which speaks of a special form of *gilgul* which can actually be seen in operation. This is the *gilgul* following the occasion of a Jewish soul being "cut off or lost" from the Jewish people.
>
> The means of separation do not seem to be important. It could have been volitional, accidental, or under duress. It could have been the result of a sin or of a mitzvah. A Jewish infant, orphaned because its parents had been killed saving the lives of others, and raised as a Gentile, or a person who had deliberately turned his back on his people and converted to a non-Jewish religion. Whatever the reason for the original separation, three, four, or more generations later, the displaced soul is reborn into the family line. The soul is reborn as its own descendant and consequently as an infant in a Gentile family. Born a Gentile, the infant is, naturally, raised and educated as a Gentile. But the yearning of the soul to return to its own people is so great that eventually it finds its way back to the Jewish religion, people, and culture.
>
> Of course, not all non-Jews who convert to Judaism are the reincarnated souls of Jews who had been separated from Judaism in former lives. There is, however, one characteristic which hints at the identification of those who are: a single Jewish ancestor in their Gentile family tree. And there is a familiar outline to their path to Judaism.
>
> The religious tradition of their birth never seems to fit them well. They cannot completely accept it. Their doubts grow. They begin searching here and there, restlessly. Finally, they are drawn to a particular Jew, or a group of Jews, and by this means gradually become part of the Jewish people. Much to their surprise, fre-

> quently such people discover after they have converted to Judaism that one of their great-grandparents had been a Jew.

He goes on to write that he has "come across at least a dozen instances of its [the *gilgul*'s] workings."

Reading the above was strangely satisfying because there are moments when I would like to understand rationally why being a Jew has brought me such absolute certainty of self-knowledge, such a deep peace and such joy! Of course, I suppose I can't equate reincarnation with rationality, especially since I do not know if I believe in reincarnation. Yet I go back to that night in the sanctuary of the Jewish Community of Amherst as I stood on the *bimah* beneath the *chuppah** and Rabbi Lander said the *kohanic* blessing and I heard my Jewish name for the first time and the undeniable physical feeling, a sudden warmth in my abdomen, and the thought: my great-grandfather is now at peace.

---

Each time I open my address book I see the folded piece of Holiday Inn stationery. Sometimes I open it and read the names and addresses of the Altschuls.

I should write them, but I am still too afraid. But for all I know there may be one member in the family who has been waiting all these years for one of Adolph's descendants to write.

I can't. They are the only link with the Jewish part of my past. In my fantasies I imagine that somewhere in an attic are my great-grandfather's *t'fillin* or *tallit*. But those probably burned when Grandmomma's house burned. I don't remember when that was, though I was living in New York at the time. Only after the house burned did Momma mention that Grandmomma had had a lot of Great-grandfather's letters which were lost in the fire. How deeply that hurts!

The only document existing in his handwriting is his will, which Momma showed me for the first time after Daddy died. He was forty-seven when he wrote it. It is an impersonal document, but two sentences contained and simultaneously hid great emotion: "To my brother Joe Altschul, my brother Morris Altschul, and my sister Jeanette Altschul, I give and bequeath one dollar each. To my wife Maggie Altschul (also not considered under the law of this state my lawful wife) which I have love and affection [sic] and consider my true and honest wife I bequeath and devise all my real estate and personal property herebefore stated . . ."

I keep my copy of his will in a special folder among my files and read it sometimes, staring at those particular sentences, hoping that the intensity of my gaze will force each letter to step forward and tell the tale of the man whose hand formed those letters. I feel both the anger and the cunning in leaving his siblings one dollar each. By doing so, he simultaneously expresses his feelings about them and makes it impossible for them to challenge his will and take the farm away from Maggie.

I had not known that he and Maggie were not legally married, though I had wondered. Knowing the anti-miscegenation laws of the South, I had never understood how they could have been married, though that is what Daddy had told me. Who was this man that he not only defied the law but affirmed his love for his "wife" in his last will and testament? He even went so far as to name her the executor of his will. And who was this woman who received that love and returned it?

But the letters have not spoken to me. Will one of the descendants of Adolph's siblings?

---

IT WORKS!

IT WORKS BETTER THAN EVER!!!

# 26

March 17, 1985

Dear Mr. Altschul,

I'm writing you in the hope that you can help me fill some gaps in my family history, or direct me to someone who could.

My name is Julius Lester. I am forty-six years old, and am a writer and a professor at the University of Massachusetts here in Amherst. The information I seek concerns my great-grandfather, Adolph Altschul, who married an ex-slave woman named Maggie Carson. He bought property on what was Sheridan Pike and is now Barraque Street in Pine Bluff. I spent many summers there with my grandmother, Emma Smith, and great-uncle, Rudolph Altschul. And I remember shopping in downtown Pine Bluff with my parents and passing an Altschul Jewelers and being told that the owner of the store was my relative, which, as a child, I found an interesting curiosity and little more.

I know very little about my great-grandfather. According to my mother, he was an immigrant from Germany who came to Arkansas as a peddler some time after the Civil War with his brothers. His marriage to my great-grandmother caused a rupture with his brothers, though on his death, his brothers claimed his body and buried him in the Jewish cemetery in Pine Bluff. I also have in my possession copies of legal documents transferring land from a Morris and Fannie Altschul to my great-grandfather in 1876.

That sums up what I have been able to learn about him. Anything you could tell me would be most welcome—where in Germany he immigrated from, what he did for a living, information about his brothers, sisters, parents, if there are photographs of him or any personal items in someone's possession I could have photographs of.

Learning about him is important to me, not only from the point of view of personal curiosity and the need to know more about my family roots, but I converted to Judaism a few years ago and having a Jewish great-grandfather was certainly a factor in that decision.

I apologize for infringing on your time in this way. I have wanted to write for several years, and didn't, not knowing if it would be worth the effort, or if any of the Altschuls remaining in Pine Bluff would be offended by receiving a letter from a very distant relative whom the Altschuls did not know existed, or had no interest in communicating with. However, my need to know has finally overcome my fears, especially since you or someone you could direct me to are the only sources for what I need to know.

Thank you for your time.

Hoping to hear from you, I am

Respectfully,

---

I hold a brown envelope in my hands and stare at the name and address in the upper-left-hand corner. "Samuel Altschul," it reads. I light a cigarette and sit at my desk, the letter opener in my right hand. I slit the envelope. Inside are a long letter and copies of old documents. I don't know what to look at first, as I want to read everything simultaneously, afraid that if I don't, I will awaken to discover that I was merely entangled in a night picture.

There is a copy of Great-grandfather's will, the page of the census record of 1880 for Adolph Altschul. By that time he and Maggie had five children, all girls. Uncle Rudolph and Uncle Charlie had not been born. I see Grandmomma's name. She was seven; Aunt Rena was nine.

Great-grandmomma's name is listed as "Annie Carter," which I know is wrong. Under the column designating "Color" are the letters "Mu." The same letters are beside the names of the five girls. I have never thought of Grandmomma as a mulatto. I suppose Momma would be considered a mulatto or quadroon, which would make me an octaroon, giraffe, or something. Although the census taker considered them mulattos, all of them, except Florence, considered themselves black. Why? None of them had Negroid features. I suspect that Great-grandmomma told them they were black, though she looked white. Momma says she never talked about slavery and when asked about it, she would merely shake her head. But she used to wear a black apron all the time, Momma told me, and every day at four o'clock she served tea and biscuits. I cannot reconcile the images—the tiny, light-skinned ex-slave with bitter memories who adopted a custom of her slaveowner. Then again, why should the images be reconciled? Am I not like a waterfall falling up a mountain?

Great-grandfather's occupation is listed as farmer and his birthplace and those of his parents is given as Bavaria. Great-grandmother's occupation is stated simply—"keep house." Her birthplace is given as Arkansas and that of her mother, Virginia. The space beneath her father's birthplace is blank. She was thirty-four in 1880. She was nineteen when the Civil War ended, old enough to have known the white man who was her father. Did she know him? Did she know his place of birth, and the blank square on the census form is her anger? Or was his existence irrelevant to her?

The final document is a copy of a newspaper clipping. On it Samuel Altschul has written "June 12, 1901." Under a heading that reads "Death Record" are the following words.

> Mr. Adolph Altschul, aged about seventy-five years, died at his country home near this city Tuesday afternoon, after a lingering illness. The deceased was a brother of Mrs. Joseph S. Altschul and F. M. Altschul, of this city, and Mr. Joe Altschul of Chicago. The remains will be interred in the Jewish cemetery this afternoon, the funeral taking place from the residence at 2 o'clock. Rev. J. S. Kornfeld will officiate.

I want to cry with joy because now I will be able to light a *Yahrzeit* candle for him.

I read the death notice again and, after doing the calculations on a perpetual calendar, learn that "Tuesday afternoon" was June 11. He was buried within twenty-four hours as mandated by Jewish law. I cannot take my eyes from one phrase, however: " . . . the funeral taking place from the residence at 2 o'clock." That means my mother was there! But I don't understand. How did Great-grandfather's brother and sister learn of his death? Did Great-grandmother send someone to town to tell them? Or did Great-grandfather reconcile with them during his "lingering illness"? Did he tell Great-grandmother that he wanted to be buried in the Jewish cemetery, or did his brother and sister convince her to let them bury him there? And why was the funeral at the house, that house sitting back from the road as if its inhabitants could belong only to one another, that house on whose top step I sat as a child, listening to Time? It was not a short drive from that house to town when I was a child. How much longer it was in 1901 in horse-drawn carriages. Did Great-grandmother go to the cemetery, or did she stand on that porch and watch as the hearse moved slowly up Sheridan Pike?

Once again I find myself hating the silence of my family. I would like to think all that silence compelled me to be a writer. That is not so, because words are another dimension of silence for me.

I smile at the reference to "Rev. J. S. Kornfeld." If his name had been Kornfield, then he would have been a "Rev.," but Kornfeld is a Jewish name. I wonder what Rabbi Kornfeld thought of the scene at that house on Sheridan Pike in Plum Bayou that day? Maybe he thought about nothing except the heat and why the God of Abraham, Isaac and Jacob had put him in Pine Bluff, Arkansas.

I read the letter. Samuel Altschul is a twenty-two-year-old student at the University of Arkansas who became interested in the history of the family when many old documents and pictures were found in the house of his great-aunt after her death. He had come across Adolph's grave in the old section of the Jewish cemetery but no one in the family knew anything about him or his descendants.

"The Altschul family," he writes, "originally came from Ober Lustadt, Rheinland-Pfalz. Ober Lustadt is a small village, and the family had lived there for many years." Adolph's parents were Samuel Altschul and Regina Behr. Samuel was born in 1816 and died in Pine Bluff in 1876. He assumes that Regina died before Samuel immigrated. He has been unable to find any record of her in America.

Adolph's grandmother was Barbara Altschul, who seems to have a story to tell. One day in 1816 Barbara appeared at the town hall in Oberlustadt to register the birth of a son, Samuel. She was accompanied only by her father, Jacob. The name of Samuel's father was not recorded, however. This would be interesting under any circumstances, but it seems that Barbara was already married, and had been for three years, to a Joseph Levy. Samuel is given his mother's maiden name, however. Three years later, in 1819, Barbara gives birth to a daughter, Rosina. Joseph Levy is recorded as the father and Rosina is given his family name.

Who was Samuel's father? Why didn't Joseph Levy give Samuel his name for the sake of appearances? After all, what married man wants it openly known that his wife had a child by another man while married to him? It may have been too much for Joseph because he died in 1822. In 1823 Barbara had another son, Jacob, and once again, no father's name is listed. I don't know if Barbara was already pregnant when Joseph died since the date of his death and the birth of the child are not mentioned in the letter, but it is possible. Later in the decade, date unknown, Barbara married Bernhard Kimpel and in 1832, they had a son, Joseph.

I do not know what to make of my great-great-great-grandmother. Did Samuel and Jacob have the same father? If so, was she somehow forced to marry a man she did not love and refuse to relinquish the man she did love? Or was she a woman who loved many and her love was stronger than the bonds of matrimony? Or was the unnamed father of two of her sons her father? After all, the second son is given his name. Well, one of these years I will go to Ober Lustadt, and find there some oral historian who carries the chronicles of the town in her or his memory and will be able to remove some of the silence from Great-great-great-grandmother.

In any event, her firstborn and my great-great grandfather, Samuel Altschul, had four children with Regina Behr: Joseph (1839–?); Adolph (1841–1901); Jeanette (1843–1923); and Morris (1851–1933). No one knows when they came to the United States, but Joseph and Adolph were in the Civil War on the side of the Confederacy. It is doubtful they did much fighting. Joseph was the Confederate Army bandleader and Adolph played in the band.

I have to laugh. Two of my ancestors were in the Confederate Army. I'm sure there are those in the Afro-Am Department who would say, "So that explains you."

Suddenly, an image comes to me. I see the members in a band walking slowly along a dusty road and into the yard of a plantation. The men sit down wearily on the porch and under trees in the yard and the slaveowner orders his servants to bring water to the men. A tiny, light-skinned slave woman ("She looked like a porcelain doll," Momma described her) brings water to one of the men. What instrument did he play? Clarinet? Trumpet? Drums? Their eyes meet and they know.

Or was there a Confederate band concert in town one Sunday afternoon, a rally to sell bonds for the Confederate cause to which Massa Carson brings his slaves and in the crowd, Adolph sees Maggie? Their eyes meet and they know.

However they met, it is obvious that Great-grandfather did not believe in the cause of the Confederacy, no matter how many times he played "Dixie."

There is more on Adolph's siblings which I skim on this first perusal of his letter. Samuel Altschul has located Altschul descendants in Europe, and it seems that one committed suicide rather than be captured by the Nazis. His wife was captured and died as a result of being injected with cancer cells. Their daughter and her husband escaped to England, where they became dollmakers and "made the only official doll of Queen Elizabeth for her coronation."

I read further and am stunned to learn that there was never an Altschul Jewelers in Pine Bluff. The Altschuls owned a confectionery and a wholesale tobacco company. However, the tobacco company did sell jewelry. From where does my memory of the sign come? I still see it clearly—the round sign, the clock in the center and the words "Altschul Jewelers" surrounding it. I wonder if there was a brief period in the mid-Forties when things were slow in wholesale tobacco and they put a clock sign outside the store advertising jewelry?

There is more Altschul family history in the letter than I can understand, but I notice that the name "Julia" appears and reappears. I was named Julius for my mother, Julia. I did not know that Julia was the name of a cousin of Adolph's father. Was it only coincidence that Adolph named one of his daughters Julia and that one of his daughters named one of her daughters Julia and that my mother named me Julius, and I, not knowing the name had been passed from generation to generation, had given David the middle name of Julius, making him the fifth generation?

I also wonder if it is only coincidence that of all the Hebrew names I could have chosen, I chose Yaacov, Jacob. Only now do I learn that it was the name of my great-great-great-great-grandfather.

The biggest shock is at the end of the letter:

> We found it interesting that you converted to Judaism while our family has gone in the other direction. My father married a Gentile and converted to Christianity when I was three or four years old. My father's brother and sister both married Gentiles. We still consider ourselves Jews even though we are not of the Jewish faith. Since you have converted to Judaism, one thing that may be of interest to you is that the Altschuls are Kohens (Kohanim), which means that they are direct descendants of Aaron. Several older members of the family have told us this fact, and many of the tombstones say this or have the Kohanim symbol.

I am the only Jew left in the family.

## June 1985

A high school graduation is such an ordinary occasion. Thousands take place in auditoriums and gymnasiums each spring, and yet it is precisely because they are so ordinary that I am thinking of dandelions and the songs of robins tonight.

What is Malcolm feeling tonight? I have no experience to help me understand. I finished high school a year early and had completed my freshman year at Fisk when my high school class graduated. I did not attend the graduation ceremony and had almost graduated from college before I thought to go by the high school and get my diploma.

Is he alternately elated, relieved, apprehensive and sad? It is the sadness I cannot imagine. I considered high school an impediment, an annoyance to be dispensed with quickly so I could enter the intellectual life of college. Malcolm enjoyed high school, especially this past year.

He was voted best all-round athlete of his class. Much of my year was spent being cold as I followed him from the football stadium to the hockey rink to the lacrosse field. It is wonderful to be awed by what your children can do. How did he learn to run so fast, to spin and change directions, leaving an opposing player hugging the ground when he was sure, and I was, too, that he had Malcolm in his grasp? He was one of the tri-captains of the hockey team, his line set a new school record for points scored in a season, and he was voted to the All Western Massachusetts Hockey Team. Watching him skate up and down the ice on Friday nights, I remembered that cold December Sunday morning when I took him to Wollman Rink in Central Park for the first time, tied the skates on his feet and, holding his hand, led him to the ice. When he stepped onto it, he released my hand, took a step, and fell. Instinctively I reached out to help him up. He ignored me, pushed himself up, and clinging to the boards, he began making his way around the rink. It was my first experience of letting him go. He needed me to help him, but he did not want me. So I stood and watched him fall, get up and watch the other skaters intently and then try to move forward again. Now he moved over the ice as effortlessly as a stream flowing through a forest.

He was one of the captains on the lacrosse team, too, considered the best in the school's history. I teased him, sometimes, about choosing sports that black people know nothing about. You can't get more white than hockey and lacrosse. He would only smile, because whenever he has asked me, "What do you think I should do?," my response has always been, "If you do what you love, you'll be all right." He has played the sports that called out his soul. I only wish his soul had been called by something played indoors, like hot-tub polo.

He was voted to the All Western Massachusetts Lacrosse Team and found himself being recruited by college football and lacrosse coaches. Although he had never seriously considered being a professional athlete, his high school athletic accomplishments were a good beginning toward a career in coaching, exercise science or something that would keep him bathed in sweat.

When we visited the college that was his first choice, I was not prepared when he said, "How would you feel if we went to the meeting for potential English majors instead of the one for phys. ed. majors?" I managed to say, "Whatever you want to do," and then held my breath for the next hour so I would not say the wrong thing; anything I said would be wrong. When the meeting ended, I released my breath and looked at him. He nodded. "I think I'll major in English."

I don't know why fathers want and even need at least one of their children to follow in their footsteps. Are we so unsure of how we have lived that we cannot know, with certainty, that we have lived well unless one of our children continues what we began? Or is it that having our children extend what we have created in the world is the male equivalent of the birth experience? As a man, do I need to feel that from my soul the souls of my children are born because I was so peripheral to their physical births?

When Jody was ten I gave her a guitar, hoping but not daring to expect that, through that instrument, she would take me into her soul and find her own. To my amazement she did. She teaches guitar, sings, writes songs, and when I listen to her, I am at peace. It is as if I have transcended the limitation of physiology which did not allow me to carry her in my body, to nurture her body through my own, but when she holds the guitar in her arms and plays it better than I ever did, I know that I gave her something as important as the breath in her lungs.

Perhaps that is what fathers need to know. It is not our fault that we could not bring you into the world physically. If we could have, we would, but we could not. But see, we can be the bridges across which you walk to reach your souls, and when we know that you choose to use us as such bridges, then we know that we have been equal participants in what will be, we hope, your unceasing act of creating yourself.

I have known for a long time that Malcolm writes well, better than I did at his age. Once or twice a year I allowed myself to say, "You write well," daring to say no more. I never expected him to know it, too, this son who was so firm in declaring that he did not want to be a writer. He says he wants to be a sports journalist. I wish I wrote as well as some of the men who write for *Sports Illustrated.* Some of the best writing in America appears in that magazine. Now that he has decided to major in English, it does not matter if he becomes a writer. He has realized that accepting his gift for language does not mean he becomes me.

After reading one of my books, my father looked at me and said, "Well, I guess you became a preacher after all. You just did it a little differently."

I smiled as tears rushed to my eyes. "Daddy, I'm so glad you know that."

I sit on the stage of the Fine Arts Center at the university, waiting for the graduation exercises to begin. I am nervous, not only because I want my son to be proud of me, but because of what he said one night several months ago.

"I'm afraid that your speaking at graduation is going to take all the attention away from me. It's my night, you know."

I was grateful for his honesty, grateful for the quick glimpse the earnest expression of his feelings had given me. What was it like to be my son? I had wanted to know so often. Sometimes it was a fear of being eclipsed. I had known that. He had chosen athletics over academics because, he said, "I want an area that's mine, that you've had nothing to do with." I remember Jody saying to me once, in exasperation, "You've done almost everything, Dad. You haven't left anything for us."

How do the children of high-achieving parents find their own identities? My children are ambivalent about their "famous" father. I am not as famous as they think I am, and yet I may be more famous than I know because I am surprised when they tell me stories of being stopped on the street by people they don't know and being asked, "What's your father working on now?" Sometimes they are flattered; sometimes they resent the intrusions into their privacy, the sudden loss of protective anonymity. Because my name and face are known to more people than I know, they are robbed of identity when they are seen as "Julius Lester's son," "Julius Lester's daughter."

I have tried to protect their separateness, perhaps too much so. I do not tell them what I am writing or when something other than a book is published. I want them to live their lives without reference to my public one. But when Malcolm says, "Why didn't you tell me you had an article in such-and-such?" publication, there is hurt in his voice, as if he thinks I want to exclude him.

It is not that. I grew up being Reverend Lester's son, which was not the same as growing up being me. Offering my children separateness from me is my way of loving them, my way of giving them the space I never had to know who I was in relation to my needs and desires and dreams. I do not want my children sacrificed on the altar of black people's needs or mine.

I fear that one day they will tell me I was wrong, that it was their task to fight for their separateness and mine to fight back.

Michael McIntosh, senior class president, the leading scorer in the history of the hockey team and one of Malcolm's linemates, is introducing me. "There are many things I could say in introducing our speaker, but I'll say only the most important. He is Malcolm Lester's father."

I know it is going to be difficult to get through this night without crying. I do not know the tears will begin as I stand and walk to the podium. The tears, which I rapidly blink away, are not of joy or sadness, but they are tears from the soul. To hear myself introduced as Malcolm's father is to be folded by the white wings of a sacred mystery, and the mystery is not that he is my son but that we are father and son together, each unknown and unknowable to the other, yet bound to each other like a star to space. And I cannot say which of us is the star and which of us is that impenetrable and eternal blackness.

# 27

## October 7, 1985

It is Simchat Torah, the night we rejoice in the Torah and complete the reading of the five books of Moses and begin again immediately with *Breshit bara Elohim et hashamayim v'et haaretz* ("When God created the heavens and the earth"). The scrolls of the Torah will be taken from the ark and, passed from person to person, carried around and around the synagogue, and we will sing and dance our joy in Torah.

I stand outside the Pennsylvania Station–Madison Square Garden complex in New York City. Twenty-four years ago the bus terminal was a part of Penn Station, and one June afternoon I stepped off a bus, guitar in one hand, suitcase in the other, typewriter beneath my right arm, walked outside, and the first building I saw was the main post office across the street. To my young eyes it was as large as all of Nashville and I turned around and went back inside the terminal to sit on a bench and wonder if I had made the right decision in coming to New York to seek fame and fortune. Since I didn't have the money for a return ticket, my decision was irrevocable, right or not. A year later I moved to the neighborhood of which Madison Square Garden and the post office were a part and they became mere edifices past which I hurried almost daily without a glance.

The sun has not gone down so I still have time to get to a synagogue, any synagogue. I remember that there is one on Twenty-third Street between Seventh and Eighth and a couple in the garment district in the Thirties on or just off Seventh Avenue. But I continue milling among the crowds of blacks lined up outside the Garden and buying tickets to hear Minister Louis Farrakhan.

A few days ago Marty Peretz, editor of *The New Republic,* called.

"I'd like you to cover the Farrakhan rally at Madison Square Garden on October 7."

My first thought was: I can't. That's Simchat Torah. But I said, "I need to think about it. Let me call you back tomorrow."

Louis Farrakhan is the tall, articulate and charismatic leader of the Nation of Islam who came to national attention with his attacks on Jews and defense of Jesse Jackson in the wake of the latter's "Hymie" gaffe. Farrakhan was news to whites, but I had been aware of him since the summer of 1960 when someone had played for me a 45 rpm record called "White Man's Heaven Is Black Man's Hell." It was a song with a calypso beat sung seductively and persuasively by a man named Louis X. That was my introduction to a view of history in which virtue was black and evil white, and there was no other reality than race. On the record I heard a truth I wished I could believe and accept. What a relief it would be to condemn all white people as unredeemable. I would be free of having to live with the uncertainty and ambiguity that was inevitable as long as I remained vulnerable to white people.

I followed Louis X's career in the black press, especially when he denounced Malcolm after his assassination. I heard rumors that Malcolm's widow considered him personally responsible for her husband's murder. After the death of Elijah Muhammad, the founder of the Nation of Islam, the Nation rejected Elijah's racial philosophy, changed its name and aligned itself with more traditional Islamic thinking and practice. Louis X, or maybe he was Louis Farrakhan by then, assumed control of the Nation.

Farrakhan delighted in shocking people, and nothing was more so than his description of Hitler as "wickedly great." I could not pretend that I could report on him objectively.

I called Marty Peretz. "I don't know if you know it, but I'm Jewish and if I cover the Farrakhan rally, I can't leave that out."

"I know you're Jewish. That's why I thought what you would have to say would be interesting."

I knew that I would have to do it because I was curious about what I would write. Would I respond to him as a Jew or would I be seduced by his charisma, his rhetoric? Would his expressions of anger and hatred be so comforting to the hurt and bleeding parts in me that I would applaud his sharp rebukes and join the laughter at his anti-white and anti-Semitic insults? I could not be sure that I wouldn't, and how humiliating it would be to have to write that.

I stand outside the press entrance to Madison Square Garden. Walking among the crowds are black men in suits, white shirts and red bow ties, billed caps on their heads with the initials FOI, Fruit of Islam. They are the elite of the Nation of Islam. Their eyes are hard with dangerous pride. Farrakhan has given them simple answers for every question, simple solutions for every problem. I look at the women of the Nation, who are dressed in long white dresses. Their heads are covered by flowing white cloths. They carry themselves with a regal arrogance as if they and only they are the owners of the future.

It has been a long time since I have been around so many blacks. I live in a beautiful New England town, and the ghosts of Emily Dickinson, Daniel Webster and Robert Frost are daily companions. I read about social problems in *The New York Times* but they do not sit at my doorstep as they would if I lived in an urban community. As I walked among the crowds earlier, I knew that I could not pretend to know them and their lives. We belong to the same race, but Harlem and Bedford-Stuyvesant are merely names to me. It is home to many of them. I look at their faces and see poverty. I look at their clothes and hands and see menial work. I have never been poor, have never worked in the garment district, a factory, or been on welfare. My hands are soft and my eyes gentle. My walk is slow and languid, as if the world is not a dangerous and threatening place and I the prey it waits for. I feel tension, fear and desperation in their bodies, even in the women in white and the Fruit of Islam. Clothes are merely a polyester shield against reality, and tomorrow despair will settle down once again like fog that can be seen but is without substance.

Once inside the Garden I look down on the main floor, which is covered with folding chairs. The seats are filling rapidly. I had hoped no one would come. What an effective repudiation of Farrakhan that would be. I am to be disappointed. Every seat is going to be taken.

Sitting in the press section, I chat casually with writers and photographers I have not seen in ten or fifteen years. Sitting next to me is a white writer from *New York* magazine. He leans over and asks, "Who's that?," directing my eyes to the stage, where a tall black man in a long, flowing white robe is talking with someone.

Whoever he is, he is quite elegant and looks like a member of some royal African family. I start to say that I don't know but out of my mouth comes "My God!" It is Stokely Carmichael.

"What's he doing here?"

"Stokely needs an audience to know he's alive and obviously he has no scruples about how he finds one."

I have not seen him since he spoke to my Civil Rights Movement class more than ten years ago, at least. Whenever it was, the year was close enough to the days of The Movement that its dying glow still infused our relationship with some warmth. But we did not have much to say to each other. If one was not female, a close relationship with Stokely depended on ideological agreement. For him the personal is political and the political personal, and as he became more nationalistic, he could not accept that I was married to a white woman, and unlike other black men so married in the late Sixties, I would not leave my wife merely because she was white. Stokely and I never talked about it, but friends told me: "Stokely has some real problems with you because of your wife." I was angered because Stokely knew my wife, had been to our apartment in New York, had eaten her cooking and sat at our dinner table, laughing and joking. But when the personal becomes political, persons cease to exist.

Looking at him sitting on the stage, I have no desire to say hello. He might greet me with one of his large hugs and his dazzling smile. Stokely and I were close once, but seeing him on the stage from which Farrakhan will speak, the personal becomes political for me. Stokely's presence on that stage is an endorsement of a man who hates Jews and Israel. All the memories of the laughter and danger Stokely and I shared are not compelling enough for me to regard him as other than my enemy.

To my consternation, one of the first speakers introduced is none other than Stokely. He calls himself Kwame Touré now and heads something called the All African People's Revolutionary Party. As he begins to speak it is as if I am watching an "I Love Lucy" rerun. His face is the same; his lines are the same: "We are not poor, we are poorly organized." "Our people don't need talk, they need guns!" I wonder how many thousands of times Stokely has said those sentences in the past twenty years and whether they have any meaning for him now or are merely taped replays to which he does not listen anymore. There is a rough desperation in his voice as he shouts and yells and receives only polite applause from the audience. They know they are poorly organized, and don't talk to them about guns; they walk the streets of their neighborhoods every day in fear of them. Only when Stokely begins attacking Israel, Zionism and Judaism does it seem that he finds what they came to hear. "Africa gave Judaism to the world," he shouts and the audience cheers and applauds. "Moses was an Egyptian! Moses was an African!" The audience is on its feet, cheering.

Looking at Stokely I realize that he is really a Las Vegas entertainer whose name used to be on the marquee as a headliner. Now he is an opening act whose role is to get the audience warmed up for the main act, all the time hoping, however, that one day he will be a headliner again. If this performance is any indication, he will not be.

Just as I am wondering if attacks on Jews, Zionism and Israel are going to be the evening's theme, a representative of the Palestinian Congress of America is introduced. He proceeds to equate Zionism with cancer, and "the supports of Zionism are cancerous." The implication is obvious: Cancer kills unless it is killed. Other speakers follow but the anti-Semitic message is the same, and the audience greets each anti-Semitic thrust by rising to its feet, cheering, arms outstretched at forty-five-degree angles, fists clenched. I feel that I have been set down in the midst of one of the Nuremberg rallies.

Finally, Farrakhan walks onto the red-carpeted stage, flanked by six women in white hats and white suits with red tassels at the shoulders. More than twenty thousand people rise, cheering and applauding, arms angled heavenward. Farrakhan steps to the edge of the stage, his arms outstretched as if he is posing as the Lamb of God.

The first half hour of his speech is a mini-lecture on Islam. Then he comes to the main item on the evening's agenda: He is the Voice of Holy Truth whom Jews are determined to silence. "Somebody has to come to separate God from Satan, slavemaster and slave, oppressor and oppressed, so they can see each other and then go to war to see who is going to rule—God or Satan." And he is that someone.

This is madness!

"Who are those who support me? The righteous! You have been deprived of justice, and if God sends a deliverer, will the oppressor love him?"

"NO!" shouts the crowd.

"Are the Jews who are angry with me righteous people?"

"NO!"

"Jesus had a controversy with the Jews. Farrakhan has a controversy with the Jews. Jesus was hated by Jews. Farrakhan is hated by Jews. Jesus was scourged by Jews in their temple. Farrakhan is scourged by Jews in their synagogues. Did Jesus care for the oppressed?"

"YES!"

"They called him a devil. They call me a devil. When Jesus raised Lazarus from the dead and fed the five thousand, it was then that the authorities began to attack him. I am resurrecting the minds of black people from the dead, and they attack Farrakhan."

The writer from *New York* magazine and I keep looking at each other and, as we busily scribble in our notebooks, ask each other, "Did he say what I thought he said?" Yet I see black reporters and photographers putting down their pens and cameras to laugh and applaud.

"I am your last chance, Jews! The scriptures charge your people with killing the prophets of God." Farrakhan goes on to contend that God has not made Jews pay for such alleged deeds. However, if something happens to him, then God will make the Jews pay for all the prophets killed from biblical times to the present. "You cannot say 'never again' to God because when God puts you in the oven, 'never again' don't mean a thing. If you fool with me, you court death itself. I will not run from you; I will run to you!"

After an hour and fifteen minutes, I leave because I am too frightened. I look around anxiously as I exit onto Eighth Avenue, feeling like a *shtetl** Jew on Good Friday. I expect to see someone point at me and yell, "He's a Jew!" and to find myself running from an angry crowd. Then I remember: My skin color is the same as theirs. It is not a consolation or a comfort.

I am a Jew now. It is one experience to read the words of political, racial and religious anti-Semitism in books; it is entirely another to hear them spoken with intensity, urgency and conviction, to hear them affirmed with cheers, the stamping of feet, laughter, applause and arms thrust toward heaven. I am afraid and enraged. How dare anyone hate the joy of my soul?

As a black I am ashamed. I do not understand what is happening to blacks that so many could revel in vicarious bloodletting. Despair, poverty, deprivation and the relentless heat of racism do not justify hatred. Those blacks inside Madison Square Garden act as if they are the first generation of blacks to make its way through the valley of the shadow of death. They are not. They are the first, however, to wear suffering as if it were the divine right of kings. They are the first to use suffering as if it gives them divine exemption from moral and ethical responsibility to the rest of humanity.

How could they not see that Farrakhan's hatred of Jews means that he hates them, too?

# 28

## Winter 1986

I look at her sitting at the table, studying Hebrew. I admire this woman whom I am blessed to also call my wife. She has the courage to walk in darkness and the faith to know that the darkness is also light. I try to imagine my life without her presence and I cannot. Sometimes such intimacy is frightening to one as solitary as I am.

Is it permissible to be in awe of one's wife? If it had been she who had plunged the marriage into the fires of Judaism, would I have sat at the Sabbath table week after week with love and respect for her and a way of being I had not chosen? Would I have continued in a marriage if she had become unfamiliar and unknown to me?

I would like to think yes, but I cannot be sure. What is certain is that she continued to say yes—to me, to us. Such love is frightening, too, sometimes. It is also humbling.

Last spring at Pesach she told me that she had decided to become a Jew. I have said little in response. I am afraid to give my joy a place in my body, afraid that joy of such magnitude will terrify her, will block the entranceway of her own joy. I need to be certain that becoming a Jew is the melody of her soul before I dare let my joy shine.

Would it have been wrong for her to become a Jew because she loves me? No. But I would not know how to receive so much love, and that is sad. I wonder how she would have responded if, four years ago, I had offered her the opportunity to join me so that we could become Jews together. I assumed that doing so would violate my separateness and hers. I think I was wrong.

Unbidden, the image comes to me of that house sitting far back from the road and of me, Momma and Grandmomma sitting on the porch in the evenings. Separateness was survival, I understand now.

When Adolph and Maggie decided to live their love in that time and that place, they separated themselves from family and community to live unto themselves by a value system which no one agreed with or approved. And that separateness was handed down, generation to generation, a blending of fear and survival, of despair and love for inner truth. There is something very Jewish about it.

Now that I am a Jew, now that we are Jews, she and I, perhaps I will eventually walk off the porch, open the gate and go outside the fence, dragging my ancestors, kicking and screaming, with me.

My wife is becoming a Jew and I am freed.

David is six now and thinks he is Jewish already. Why wouldn't he? He has grown up with the smell of challah baking every Thursday night or Friday morning. During the eight days of Passover he does not eat *chametz*—cereal, bread, etc. He has never eaten pork or shellfish. I have taught him the *alef-bet* and he is learning to read Hebrew as he learns to read English. Sometimes when he is playing by himself, we hear him singing under his breath, and listening closely, we hear *"Sh'ma Yisrael Adonai Elohenu Adonai Ehad."* Last spring when we met with his kindergarten teacher for our regularly scheduled end-of-the-year conference, I noticed on the blackboard in the classroom a number of words beginning with *z*. Among them was *zayin*, the name of the one of the letters of the Hebrew alphabet.

"Was *zayin* David's contribution of a *z* word?" I asked Nomi, one of his teachers and the daughter of Haim and Yaffa Gunner.

She said, "Yes," and then chuckled. "Let me tell you a story. One day we were discussing names and what they mean. One boy, I don't remember who, said his name and said it was a Hebrew name and meant such-and-such. Up went David's hand. I called on him and he said, 'My God speaks Hebrew,' and that was all."

On the wall next to my computer is a short essay David wrote a few weeks ago in school. The assignment was to write a few sentences about their dreams, not the night pictures, but their wishes for the world. David wrote: "I dream that Hitlr was navr alive. Be cos he got clos to kiling avre Jew."

The other children show no interest in Judaism, or any religion. I do not mind. To force Judaism on them is to guarantee their antipathy. David has a love for Judaism, however, which surprises and startles me. After my wife becomes officially Jewish, we will have him converted. His only regret is in giving up Christmas. Last December was the first time there was not a Christmas tree in the house. How pure the house was for me without it. I did not like Christmas even as a child.

Now I resent it, and the store clerks and strangers wishing me a "Merry Christmas." Sometimes I say nothing. Other times I say, "I'm Jewish." Saying nothing I feel like a traitor, but when I say that I'm Jewish, a "Happy Chanukah" covered with Christmas tinsel is thrown at me. I think I will wear a Star of David from the first of November through Christmas every year. Maybe that will force Gentiles to limit their greetings to "Hello."

On Christmas Day, the children said they were glad not to be celebrating it. Elena found that she was released from the monumental expectations Christmas creates as well as the anxieties of not having those expectations met.

Adin Steinsalz has written that it takes three generations to make a Jew. I hope my wife and I live to be called to the *bimah* for an *aliyah* on the bar or bat mitzvah of a grandchild. I fantasize about such a day and wonder who I will be then. I would like to be living in Israel, in the desert or in Jerusalem. It used to be the custom for Jewish males to write out their own copies of the Torah. That is how I would like to spend my old age, slowly, reverently meditating on each letter of the Hebrew alphabet, each one a holy picture delineating my soul and the face of God. I want my last years to be lived in holy silence, opening my lips only to sing the prayers of worship. A Jew is created in silence and song. The two are one and interchangeable when joy burns the earth and scorches the stars.

Last June I attended a three-day seminar on cantorial music and the cantorate as a profession at the University of Hartford. I was afraid to know if I had wasted my life by not becoming a Jew twenty-five years ago. But my wife urged me to have the courage to find out.

The seminar was sponsored by the Cantors Institute, which is part of the Jewish Theological Seminary, the educational center of Conservative Judaism. Twenty-five people were enrolled in the seminar, and only one was older than me, a man who served as cantor in a small Connecticut town and had come because he felt the lack of formal cantorial training.

I did not know what to expect. As much as I love Judaism, it was still not easy for me to venture into the world of Jews. Many of them have mixed feelings about converts and some are not shy about expressing those feelings.

The comment I hear most often is "Didn't you have enough problems being black?" The remark startles me because what the person is really saying is that he has problems being Jewish. I generally respond by saying, "Being Jewish is a joy for me."

There was a woman who said sweetly, "Oh, you're like Sammy Davis, Jr." I said, "I wouldn't know. I never met him." Rabbi Lander told me that I was too polite. "You should've said, 'Oh, and you're like Mrs. Portnoy.' "

I was not polite to the woman who said to me, "Well, you're not really Jewish, you know." I looked at her with Grandmomma's eyes and said angrily, "How dare you!" Many Jews (and Gentiles) feel that if you're not born Jewish, then you aren't *really* a Jew. I am learning, however, that the more religious the Jew, the less intense his problem. Only secularly identified Jews cannot accept that I, too, am a Jew.

No one at the seminar gave me a second look, or asked if I was looking for the jazz seminar, or if I was a convert. It was assumed that I was there because I loved being Jewish and wanted to know if God had called me to express my love in song.

For three days I listened to cantors talk about prayer, what it is, what it is supposed to do, what it means in the Jewish tradition. For three days I was with Jews who cared about prayer, who cared about the enormous responsibility and unique expression which Jewish prayer is.

On the last morning I asked the older man if he was going to apply for admission to the Cantors Institute. He shook his head. "It's too late for me," he said, bowing his head.

Me, too. I had listened to the young people sing, many of whom were still in college. They were music majors, had taken voice lessons, studied music theory, sight-singing, and were, in essence, trained musicians. Even though I had recorded two albums of original songs in the mid-Sixties, my voice was untrained and it no longer had the richness and purity of twenty years ago.

Later that day I talked with a young woman from Delaware with whom I had become friendly and asked, "Why do you want to be a cantor?"

She smiled. "My synagogue has given me so much. You know? I just love to go to synagogue. Because it has given me so much, I want to give something back."

I nodded and thought, Yes, Judaism has given me so much. I, too, must give something back. But how? At the seminar I learned the term I needed for who I wanted to be—a *baal t'filah.* These people were men in the *shtetls* of Eastern Europe who prayed to God for the congregation. They were untrained musicians, but the sacredness they brought to the prayers caused them to be chosen by their congregations to pray in song. That was who I wanted to be—a *baal t'filah,* a "master of prayer."

At the end of the seminar, I knew I could no longer stay at home on Shabbat mornings and be happy studying Torah. I needed to be in synagogue, needed to be with other Jews, singing prayers to God. I had continued studying Hebrew at the university and had just completed a year of biblical Hebrew to complement the year of modern I had had. Although I could not read it rapidly and fluently, I could follow someone else's reading comfortably. So the following Saturday David and I drove the ten miles to the synagogue in Northampton.

From the beginning of the preliminary service I knew that I had found my home. The synagogue had no cantor, but the rabbi, Edward Friedman, had a strong tenor voice and, most important, knew that his voice and the music were vehicles for prayer. And there was a young woman in the congregation, Laurel Zar-Kessler, who *davened** the Torah service and brought tears to my eyes.

If I had had any doubts that B'nai Israel was truly my home, they were banished when the *gabbai,* the man who passes out the *aliyot,* whispered in my ear during the repetition of the *amidah,** "*Kohen* or *levi?*"

"Israel," I responded.

"*Shlishi,*" he responded. "What's your Hebrew name?"

"Yaakov ben Avraham."

He patted me on the shoulder and continued around the congregation.

Traditionally the first two persons called to the *bimah* to read the Torah are descendants of the priestly and levitical lines. Though my great-grandfather had been a *kohen*, Orthodox and Conservative Judaism recognize only matrilineal descent, so I could not claim to be a *kohen*. I do not know, even now, whether the man, whom I came to know as Mel Prouser, assumed I was a Jew, or whether asking me if I was *kohen* or *levi* was his way of finding out, because a non-Jew would not know what was being asked. But I will always be grateful to him for addressing me as if I were a Jew instead of asking.

A few months after I started attending B'nai Israel I told Rabbi Friedman that I wanted to have my conversion done Halachically,* since I had not been circumcised before. I did not know if he would ask me to study with him for another year or what he would say, but I told him I would be willing to do that if he thought it was necessary.

He smiled. "Oh, you know more about Judaism already than many people in the congregation. When would you like to do it?"

The next week I met him and two other rabbis at the *mikveh** in Springfield. The *mohel** took a sharp instrument (I was too scared to look) and drew a drop of blood from my circumcised penis. I immersed myself in the ritual bath, said the appropriate blessings, and it was done.

## May 10, 1986

It is Shabbat, the first of Iyyar 5746, the 16th day of the Omer and the second day of Rosh Chodesh, the New Moon. My wife, David and I sit at the rear of the sanctuary of B'nai Israel.

A brown velvet *kippah* is on my head, my multi-colored *tallit* wrapped around me and flowing down to my hips. I am nervous, as I have been since the Saturday morning early in the spring when Rabbi Friedman said casually to me after services, "When are we going to get that bass voice of yours up on the *bimah?*"

I had not been aware that he could hear my voice. I know it is deep and loud, which is why I tried to sing quietly. But there had been Saturday mornings when joy banished timidity, especially during the repetition of the *amidah* when we sang "*Yismach Moshe*" and "*Sim Shalom.*"

In a few moments the repetition of the *amidah* will be finished and Rabbi Friedman will say, "Julius Lester will lead us in the *Hallel.*" I will rise, walk to the *bimah* and begin to sing Psalms 113 to 118, those special psalms of praise that are only sung on holidays and when Rosh Chodesh coincides with the Sabbath. At long last I will stand in a synagogue and sing Jewish liturgical music as a Jew. What if I fail? What if I forget the melodies?

I remember what we were told at the seminar last summer: "Sing sweetly. Sing sweetly." I will not be going to the *bimah* to perform but to lead the congregation in prayers of praise to HaShem. That will be my only function.

"Julius Lester will lead us in *Hallel.* Please rise."

I squeeze my wife's hand, and taking her smile with me, walk slowly down the side aisle, ascend the steps to the *bimah* and stand behind the broad table on which the Torah scrolls are laid. I close my eyes and begin to chant the opening blessing: "*Baruch ata Adonai Elohenu melech ha olam asher kidshanu b'mitzvotav v'tzivanu likro et ha hallel.*" ("Blessed are You, O Lord our God, Ruler of the Universe, who has sanctified us by Your precepts and enjoined upon us the reading of the *Hallel.*") The melody is my own and it is simultaneously joyous and mournful, because that is the essence of Chosenness.

As I hear the voices from the congregation rising to meet mine, there is no separateness between me and them. We have become music; we are embodied prayer. When I begin the up-tempo and very rhythmic melody for Psalm 115, I hear a soprano voice from the congregation doing an ascending obbligato at the end of each line and I smile, recognizing the voice of Janice Friedman, the rabbi's wife, and I think about the words we are singing: "*Ha shamayim shamayim l'adonai, v'haaretz natan livne adam*" ("The heavens are the heavens of the Lord, but the earth He has given to children of men"), and it is as if our voices are fusing the two into one so that heaven has now become earth and earth is heaven and the two are one as God is One.

I know now. At long last I know what my voice was meant to sing. All those years I sang folk songs, spirituals, blues, work songs, and always knew that something was absent, that as much as I loved spirituals, I was not wholly present when I sang them. Now I know why. It is this music my voice was meant to sing. It is this music of praise and love that releases my soul into my voice, and I have known that ever since I was seven years old and sat at the piano playing "*Kol Nidre*" over and over. I knew. It took only forty years for me to believe in what I knew.

All too soon it is over and I descend the *bimah* and begin walking up the aisle to return to my seat in the back of the synagogue. The oldest member of the synagogue offers me his hand and says, "*Yasher koach.*" ("More strength to you.") There are tears in his eyes and I want to cry in my joy.

I know now who I am. I am a Jew and I am a lovesong to the God of Abraham, Isaac and Jacob, a praisesong to the God of Sarah, Rebecca, Rachel and Leah.

That is all the 613 *mitzvot* are, the *midrashim*, the Talmud, the Torah, *kashrut*, *tzdekah*, and everything else in Judaism. They are lovesongs to HaShem.

And so am I.

13 Elul 5746

# Glossary

**Aliyah (Aliyot,** plural) Hebrew. To go up. It is used to describe the honor of being asked to go up to the *bimah* in synagogue and sing the blessing over the Torah before and after it is read. The word also means to immigrate to Israel, "to make *aliyah.*"

**Amidah** Hebrew. Standing. It refers to the prayer said silently, while standing, at every service.

**Baal Korei** Hebrew. Master reader, the person who reads from the Torah scroll for and to the congregation.

**Bet Din** Hebrew. The Jewish religious or civil court of law.

**Bimah** Hebrew. The elevated platform in a synagogue where the reading desk stands from which the Torah is raised.

**Bris** Hebrew. Also called *brith milah.* The ritual of circumcision performed on the eighth day after the birth of a Jewish male.

**Chanukah** Hebrew. Dedication. The holiday begins on the twenty-fifth of the Hebrew month of Kislev and continues for eight days. It commemorates the victory of the Maccabees over the Syrians in 165 B.C.E. (Before the Common Era). Antiochus, king of Syria, attempted to force Jews to give up their religion for paganism. Thus Chanukah commemorates what was probably the first struggle for religious freedom in history.

The lighting of one candle a night for eight nights is a reminder of the miracle which occurred when the Jews recaptured the temple and found only enough oil to burn in the lamp for one night. Miraculously, the oil burned for eight days and nights, time enough for more oil to be pressed and made ready.

**Chasid (Chasidim,** plural) Hebrew. A member of any one of a number of ultra-Orthodox Jewish religious groups originating in Eastern Europe in the eighteenth century. *Chasidim* are known for their strict and literal adherence to Jewish Law as well as for the distinctive black garb worn by some.

**Chuppah** Hebrew. The canopy under which a Jewish couple is married.

**Daven** Yiddish, the origins of which are unclear. Some associate it with the Latin *divinus.* It means to pray to the Divine.

**Erev** Hebrew. Evening. However, when used in connection with a religious holiday, it means the day before. Thus, because Shabbat is Saturday, erev Shabbat is Friday.

**Gemara** Aramaic. *See Talmud.*

**Haggadah** Hebrew. The book read out loud at the Passover seder. It contains the story of the Exodus from Egypt, rabbinic commentary, explanations of the symbolic objects on the seder plate, prayers, psalms and songs.

**Halachic** Hebrew. According to Jewish Law.

**Kashrut** Hebrew. Fit, legitimate. This word usually applies to foods, sacred objects, but the concept can cover any aspect of an observant Jew's life.

**Kiddush** Hebrew. Sanctification. It is the benediction and prayer said over the cup of wine or bread that begins the Sabbath or a festival.

**Kohanic** Referring to the *kohanim* (plural of *kohen),* the priestly class, descendants of Aaron.

**Lubavitcher** Yiddish. One of the largest and most active of Chasidic groups.

**Mensch** Yiddish. There is perhaps no higher compliment one can give or receive in Jewish life. To define it as a person of the highest character cannot give a full sense of the love and respect that permeate this word.

**Meshugge** Yiddish, crazy, not right in the head.

**Mezuzah** Hebrew. Literally, doorpost. The word refers to the small case affixed to the right side of the doorposts of Jewish homes and to the right of rooms inside the home used for living purposes. Inside the case is a small parchment on which is inscribed the first two sections of the *Sh'ma* (Deuteronomy 6:4–9 and 11:13–21). The other side of the parchment is inscribed with the Hebrew word *Shaddai,* Almighty, and the parchment is rolled in such a way that the three Hebrew letters for *Shaddai* are visible through the opening in the case.

**Midrash (midrashim,** plural) Hebrew. A method of studying and interpreting a Biblical text.

**Mikveh** Hebrew. Gathering of water. The term refers to the ritual bath.

**Minyan** Hebrew. Number. The term refers to the minimum number of Jewish males over thirteen required for a public service. Non-Orthodox Jews include women in the counting for a *minyan.*

**Mishnah** Hebrew. *See Talmud.*

**Mitzvah (Mitzvot,** plural) Hebrew. Religious and moral obligation as indicated by the commandments, statues, ordinances, observances and teachings. Traditionally, there are 613. Of these, 248 are positive commandments, i.e., acts one is supposed to do, and 365 are negative ones, acts one is not supposed to do.

**Mohel** Hebrew. Ritual circumciser.

**Omer** Hebrew. A measure. In Leviticus 23:15–21, Jews were commanded to count fifty days from the second day of Passover, at which time an offering of new grain was to be made to God. The practice of counting the days from the second day of Passover continues. The end of the Omer period is the festival of Shavuot, the celebration of the Revelation of the Torah at Sinai.

**Oy Gevalt!** Yiddish. An exclamation that is untranslatable.

**Parashah** Hebrew, referring to the portion of the Torah read at services and studied each week.

**Payess** Hebrew. Earlocks or side curls worn by ultra-Orthodox Jews.

**Rashi** An eleventh-century biblical and Talmudic commentator.

**Rebbe** Yiddish. Chasidic religious leader.

**Sefer Torah** Hebrew. Literally Book of the Torah. The term applies to the Torah Scrolls on which are written the Five Books of Moses.

**Sephardim** Hebrew. Jews of Spanish and Portuguese origin.

**Shemini Atzeret** Hebrew. The eighth day of the festival of Succoth.

**Shivah** Hebrew. Seven, and referring to the first seven days of mourning after the burial of a close relative.

**Sh'ma** Hebrew. Hear. The word is short for the central prayer in Judaism, and derives from the opening line of the prayer *Sh'ma Yisrael Adonai Elohenu Adonai Ehad.*

**Shtetl** Yiddish. Little town. The Jewish villages or Jewish sections of towns of pre-Holocaust Eastern Europe.

**Shul** Yiddish. Synagogue.

**Siddur (Siddurim,** plural) Hebrew. Prayerbook.

**Simchat Torah** Hebrew. Joy of the Torah. It is the festival celebrating with singing and dancing the yearly completion of the reading of the Five Books of Moses and the beginning again of the cycle.

**Tallit** Hebrew. Prayer shawl.

**Talmud** Hebrew. Study. The Talmud is the cornerstone of Judaism and Jewish life. It consists of two parts: (1) The *Mishnah,* which is the code of laws extrapolated from Biblical texts, and (2) the *Gemara,* which is the commentary and discussion of the *Mishnah.* The commentary and discussion include stories, science, history and folklore. *Talmud* and *Gemara* are used interchangeably.

The Babylonian Talmud, the one most widely used today, achieved final form around 500 C.E. The Palestinian Talmud achieved final form around 425 C.E.

**T'fillin** Hebrew. The two black leather cubes with long leather straps worn on the forehead and upper arm by Jewish males at the morning service except on Shabbat.

**Trayf** Hebrew. Literally, torn by beasts. The term has come to mean anything that is not kosher, that is unfit, not proper according to Jewish Law.

**Tzedakah** Hebrew. Righteousness. In general usage, the term means charity, because to give charity is an act of righteousness.

**Yahrzeit** Yiddish. The anniversary of the death of a relative, which is observed by the burning of a candle for twenty-four hours.

**Yiddishkeit** Yiddish. The culture of Eastern European Jewry.

(Reference: *The New Jewish Encyclopedia,* edited by David Bridger in association with Samuel Wolk. New York: Behrman House, Inc., 1976.)